REPORTING INDONESIA

THE JAKARTA POST STORY

BILL TARRANT

REPORTING INDONESIA
THE JAKARTA POST STORY

EQUINOX
PUBLISHING
JAKARTA · SINGAPORE

Equinox Publishing (Asia) Pte Ltd
No 3. Shenton Way
#10-05 Shenton House
Singapore 068805

www.equinox.asia

Reporting Indonesia: The Jakarta Post Story
by Bill Tarrant

ISBN 978-979-3780-69-6

First Equinox Edition 2008

Printed in the United States

1 3 5 7 9 10 8 6 4 2

TABLE OF CONTENTS

FOREWORD

It is a story very much worth telling: how *The Jakarta Post* rose from its humble birth in an empty warehouse a quarter of a century ago to what it is today – a prestigious independent broadsheet with extensive national and international influence.

That influence is due to the professionalism of its reportage – done in English, the official language of ASEAN and the lingua franca of the world – and the high quality of its loyal readership of English-literate Indonesians and most of the large expatriate community in Jakarta.

The story is well told because the book goes beyond recounting a series of important events in the life of the newspaper. In fact, this is the collective memoir of brave men and women who over the years struggled to exercise that fundamental civic freedom, freedom of the press, even under the most inauspicious circumstances.

As such, it tells its story in terms of human experience, with a great deal of élan, pathos and good-natured humor. It tells, for instance, of how the *Post* editors and reporters played hide-and-seek with and in interesting ways battled the censors of the New Order era. That makes this book a good read.

But apart from enjoying the book, we must pay tribute to the struggle that it tells. Personal fortunes, careers and even lives were risked in the course of waging that struggle, which is an important part of the larger endeavor of the Indonesian people for freedom from the grip of authoritarian rule. Thus there were forces for reform at work even during those repressive times and they included journalists all over Indonesia.

Thanks to these forces Indonesia has made its transition to a more fully democratic system. The press in Indonesia today is free and untrammeled.

New pressures, however, are now being exerted on the *Post*. It has to cope with enormous competition from the electronic media. It must at least partially migrate to the cyber world.

Yet its relevance to the national life remains unchanged. It continues to serve as both mirror and window to the realities and the march of daily events in Indonesia. Through its reportage, its readers – both Indonesian and foreign – make sense of these local and national events and their impact on a globalized international community. In that way it engages in "popular geopolitics" which complements the "practical geopolitics" that is carried out by Indonesia's leaders and corps of diplomats.

Both the *Post* and the Department of Foreign Affairs are therefore in the service of Indonesia's national interests. That is the rationale behind the Department's regular breakfast dialogue on foreign affairs with members of the national press. And that explains how two former editors of the *Post* have served with distinction as Indonesian ambassadors: Mr. Sabam Siagian to Australia and Mr. Susanto Pudjomartono to the Russian Federation.

This does not mean that the *Post* and the Department always see eye-to-eye on what the national interests are and how they should be pursued. The *Post* can be very vocal in its critique of Indonesian foreign policy and diplomacy. But that is both natural and good. It livens up the dialogue. Two heads, after all, are better than one if they sometimes disagree.

Of course, in the practice of a demanding profession, there will be occasions when a reporter, perhaps under pressure of deadline or a family problem, files a story that is distorted by an inaccuracy, or in a moment of inattention omits an essential fact. On those occasions, the fury of our concerned officials will be expressed in loud and colorful language. But we will be quick to forgive, forget and move on.

The devil may be in the details but the important thing is that we never lose sight of the national interest and we never differ on matters of principle. I have always been sure of this through all the years that I interacted with the editors and reporters of the *Post*. Anyone who reads *Reporting Indonesia: The Jakarta Post Story* will be just as certain.

This is therefore an important book not only to Indonesian diplomats but also to all Indonesians. With its publication in English, only one more thing needs to be done. The story of *The Jakarta Post* is too good not to be told also in the Indonesian language.

I look forward to the publication of its version in Bahasa Indonesia.

Jakarta, 14 October 2008

Dr. N. Hassan Wirajuda
Minister of Foreign Affairs
Republic of Indonesia

PREFACE

I cannot think of a greater gift to mark the Silver Jubilee of *The Jakarta Post* this year than a book that chronicles the journey of this great newspaper for the last 25 years. As important as the receptions, seminars and other events we held to celebrate the occasion throughout this year, none beats a book when it comes to sharing the joy that we feel with our 25th anniversary with as many people as we can.

We are looking at a book that tells the story of the company, how it all started, and the vision of its founders for setting up an English language newspaper that becomes known as *The Jakarta Post*. We want a book that tells the aspirations of those involved, and the struggle as well as the ups and downs of the newspaper in the constantly changing political and business environments. We want a book that tells about the directors, the editors, the journalists, the business managers and every one else involved, about how they see their role in all this, and may be a little bit about the back office politics to help illustrate the dynamics of a modern newspaper company.

If one generation is said to last 25 years, this book is about the first generation of *The Jakarta Post*. Of course, a newspaper is much more dynamic and generational changes occur all the time. We have had four editors-in-chief between 1983 and 2008.

The first 25 years is nevertheless important for the story to be told in a book. This is true especially since the challenges for the next 25 years will be significantly different. This is not to say that the story in this book is ancient and has no relevance to the present and future of *The Jakarta Post*. Precisely because we feel that there is value in the story to the present and next "generations" that we commissioned this book.

We are thus grateful to Mark Hanusz of Equinox Publishing for collaborating with *The Jakarta Post* in the making of this book. We have picked Bill Tarrant, a senior Reuters journalist with long service in Asia, to undertake the monumental task of writing of the book. Bill was involved in the first years of newspaper to know enough about the background, but left in 1984, long enough to be emotionally detached from the subject he is writing on.

We have made it a point to have a book that is independently written, and for the story of *The Jakarta Post* to be told as truthfully as possible. For the book to be of any value to anyone, this book could not be made into an ego trip of some of the people written about.

The greatest gift that we can give for our 25th anniversary is this book, one that tells in an honest and humble way, the history of the newspaper which is inextricably linked to the fate of the city and the country it calls home, and one that tells about 25 years of constant dedication in public services through newspaper journalism.

Jakarta, 27 October 2008

Endy M. Bayuni
Chief Editor
The Jakarta Post

WELCOME TO INDOPLANET

I was wandering around town in Bandung, looking for a place that might sell foreign newspapers, when I met Bambang Harymurti. My story on the erupting Galunggung volcano in West Java had been published in *Asia Magazine,* then a Sunday supplement for various newspapers around Asia, including the *South China Morning Post,* the paper I was looking for. I was eager to see if my story had made the cover (it had not).

I had barged into *Tempo* magazine's Bandung bureau under the mistaken impression that it was an establishment selling newspapers and magazines, a notion conveyed by the "news agency" signage on the storefront. Bambang, back then in December 1982, was a newly minted graduate of the prestigious Institute of Technology Bandung (ITB), and *Tempo's* bureau chief. He laughed politely when I asked him, dubiously by now, if he possibly had any newspapers to sell.

He cheerfully assured me I had a snowball's chance in Galunggung's hellish crater of finding any foreign newspapers in Bandung and then proceeded to interview me. We talked for a long time. Bambang, *Tempo's* future chief editor, was lively, funny and articulate and I was excited to finally meet a fellow journalist five months into my Indonesian sojourn. My brother's aid and development crowd was great, if a little pointy-headed, but here was a comrade-in-arms, a kindred spirit. "Say," Bambang said at one point. "You know you should go meet my boss in Jakarta. *Tempo* and some other media groups are starting up a new English language newspaper, and it's going to be called the *Post*, too. *The Jakarta Post*."

It was a tantalizing proposition. But wasn't I supposed to be just visiting my brother in Indonesia? My mother was expecting me home in Pittsburgh for Christmas.

I could see my brother Jim, wearing a Panama hat and a Hawaiian shirt – maybe it was batik, I wouldn't have known the difference then – doing a comical *luau* dance in the arrival hall of Jakarta's old Halim airport. "Welcome to Indoplanet!" he cried.

It was July 14, 1982, the day the people of Paris stormed Bastille prison to free political prisoners during the French Revolution. I'm in flight myself both literally and metaphysically, having just stumbled out of a Singapore Airlines plane from San Francisco and before that a long journey from Pittsburgh across America, mostly by Greyhound Bus. I had only meant to visit Indonesia for a few weeks, but more than a quarter-century later I have not returned to live in America. One thing just led to another, as things often do in the Orient.

Jim led me imperturbably through the "hey mister" chorus, swarming around us grabbing for my big, ugly second-hand suitcase from hell, to a rank of yellow President taxicabs that looked like they had recently take part in a particularly vicious Demolition Derby. We piled into one which had a gaping hole in the back seat, windows that couldn't wind down, and no air-conditioning. The top of the front windscreen was largely obscured by a Marlboro decal. My brother, who is 51 weeks older than me (a phenomenon sometimes referred to as Irish Catholic twins) had been writing to me for months about his strange and wondrous life in Bandung, an old Dutch colonial hill station and university town nestled in the volcanic hills of West Java.

The East Indies! Smoking volcanoes and chocolate-skinned women in batik sarongs. Teeming markets selling strange vegetables and concoctions. Water buffalo plowing verdant rice fields. Stilt villages under plunging waterfalls. Children in native attire performing traditional dances and village ceremonies. Primitive tribesmen with magical weapons. These were the Spice Islands that

Columbus was trying to find when he set sail in 1492, and whose fabulous treasures the British, Dutch and Portuguese fought over for centuries. A weird, wonderful place where expats lived in bungalows set amid lush gardens of banana, rambutan, jackfruit, avocado and mango trees, with servants tripping over each other to provide *Tuan* with all the creature comforts.

The President taxi took us on a tilt-a-whirl ride into Jakarta's cacophonous traffic: buses belching like volcanoes; families on motorcycles; three-wheeler Bajaj "taxis" – a Halloweenish orange and black shell covering a motorcycle – buzzing noisily through traffic like giant insects; children selling newspapers and clove cigarettes, wearing pathetic expressions and pressing their faces onto the windows at traffic lights; dirty beggars jostling them for importuning space.

Cars seemed to be coming straight at us at high speed, swerving and braking like some madcap video arcade game. Except this game was all too real and I slithered down the seat, unable to watch, my nerves already shot from a journey halfway across the world. We drove by broad canals smelling like sewers, naked little boys splashing happily in the flotsam and huge socialist-surrealism monuments that Sukarno erected in the 1950s to glorify the working class hero. The *eau de Jakarta* that wafted through the taxi windows was a mélange of cooking fires, turds, vehicle exhaust, rotting food and sweet tree blossoms.

We were heading for the U.S. embassy because my brother, then working for the U.S. Agency for International Development (USAID), needed to change money to pay bills for the week. It was pretty much a cash economy, with few foreign banks operating in Indonesia a quarter-century ago. Nobody had checking accounts or used credit cards. People walked around with bulging wallets and bank envelopes stuffed with cash looking furtively over their shoulders – Jakarta's pick-pockets were magicians at their trade.

Police barricades around the embassy forced the taxi to drop us off a couple blocks away. Army trucks rumbled past, discharging soldiers who leisurely took up positions around the front gates. Frank Sinatra's "Strangers in the Night" sounded above the traffic din and a battered city bus with people hanging out the doors flashed by.

"It's a claxon horn," Jim explained. "It plays music instead of going beep, beep. People love to use horns here." Indeed, I would soon discover it was not unusual to hear "Greensleeves," Beethoven's "Für Elise" or even "Jingle Bells" above the traffic din.

We were now wading through a growing crowd around the embassy that was shouting anti-American slogans and admiring the colorfully painted banners they had just draped along the iron railings. I wondered if perhaps we should take the back entrance.

My brother assured me there was nothing to fear. The United States had sent the Marines into Lebanon a few weeks earlier and we were witnessing the daily pro-forma protest in predominantly Muslim Indonesia. This was Suharto's Indonesia. Nobody could assemble on the street in more than a handful of numbers without the express permission of the authorities. Suharto was staunchly anti-communist and pro-American, coming after the mercurial and pro-China Sukarno. Billions of dollars in aid was flowing into the country through the World Bank and other institutions under Washington's sway.

The demonstrators at the U.S. embassy were probably from Golkar, Jim explained, referring to the government party made up of civil servants, tame unions, the army and intellectuals – or more likely they were the street lumpen Golkar usually employed when a little crowd noise and muscle was needed. By now, jet-lagged and culture-shocked, I could only nod dumbly.

"You're not in Kansas anymore, Dorothy," Jim laughed, deploying a line from the "Wizard of Oz" he would often use in the months ahead.

The train to Bandung chugged past miles of shanty-towns and garbage, new factories and old colonial homes. A woman, dirty and disheveled, stared vacantly at the passing train, nursing her naked baby. The train was called the Parahiangan Express, named after the ancient Preanger Kingdom of the Sundanese people of upland West Java. Yet, while it had few stops once it left Jakarta, the train was hardly an express.

The jumbled built-up cityscape of Jakarta abruptly ended and, like the next click of a slide show, the scene suddenly changed to women in straw hats and water buffalo pulling plows in verdant rice fields. The jungle was interrupted now and again by dense woodlots and home gardens, where children rolled tires with sticks or played with goats. And, shimmering through the heat haze in the distance, conical volcanoes. Even on the steep slopes of these brooding hulks, rice was being cultivated on glimmering, terraced paddies. Yes, this was the fantastic Spice Islands and what a swell train was this Parahiangan Express to Bandung.

Jim was telling me that I could stay as long as I wanted in his bungalow, but I had one job to do: sweep the veranda and driveway of volcanic ash from Mount Galunggung's diurnal eruptions. The servant might have done that, except Jim had fired him for stealing his traveler's checks. That crime came to light when the local constabulary came to the house with the evidence in question and informed Jim his manservant had done a dismal job of masquerading as a U.S. Embassy aid consultant and forging his signature.

I already knew about Galunggung. Singapore Airlines had warned us of a possible flight delay to Jakarta because of the huge clouds of volcanic ash it was spewing out over West Java. Months earlier, a British Airways 747 plunged 25,000 feet when its four engines cut out after it flew through an ash cloud. A Singapore Airlines jet had had a similar experience. Each airliner made a miraculous landing with terrified passengers. The unceasing eruptions had killed more than a hundred and left more than 50,000 homeless in the city of Tasikmalaya, about 65 km southeast of Bandung. Dry season trade winds pushed the ash clouds over Bandung.

I awoke one morning, a few days after my arrival, to find day had turned to night. It was pitch black outside and car headlights shone on what looked like a blizzard. Galunggung had erupted again. A canopy of white dust lay on the landscape like newly fallen snow. By midday, night had turned to a London fog. Dust clouds swirled from ash-covered vehicles. Bambang, the rooster my brother kept, crowed the whole morning announcing the false dawns. Now I knew what Jim meant. I grabbed a shovel and an Indonesian stick broom, wrapped a bandana around my face and trudged out to the veranda. It was like shoveling snow as a kid in my hometown of Pittsburgh.

Jim was involved in setting up an environmental studies center at the Bandung Institute of Technology (ITB), part of a USAID grant program. Not long after I arrived, Jim informed me that his co-workers at ITB had arranged a traditional party to welcome newcomers to their community. The party, he said, was called "Hello Bill, Hello!" in my honor. Though this sounded a bit unusual, I had already discovered nothing was too strange on Indoplanet. The hard plastic contact from my right eye had shattered in its case the night before, which I attributed to sensory overload, and so I went to the picnic half-blind and totally bamboozled.

It was a traditional celebration, alright, but rather than "Hello, Bill, Hello" it was a *halal bihal* feast, which companies usually organize for their employees in Indonesia within a month of the Muslim *Idul-fitri* festival marking the end of the Ramadan fasting month. Indonesians like nothing better than a joke, and people at the picnic gladly greeted me with shouts of "Hello Bill, Hello." Jim introduced me to the environment minister, Emil Salim, who was among the so-called "Berkeley Mafia," a cohort of Indonesian economists who had studied at the University of California at Berkeley and whom Suharto brought into his cabinet to reform Indonesia's socialist economy after easing Sukarno from power in 1967. Jim was a big admirer of "Pak" Emil and didn't clue him into the joke at the picnic.

My brother was the only *bule* (meaning albino and common slang for a Caucasian) on his USAID project. Though he had a Jeep at his disposal, it was mostly used for field projects and ferrying around the Indonesian project head. Jim was unenthusiastic about driving in the barely controlled chaos of Java's roads. And as a former Peace Corps volunteer in Ethiopia, he preferred to go native as much as possible.

Jim introduced me to Bandung's astonishing variety of public transport, which included an ancient fleet of public buses, *opelets*, *bemos*, "Hondas" and *becaks*. *Bemos* were tiny three-wheeled group taxis that looked like the head of grasshopper. Hondas were simply small pick-up trucks with enclosed bays and bench seats, and *becaks* were bicycle rickshaws. But the most curious were *opelets*. The *opelet* is Indonesia's oldest public taxi, appearing in the early 1940s. It is the jitney of Indonesia, usually a nine-passenger station-wagon built up with wood from an old Austin chassis. The name actually comes from the few vehicles that were built up from GMC Opels. All of them had been remodeled – apparently by sledgehammer – in order to accommodate as many seats and passengers as possible. Many had no side doors, which facilitated entrance and sometimes unintentional egress, while the dreadful exhaust system caused petrol fumes to swirl through the passenger compartment. All forms of public transport featured a *kenek* – Dutch slang for conductor – usually young boys who hung off the back bumper soliciting passengers. Vehicles abruptly lurched to the side of the road anywhere at a raised finger or toss of the head.

Bandung sits on a high plateau, 700 meters above sea level and surrounded by volcanic hills draped in tea plantations, protected forests and the ubiquitous rice terraces. Thousands of years ago, the valley in which Bandung sat was once a naturally dammed lake that then drained away after an earthquake. The name Bandung, in fact, is a variant of *bendung*, meaning "dam."

Bandung was still wistfully referred as the "Paris of Java" because the city's tree-lined streets north of the railroad tracks were lined with old, Dutch colonial homes, many schools, universities and cultural attractions, evoking an old-world civilized air. The cool climate drew Dutch planters to settle here rather than in densely populated, fetid old Batavia in the early 19th century. Indeed, the Dutch had planned to build up Bandung as the colony's administrative capital but these plans were never realized due to the Great Depression and World War II.

My brother's house on Jalan Dago was of the Dutch colonial style that had outdoor *mandis*, chest high concrete and tile enclosures with great views of the city below and a *bak*, or small concrete tank, filled with water made icy in Bandung's briskly cool early mornings. I would ladle the water over myself, yelping at the shock of cold water, which Bambang seemed to think was a call to his ladies (Mimi and Tin were our hens) and would crow back in protest.

I used to be a late sleeper, but *kampung* life soon cured me of that. The mosquito flying around my ear was the first sound to pull me to consciousness my first night in Indonesia. But what really caused me to bolt upright in bed was the sound of someone repeatedly clearing his throat in a speaker system, sounding like he was in his death throes. But what then followed was possibly one of the most beautiful things I have ever heard in my life, the stirring opening stanzas of the Muslim call to prayer from the mosque behind our house, which were soon echoed by hundreds of other mosques across the city.

The imam's *azan* prayer prompted Bambang to perform his own morning call, which set all the dogs in the neighborhood to bark monotonously at each other, waking up at least two babies who quickly chimed into the morning din. Whining scooters heralded the beginning of another day of road chaos, and Jim's West German grandfather clock in the living room musically intoned the fifth hour of the day.

I met my first *bule*, other than my brother, a few weeks after arriving in Indonesia, and for that reason alone Jeremy Allan seemed exotic.[1] A scrawny Canadian with a red goatee, he made a grand entrance at the house on a 1962, 900cc Harley Davidson Sportster, which we heard long before it eased into the driveway.

Jeremy was a "seismic engineer" for an oil company in East Kalimantan on Indonesia's part of Borneo island. That meant he and his Indonesian crew traipsed about the jungle with explosives blowing holes in the ground in order to sample the "mud" for possible evidence of oil. At least that's how he explained it. Jeremy loved his job.

He was about to embark on a trip across Java to Bali on the Harley and I begged him to take me along, which he reluctantly agreed to do. I soon learned why. Harleys are temperamental beasts, and 20-year ones are demented and diabolical.

We inaugurated the trip with ritualistic attendance at a *wayang golek* performance, a puppet show depicting ancient Indian epics that had been staged in Indonesia centuries before Islam started to spread through Java around the 14th century. The show lasted all night, and

---

1   Jeremy Allan, the author of *Jakarta Jive* and *Bali Blues*, makes his home in Bali.

as such, was a place where folks could hang out and make the scene on Saturday night. The auditorium was packed. People wandered in and out, alternately snoozing and guffawing at the antics of the puppets.

Wayang can have a hypnotic effect, particularly for the uninitiated. The *dalang* or puppeteer enthusiastically narrated the story in the Sundanese dialect, while manipulating the puppets behind the stage; the gamelan orchestra behind him laid on the sound effects and mood music with gongs and chimes; the smell of clove cigarettes hung heavy in the stuffy air of the auditorium.

Fifty exotically costumed puppets constituting the cast of characters in the *wayang* stories were arrayed along the front of the auditorium stage, while the featured puppets glided eerily across the puppet theatre, like a cartoon come alive, under the practiced hands of the *dalang*.

I dozed off into a dream, only to awake in a hallucination of clashing puppets, urgent gongs and a thunderous *dalang* voice like god on high. The *dalang* was telling one of the tales from the Mahabharata, the great Indian epic of warring families, whose central episode is the Bhagavad-Gita, the Hindu bible.[2] The fact that Hindu mythology was popular entertainment in predominantly Muslim Indonesia was just one of the many wonderful things I was discovering about Indonesia.

The audience laughed and cheered at the antics of the puppets, particularly when one pot-bellied character with a shit-eating grin appeared. This, I later learned, was Semar, a distinctly Javanese character, who was the "wise fool" and "guardian of Java." The *dalang* had slyly used Semar to introduce some political satire into the story. (Semar was the favorite *wayang* character of Suharto, also known as "the smiling general".) In Suharto's Indonesia, a controlled press and muffled opposition allowed little in the way of dissent, let alone ridicule. *Wayang* had to do that work.

An election in May had given Golkar another landslide in what

---

2   A grand statue depicting the opening scene of the Bhagavad-Gita, in which Lord Krishna imparts wisdom to Arjuna as he rides into battle, stands at the entrance to Medan Merdeka, or Freedom Square, in Central Jakarta.

everybody assumed were rigged elections, but at least 18 people were killed, hundreds injured and dozens of cars burnt when Golkar staged its first (and last) public rally in Jakarta in March, an indication that all was not quite well in Suharto's New Order. Growing dissatisfaction with his development strategy, which emphasized big infrastructure projects and top down-industrialization financed by massive amounts of foreign aid, began to boil after OPEC member Indonesia abruptly announced a 60 percent across-the-board increase in the price of subsidized oil products. It had to be done – international oil prices had risen to $36 a barrel and the subsidies the government was paying amounted to around 5 percent of GDP – but spin-doctoring and public relations were not a hallmark of the regime. The *wayang* that night was ridiculing all this, Jeremy's Indonesian friends told us.

Jeremy said the *wayang* was the soul of Java, and that I couldn't understand what the road was like if I didn't understand the performance. I didn't understand the performance. But its psychedelic drama seemed an appropriate prelude to our own surreal trip across Java.

We embarked on our journey on a vehicle as odd and recalcitrant as many of the other conveyances on the road. The Harley's engine, when kicked over, sounded like a Galunggung eruption. When it kicked over at all, that is to say. Because, in keeping with the tenor of Javanese road life, the Harley had something mystifyingly wrong with its powerful engine that caused it to stall out and die in the middle of nowhere, or precisely in the middle of town during rush hour. We stopped at the Bandung Harley-Davidson club – oddly enough, one of the largest outside the United States at the time – to get the engine timed, Jeremy explained. That should have tipped me off from the start.

Trouble first hit on our way to Tasikmalaya, a lively market town southeast of Bandung that had the misfortune of lying at the foot of Mt. Galunggung, which had already erupted violently dozens of times since April. It had staged a major eruption the day before we set out and it wasn't long before we slammed into a choking ash blizzard that lasted a good 50 km. Visibility was only a few feet at the most, and the only way we knew we were following a gas truck was the acrid, suffocating smell of the fumes it was spewing from its exhaust pipes as it crawled up the torturous mountain roads between Bandung and Tasikmalaya.

Just outside Tasikmalaya, we took a wrong turn – the right turn, as it turned out, for two ash-drenched bikers. The Harley, like an old mule, seemed to have its own idea of navigation and was making a bee-line for Pangandaran, a peaceful fishing village on the Indian Ocean. We arrived just in time to witness the sun setting in a conflagration of reds, purples and gold, enhanced by a plume of volcanic dust in the distance, while dining on durians, mangosteens and beer. It was my first encounter with the "king of fruits," which to me tasted of limburger cheese and vanilla ice cream. Jeremy warned me that durians and alcohol can have a hallucinogenic effect, but at that point I thought: How could either of us possibly tell?

We left Pangandaran at sunrise, hoping to get a good jump on the marathon leg to Solo, in Central Java, a good 10-hour ride on hard roads – really hard roads. We were numb and bleary when we dismounted a couple of hours later for breakfast, only to discover we had been riding on a flat back tire. The road east across Java runs parallel with a virtually unbroken line of volcanic mountains, whose odd shapes and contours – conical, elliptical, round, soft and greenish blue – look like an illustration from a J.R.R. Tolkien book. Most Javanese live and die within sight of a volcano, as more than 100 cones and craters form a rugged backbone across the middle of the island, 35 of them still active.

The Harley quit on us early in the afternoon in Gembong village, the first of many such episodes on this trip. Jeremy joked the bike, like many Indonesians, customarily napped in the afternoon. He would lose his sense of humor about the mulish Harley as the trip unfolded. We hung out at a *warung* while Jeremy tinkered with the bike. Within its dark confines were tables set with bowls of food: buffalo meat, stir-fried veggies, spicy fried chicken, *rendang* beef marinated in coconut sauce, *tempe*, peanut sauce, fish crackers, boiled eggs, rice, and a squadron of flies patrolling the food plains below.

We picked from among the bowls to fashion our meal, trying

not to mind the fact that everybody in the joint was staring at us in disbelief. Westerners were a novelty in an Indonesian village those days, before commercial television and the global village, and they found it something of a marvel that Westerners ate rice, too. The Harley and its sooted warriors only added to the spectacle.

As we journeyed into Central Java, the countryside flattened out, opening up Java's rice bowl lands. Towns and villages are smaller, the fields larger, occasionally interrupted by dense rubber and teak tree plantations. Animals wandered all over the road – oxen, water buffalo, goats, ram, sheep, ducks, turkeys, chickens – usually tended to by scampering children: one of Java's many ways of forcing you to interpenetrate its life, even if it involves screeching perilously off the road to avoid hitting random, roaming fauna.

In Solo, we stayed at a palace: a little down-at-heel, but a sumptuous sight for sore eyes and butts nonetheless. It once belonged to a prince of the Solonese Sultanate, which was dissolved when Indonesia became a republic in 1950. Part of it was now being maintained by a group of Westerners, who were devotees of the Sumarah Meditation Center, a mystical fraternity founded by an Indonesian bank clerk in 1937. Loosely based on Hindu and Sufi teachings, followers strove to create a world "filled with light, but no shadows," opening up the powers of the mind. Our simple rooms had both light and shadows, and mosquito nets too, because no power of the mind has been discovered that will keep these pests at a distance.

Solo had many such religious, mystical and meditation centers. Perhaps it had something to do with the fact that Solo is in the exact geographic centre of Java, is the island's oldest cultural centre and is its least Westernized city – the prehistoric bones of "Java man" were found interred in the Solo river. Pressure from the Islamic right wing made these sorts of syncretism cults politically incorrect in the decades to come. Solo would become known after the Sept. 11 attacks in the United States as home to Abu Bakar Bashir's *pesantren* (Islamic school) and a stronghold of the militant Islamic network, Jemaah Islamiyah.

Ever the optimists, we left Solo after fixing another flat only to stall out again an hour later by a rice field, and not a building in sight. The Harley had been running like this ever since we went through Galunggung's ash gauntlet – sputtering, lurching, stalling. Jeremy had been insisting this was the existential state of Harleys: "always running broke." But now even he was beginning to have doubts. Stalled vehicles are the norm on Java's roads and account for the proliferation of small *bengkel* workshops across the land. In these shops, by some sort of Javanese alchemy, 40- and 50-year old Pontiacs, Kaisers, Hudsons and Packards – not to mention the ubiquitous Japanese cars and motorcycles – were given new life. Parts were cannibalized and forged anew to create Frankensteinian vehicles that at least got you where you needed to go. But this time, no bengkel was in sight. So with the aid of two bemused farmers, we push-started the Harley, resuming our limping journey to Madiun, about a two-hour drive into East Java.

Following our usual pattern, we gasped into town at sunset – just in time to get swallowed up in a long parade of marching schoolchildren and bands, which was proceeding down the main drag to kick off a big, scholastic soccer match. We had already discovered that marching down the main street for whatever reason seemed to be popular on Java. Just as we threaded our way to the head of the parade – and getting loudly cheered for our efforts – the Harley, sounding an ominous death rattle, gave up the ghost. Jeremy was now muttering about putting the "thing" on a train and continuing our journey by rail, so I knew our plight was pretty grim.

But he was inspired to ask a traffic cop, if by chance, Madiun had a Harley-Davidson club. And sure enough, the club was not more than 100 meters from where we were marooned, and its members greeted us with an outpouring of goodwill. A mechanic came to fiddle with the bike, and then somewhat incongruously, we mounted their Japanese motor scooters for a tour of Madiun's raucous nightlife. Indonesians are often like that – spontaneous, affectionate, helpful, extroverted, sometimes even a little goofy.

Violent crime (unless instigated by the authorities) was unusual in Java then, though pick-pocketing was a high art form. Probably because so many people live so close together – Java's population of well over 100 million at the time lived on an island the size of the state of Louisiana – the people had evolved an ad hoc, give and take, share the poverty, cooperative form of society. This is encapsulated in the *gotong royong* (community self-help) ethic in Indonesian society.

The terrain became mountainous again on the road through East Java, and steadily worse, too. Rice fields gave way to tall sugar fields, and teak and mahogany forests. Tiny box cars full of cane, ran along narrow-gauge rail lines, sometimes powered by tiny, ancient steam locomotives, but more often pulled by teams of oxen. Jeremy was expert at deftly moving off to the shoulder and going around the raucous parade of vehicles on Java's narrow, twisting, rocky roads, telling me in the midst of one of these maneuvers about the time a friend took his Kawasaki 1000 on an unscheduled tour of four food stalls at 140 clicks after losing control trying to make one such detour. We staged our usual evening breakdown in the main square of Malang at the far eastern end of Java during rush hour, drawing a record crowd this time of 62 concerned citizens, mesmerized at the spectacle of Jeremy, in aviator sunglasses and infantry jacket, flinging all of his 125 pounds on the unresponsive kick starter – to no avail.

By now, the Harley had gone through a complete engine overhaul and was staggering along, bandaged and bruised, quite literally Jerry-rigged. The blown head gasket was only its latest malady and that was easily ameliorated with a borrowed rag and stereo wire. I really didn't want to know how.

Malang was a welcome respite from the tribulations of the road, a cool, clean city surrounded by volcanic hills with pretty squares and parks, large, old Dutch villas and a riotous *pasar besar* (big market) even by Java's standards. The market sprawled over several city centre blocks, with scenes that struck me at the time as something out of a Hieronymus Bosch painting, but were probably not that much different from what you might find in any Asian city at the time. Vendors of clothing, jewelry, food, housewares and pure junk beseeched me (*"mister, mister"*); hands clawed at my shirt as I stumbled through the crowd. Loudspeakers from music stores and *warungs* blared a medley of South American jazz, gamelan music and rock and roll. A sidewalk sharpie dispensed pornography under the guise of a medical anatomy lesson to an ogling crowd of bumpkins, while quadriplegics in rags writhed on the sidewalk for spare change.

The next morning, Jeremy cockily announced the Harley was rehabilitated enough to "bomb all the way to Bali today." Clearly, he was referring to the road, which appeared to have been inflicted with a carpet bombing attack by B-52s – huge craters pockmarked its surface. That made it hard to focus on the stunning panorama unfolding before us of pine and teaks forests, coffee plantations, waterfalls and old rickety bridges, dramatically ascending rice terraces, hair-raising mountain passes and plunging river gorges. We slowly ascended Java's "mother volcano," Mount Semeru, the magic mountain and abode of gods, reputedly the world's most beautiful volcanic peak, and the highest (3,680 meters) on Java. Legend has it that Semeru was dispatched from the Himalayas, because the Hindu gods there wanted a guest house on Java. But Semeru swept so fast through Java, (this was of course before roads were built to slow things down) huge chunks fell from it to create the volcanic mountain chain that bisects the island.

The Harley, much to our amazement, made it over this mother of a mountain and we were on smooth road through tobacco, rubber and teak tree plantations, on the last 100 km to the ferry to Bali. We caught the ferry as the dying rays of the setting sun cast a pinkish glow on the hills of Bali, only two km across the Bali Strait. We pushed on into the night through the southern tier of Bali, and no sooner had we passed a procession of school girls in uniform carrying torches, then the Harley was veering all over the road like a balloon when the air is let out – having blown a tire once again. Yet even in the pitch darkness, far from the nearest town, first one and soon a dozen Balinese children appeared in the night, squealing and hopping about in delight at discovering this odd development in their neighborhood. They led us to a nearby farmhouse, where we stashed the bike in a shed, and called it a night at the local *losmen* (guest house.)

On the final leg of our long, erratic journey to Kuta beach, the day was snappy clear and the road was smooth. We stopped at a rest spot, where a Hindu priest was blessing travelers, so the Harley could get its benediction; better late than never. We finally made it to Kuta beach after six days and nights across some of the worst roads in the world. I'm one of those annoying people who can say: "Yeah, but you should have seen Bali 25 years ago." But in many ways, it's a lot nicer today, especially for families. It was pretty much a backpacker's haven then – psilocybin mushrooms in the pancakes and that sort of thing.

I had discovered on this trip that Indonesia has great capacity for accommodation and adaptation, no matter how strange the people and their contrivances and contraptions. The national motto "Unity Through Diversity" refers to the admixture of Muslim, Christian, Buddhist, Hindu, and other religious beliefs; the hundreds of ethnic groups and their languages, from stone age tribes in Indonesian New Guinea to the purist Islamic culture of Aceh, dispersed across the 17,508 islands of the archipelago. Java's road life is a living portrait of this diverse unity: women swaying under wide baskets of fruit and vegetables; men quick-stepping gingerly with huge loads in their shoulder baskets; squads of marching schoolchildren; inter-city buses jam-packed with indifferent passengers careening wildly down twisting, mountain roads; the percussive strains of gamelan music wafting through the air; breathtaking views of ancient Hindu and Buddhist ruins, erupting volcanoes and tropical beaches; oxen cars, push carts, pedicabs, impossibly loaded trucks, fowls a-flocking and water buffalo bathing, pre-war Chevrolets and millions of Japanese motor scooters all vying for space on the mind-boggling roadscape. I had all the work I could handle teaching English at one of the many English-language tuition centers in Bandung after my excellent adventure across Java. It had a slightly ominous name: Triad. But the three kind and elderly university professors that ran the school were a far cry from Chinese gangsters. They also arranged for me to teach at Maranantha Christian University, a Protestant-affiliated school with some 3,000 students. The university seemed to be freeze-framed in 1950s. My first class of freshmen all had shaved heads and wore white uniforms, and outside of class were made to do ignominious deeds by their gleeful seniors.

As a young American male, I was a hot commodity on the English-language teaching circuit. At least that's what the Triad gentlemen told me. Most of their students were young women wanting an American-style language course because they hoped to study in the United States. Native speakers define the prestige of these schools, and men were especially prized because almost all the native speakers available in Bandung tended to be wives of consultants on Indonesia's many and various development projects.

Teaching was easy. The books all had self-contained lesson plans, so it was very easy to prepare for class. Because they were going to these classes in their spare time, the students were very attentive and motivated, and seemed to enjoy my somewhat animated performances, even if they didn't always understand them.

Some wanted private lessons and we soon had a steady procession of (mostly) young women coming to the house on Jalan Dago, along with the "antique" sellers, random house guests and the odd passers-by looking for pizza. (Jim had painted in large, black lettering along the wall out front a sign for "Joe's Pizza", so people would be better able to find his house, though, in fact, he also made pretty decent pizza.). By October, the rainy season had begun to set in, sweeping away Galunggung's ash that had piled up along streets and lawns, turning the city into a mud bowl.

Jim and I were returning home one night in drenching rain from visiting his Sundanese girlfriend and *pencak silat* teacher, Rita, who also had a gorgeous younger sister that I was introduced to under the glowering eye of her father, the Master of the Mande Muda *pencak silat* school. (*Pencak silat* is an Indonesian martial art similar to kung fu.) We were discussing the wisdom of getting involved with a family – any of whose members could easily beat the crap out of both us with one arm tied behind their back should relationships sour – when I suddenly disappeared. The storm canals, choked with Galunggung's ash, had overflowed and the flooded sidewalk was no longer distinguishable from the ditch beside it. I was floundering under the filthy water for a while, before my brother realized he was talking to himself (itself not an unusual occurrence) and fished me out.

I had badly scraped my arm during the fall and the following day

I had a raging fever that lasted for days after the wound turned septic. Even after the fever broke, I was sick for weeks with gastric distress and diarrhea. I was sure I had a parasite, some exotic Indoplanet bug. But a doctor at Bandung General Hospital told me that my system was merely suffering "culture shock." I begged to differ with her. I had travelled across Java on an old motorcycle. I was living a great life in an old Dutch bungalow. I had a nice job teaching English at a college. I was meeting many girls who seemed to be flirting all the time with me. I was having fun! Except for this pesky parasite. She said all that may be true, but my stomach was not happy and it had stopped digesting food. She gave me peristalsis pills to kick start the old digestive juices and that cleared it up right away. In fact, I've never hosted a parasite in all my quarter-century of travels in Asia.

> The traveller soon comes to look upon this region as one apart from the rest of the world, with its own races of men and its own aspects of nature; with its own ideas, feelings, customs and modes of speech, and with a climate, vegetation, and animated life altogether peculiar to itself.
>
> Alfred Russel Wallace, *The Malay Archipelago*

We were making do without servants in Indonesian *gotong royong* (everybody pitches in) style. Betsy, a recently divorced West Sumatran who my brother met on an *opelet* ride, had moved into the servant's quarters out back and was doing the housework and some cooking in exchange for her board. I was taking care of the yard, which was a more manageable job now that Galunggung wasn't coughing up a storm every afternoon. Jim did most of the cooking.

Bandung had few bars or nightclubs and the city pretty much rolled up the sidewalks after sunset. My brother whiled the time away building a life-size sculpture of a voluptuous and naked mermaid, his Nyai Loro Kidul, or "Queen of the South Seas", by the garden pond out back, which fortunately was well hidden from neighboring eyes by large mango and avocado trees. He also rigged up a solar water heater contraption so we could have warm water for our morning *mandi.* Occasionally it actually worked.

In the evening we sat in the living room, filled with Jim's antiques – *goleks* peering at us from dark corners, *kris* swords and huge batik paintings on the wall, sipping whiskey and listening to the BBC on his Sony short-wave radio. We had no TV, and there was nothing to see on it anyway. Commercial-free TVRI showed endless talking head shows, though what they found to talk about in the depoliticized world of the New Order was barely disguised propaganda. Cheap melodramas and old Indonesian films rounded out the limited fare.

We read the English-language dailies, mostly for laughs. "Indonesia exports 500,000 tons of semen to China" went one memorable headline in *The Indonesia Observer (semen* being the Indonesian word for cement.) The newspaper had a columnist, Professor Suryabrata, that Jim especially enjoyed reading aloud for his sheer daftness and circular reasoning.

"It is a pity that we don't have an Indonesian word for 'humaniora,'" the professor began one column. "I am sure there is one, and if we can't find it, we should make one up. For the time being, however, we use this word humaniora. It sounds ministerial and old European." "Too bad there's no English word humaniora, either, professor," Jim commented dryly.

Sometimes Jim would slip into his alter ego, Percy Bathos, a 19th century naturalist and colleague of Sir Alfred Russel Wallace, creator of the Wallace Line, an imaginary boundary that runs through the middle of Sulawesi and between the islands of Lombok and Bali which separates Asian flora and fauna from Australian ones.

"Bathos" would engage me in conversation. "Good evening, old bean. How goes the education of the natives? Trust you're ennobling their spirits. Yes, quite. Well I was having tea today at the Savoy with Reginald Flambam of the U.S. Geological Service. You must have heard about his brother Roger. Met an untimely end under the wheels of a trishaw, poor sod. Told me some amazing stuff, indeed, about the Jupiter Effect[3]. The influence of this planet is having the

---

3 *The Jupiter Effect* was a best-selling book in 1974 that predicted that a close alignment of the Planets in March of 1982 would create a number of disasters, including earthquakes and volcanic eruptions.

most extraordinary effect on the fault lines and volcanoes here in the Dutch Indies, you understand. All the magma, it seems, is rolling up to one side and farting and belching through the pliant crust." He blew smoke rings from a cigarette to demonstrate.

Betsy cackled at the impromptu skit and Bambang, outraged as always when someone besides him shrieked in the house, crowed in protest. Betsy scolded him bitterly and chased the bantam fool out of the house with a stick broom. Bambang had become a permanent house guest and had taken to roosting in the dining room, stalking and squawking at anybody in his way. One day, Betsy chopped off his head and served him for dinner. He tasted awful. You can't eat an animal that you've named.

Indonesia was getting under my skin, and it was a writer's paradise, if only I could find someone to publish my freelance work. I was keen to get back to journalism. I had joined the *Boca Raton News* in Florida as a reporter a few years earlier. But after an argument with the editor, I impetuously typed up a letter of resignation, which he promptly accepted. Note to self: never write an angry letter of resignation without having another job lined up.

I eventually joined an advertising and public relations agency and then one of my clients hired me to be their Southeast U.S. manager. This was in the fall of 1981. A year later, I would be Southeast, alright, but in Southeast Asia. Ronald Reagan became president, the United States fell into recession, and I got laid off. That's when I sold everything I had and bought a ticket to Indonesia. I had come to Indonesia with hardly a nickel to my name. My plan was to work my way home.

I was taking *pencak silat* classes from a young mystic, who spoke to me only in Bahasa Indonesia. He said he imbibed many of his martial arts moves after communing for days with the Queen of the South Seas, sitting in the surf on Pangandaran beach. He was scary strange, one of those chaps who chew glass and cuts open his stomach to wash his intestines – or so he claimed – but his school was kind enough to sponsor my visa, when the gentlemen from Triad no longer had juice with the folks in *Immigrasi* (Immigration).

By December, I had saved enough money from my teaching gigs to buy a plane ticket home. But I kept putting it off, much to my mother's dismay. The U.S. was still in recession and...I was having a ball on Indoplanet. I wrote a letter to my parents back in Pittsburgh. "I am still thrilling to the circumstance of being in a foreign culture. It is very stimulating and educational for me. And unlike the U.S., there are many more opportunities for the likes of someone like me in the Indo-Singapore-Hong Kong-Tokyo stream of things. To tell you the truth, I'm preparing to make contacts with magazines and newspapers in these areas, to get my writing career on track again."

That was when I had my fateful introduction to Bambang Harymurti. But before I went off to meet his boss Amir Daud, a senior editor at *Tempo* and soon to be managing editor at *The Jakarta Post*, I consulted the *I Ching*, or Book of Changes. This was something I had been doing for years, ever since college. I found it to be a good meditation exercise, particularly when weighing new courses. That night, at Joe's Pizza on Jalan Dago, I tossed three coins six times in the prescribed manner and produced the hexagram "Introspection" in the *I Ching*. "You are in a position to set a good example for others by the value you hold and the beneficial actions you take... others will see clearly that your actions are in harmony with All-That-Is, and they will look up to you as a role model."

"Good grief!" I thought to myself. "I just want to write some stories."

᷒᷒

CHAPTER ONE
CREATING A NEW ORDER

Jusuf Wanandi took his place in the line outside Minister of Information Ali Murtopo's office in Jakarta one hot July morning in 1982. After 18 years working with Murtopo, he was not surprised by the parade of leftist intellectuals, jihadists, gangsters, double-dealers, teachers, preachers, journalists, tribalists, union leaders, shamus and finks, also waiting their turn. This was Murtopo's intelligence network – a motley group that Indonesians had long called "the Murtopo Zoo."

Eventually Jusuf was ushered in. He was struck, as always, by how unadorned Murtopo's office was, how simple and unpretentious. His staff consisted of one aide-de-camp with a typewriter on a table piled high with files. Murtopo himself sat behind a desk devoid of paper, peering owlishly from behind black, horn-rimmed spectacles – Jusuf had convinced him years ago to abandon the tinted glasses that made him look like a tinpot generalissimo. The office was no longer smoke filled, either. He had quit chain-smoking unfiltered clove cigarettes since his massive coronary a few years earlier. Wanandi sat down, eager to discuss his new idea: a newspaper that would explain the New Order to the world.

Ali Murtopo had been President Suharto's right-hand man for nearly 25 years and by 1982 he was nearing the end of his career. Born on September 23, 1924 in Blora, Central Java, he had left school at 15 to join Hizbullah, a Muslim militia organized by the Japanese occupiers during World War II, and, after the war, the staff of Ahmad Yani, future leader of Indonesia's armed forces. Murtopo had risen to commander in Yani's Banteng Raiders, a special force created to battle insurgency in Central Java in the 1950s.

In 1956, still in command of his Banteng unit, he was approached by a young officer called Suharto, who had just been appointed commander of the prestigious Diponegoro Command in Central Java. Later in 1958, the province was put under martial law making Suharto the military governor. He recruited Murtopo to be his political assistant, joining Yoga Sugama his intelligence chief and a Javanese mystic called Sudjono Humardhani, who was put in charge of finance. The four of them would constitute Suharto's "kitchen cabinet" during the early years of the New Order – the heart of his regime.

It was not, however, to be smooth sailing. While it was common for army commanders to supplement meager budget allocations with some local business arrangements, Suharto apparently went above and beyond the call of duty with two ethnic Chinese businessmen, Bob Hasan and Liem Sioe Liong, who would remain close to him for the next four decades. His army superiors accused him in 1960 of smuggling and illegal trading. The group was broken up, and the military men exiled in disgrace to training colleges around Java.

Jusuf Wanandi first met Murtopo, the man who was to change his life, in 1963 at a seminar sponsored by the Army's Strategic Reserve Command or Kostrad, which Suharto was now heading, having done his penance at staff college. Jusuf had argued at the seminar that Indonesia was better off aligning with the West rather than China – which President Sukarno was tilting towards. Jusuf was teaching law at the University of Indonesia, the most prestigious law faculty in the country. He also headed the Catholic Student Union, one of several student groups leading protests against the increasingly authoritarian rule of Sukarno and his perceived bias toward the pro-Chinese communist party.

Born Lim Bian Kie in the West Sumatran coal-mining town of

Sawahlunto in 1937,[1] Jusuf Wanandi had Chinese blood in his veins, but that was almost his only surviving connection to China. His great-grandfather, a member of the Lim clan, was born in Fujian province and his grandfather had attended school in China. But his father and mother both went to Dutch Catholic schools in Indonesia and converted to Catholicism. Chinese was not even spoken at home. The young Bian Kie and his brothers were sent to the Jesuit Canisius High School in Jakarta.

In March 1964, when Jusuf was a teacher and activist, Sukarno was at the height of his anti-Western rhetoric. His "Guided Democracy," his pro-China stance and his call for Indonesia to be self-sufficient were bankrupting the country and alienating the West. In an iconic speech that month he told the United States to "go to hell with your aid." He then launched his "Confrontation" campaign against the creation of Malaysia, a union of the old British colonies on the Malay Peninsula with those on the island of Borneo. This new state, he thundered, was a "neo-colonial puppet," and called on the army and the PKI to resist it.

Confrontation was a mess. A few hapless volunteers parachuted onto the Malayan peninsula but were quickly rounded up before they could do much harm. On Borneo, the eastern half of the new state, the Indonesian army was dragged into a series of messy jungle forays, fighting British and Australian forces allied to Malaysia.

The generals wanted out, and Yani, now army commander, turned to his former comrade-in-arms Murtopo to forge secret contacts with Malaysia. "Yani," Jusuf recalls, "was worried that Confrontation was the wrong thing to do, because that would only increase our dependence on China and enmity against the USA." He also feared that with so many of his troops spread around Malaysia, the main island of Java was vulnerable to a takeover by the PKI. Murtopo, Jusuf recalls, was blunt. "'Then why don't you stop it?' Ali said. And

---

1 In 1966, the Suharto regime ordered that all Chinese, some of whom it suspected of supporting the Communist Party of Indonesia, or PKI, change their names to Indonesian-sounding ones. Wana means forest in Javanese, which is also what Lim means in Chinese. Yusuf's younger brother Lim Bian Koen was in Sofia, Bulgaria when the order came down and so he chose the name of the Bulgarian capital as the basis for his new first name, Sofyan, and, along with his brothers, Wanandi for his surname.

Yani said 'How can I?' And Ali said, 'Give me the chance and I will stop it.'"

Yani gave Murtopo his chance, and *Operasi Khusus* (special operations) was established, with Suharto in command, and Murtopo as project officer. "Opsus," as it came to be called, was to become Murtopo's all-purpose covert operations and intelligence unit for the next decade.

Murtopo quickly got to work. He contacted separatist guerrillas in Sumatra – the same ones he had once fought and who were now siding with Kuala Lumpur – and asked them to act as go-betweens in contacting the Malaysians. Secret meetings were arranged between representatives of the two countries in Hong Kong and Bangkok at the end of 1964.

Leonardus Benyamin "Benny" Murdani, then a military intelligence officer in Kostrad and later a powerful armed forces commander in the Suharto regime, pretended to be a Garuda Airlines representative as his cover at the clandestine talks. Neither Sukarno nor Malaysian Prime Minister Tunku Abdul Rahman were aware of the backdoor talks. "The unconventionality of this man!" Jusuf says of his mentor Murtopo. "He was bright and brave and unorthodox." Murtopo's critics, however, saw a ruthless Machiavellianism behind the bright, unorthodox façade.

Sukarno's lurch to the left was angering anti-communist student groups like Wanandi's as the Year of Living Dangerously unfolded in 1965. "He was becoming more anti-capitalist and anti-West as well, and so it became a problem for all the right-wing students, especially in our (student union)," Jusuf says. In August, Sukarno announced Indonesia, which had already stormed out of the United Nations, was withdrawing from the International Monetary Fund and the World Bank as well. In his Independence Day speech on August 17, Sukarno proclaimed an alliance with Asian communist nations: what he called the "Jakarta-Phnom Penh-Hanoi-Peking-Pyongyang Axis."

As the situation unraveled, the military found itself at the center of attention, courted by both the Soviet Union, anxious to curb China's influence on the PKI, and the United States, which was concerned about the spread of Communism in Indonesia at the peak of its military build-up in Vietnam. Meanwhile, inflation was running at 600 percent, rice and key commodities were running short, and Sukarno himself was chronically ill, causing some on the left to fret that he would die and leave them exposed to the wrath of the military. Sukarno's proposed new "fifth force," comprising a million peasants and workers, to join Confrontation, appeared a direct threat to the army's position, angering Yani and Defense Minister Gen. Nasution

By then Suharto and his team were back in favor after two years of penance at military training college. In 1962, Suharto had been put in command of the campaign to liberate West New Guinea (Irian Jaya), his plans for an invasion thwarted by the Dutch, who, with some arm-twisting from Washington, agreed to withdraw. Suharto was promoted to major-general and made commander of Kostrad, a little known but elite strategic reserve command based in Jakarta.

His career, however, seemed to be going nowhere when a group of leftist officers launched their coup attempt on the night of September 30, 1965. Kidnapping and killing six top generals, including Yani who was shot at his home, the rebels set up a base at Halim Air Force Base south of Jakarta. Somehow spared, Suharto led the counter-coup and emerged victorious, blaming the PKI and overseeing a pogrom that saw hundreds of thousands of communists and suspected communists murdered. Sukarno, despite being weakened by the scourge, remained in power.

Suharto and his team could not confront Sukarno directly; for that they turned to the students. "Suharto couldn't move openly with the army against Sukarno, because Sukarno was still too powerful," Jusuf recalls. "And if he was going to start to move, it would be considered a coup. Number two, Suharto at this time was politically nothing compared to Sukarno." Jusuf admired Suharto because he had been the only one willing to confront Sukarno from the start. "But he couldn't do it openly or too blatantly. So we had to be literally his shock troops. We were on the streets every day agitating to get rid of the communists."

And the students needed Suharto to protect them. Sukarno still had some troops and police loyal to him and they were looking to round up student leaders, including Jusuf and his younger brother, Sofyan, the Catholic Student Union leaders. Behind them was a growing alliance with Suharto's key advisors: Murtopo and Gen. Sudjono Humardhani, Benny Murdani, Yoga Sugama, Kemal Idris, Sarwo Edhie – the latter two known as 'red barons', the paratroopers identified by their red berets. "During that period, I always had two or three red baron guards with me all the time," Sofyan said.

Day after day, Jusuf, Sofyan and other student leaders who had come together in the Indonesian Student Action Front (KAMI) poured tens of thousands of students onto the streets of Jakarta. With other supporters from the "Pancasila Front", consisting of political parties and other organizations including Nahdlatul Ulama and the Catholic Party, they stopped hundreds of cars, deflating the tires, in order to snarl traffic and paralyze the capital. They spray-painted slogans along walls and buildings denouncing the communist party.

With the help of Suharto's troops, the demonstrations became bigger and more explosive at the start of 1966. And because so many of the students were children of the educated middle class, the movement acquired broad support among the elite and influential. Hardly a home in Jakarta was unaffected. Even small children were skipping school and their older brothers and sisters would be gone for days.[2] "Students were very critical to Suharto's rise to the Presidency," Jusuf said. "He needed the students, actually; they were willing to do the job on the streets for him and put pressure on Sukarno."

For the ardently anti-communist Wanandi brothers those were heady days.

"We put pressure on him to disband [the PKI], but he was always resistant to that and always wanted to protect them," Jusuf said. "So at the end, we had to get rid of Sukarno."

On March 8, the student movement took a fateful turn when, early that morning, they stormed into the foreign ministry, ransacked it, and held it for around five hours before police expelled them with tear gas. One of the chief demands of the student movement was to put Foreign Minister Subandrio on trial as a pro-Beijing communist sympathizer. A free-for-all rumble ensued on the lawns

---

2   John Hughes, *The End of Sukarno*, Archipelago Press, p. 230

of the ministry after pro-Sukarno students swept in to protect the ministry. That same day, leftist students swarmed over the gates at the American embassy and bombarded it with rocks and Molotov cocktails, or gasoline bombs.

The following day, it was the Chinese mission's turn to defend itself. The Wanandi brothers helped lead an attack on the villa housing the official New China News Agency and on March 10 the students overran the Chinese consulate-general and a house used by the commercial attaché. They made a bonfire of the furniture and files on the lawns outside.

Jusuf said this was a tactic to keep hot-heads from marching into Chinatown to burn shops belonging to Indonesia's ethnic Chinese. "So the Chinese (mission) was on the way, and instead of burning our own people's shops, we burned their embassy," Jusuf says.

With Jakarta on the brink of anarchy, Sofyan and other student leaders hid out at Ali Murtopo's headquarters in a white, Dutch colonial mansion not far from Independence Square, the epicenter of the protests. "They were looking for us. And the military was hiding us here," said Sofyan, now 66, in an interview at the house, which he bought and restored years later to be the corporate headquarters of his Gemala conglomerate. "There were at least 20 of us hiding here until the 11th of March."

That's when Sukarno, who had earlier that day retreated to his palace in Bogor, was forced to sign the so-called *Supersemar* document that handed emergency powers to Suharto, and guaranteed the safety of the president and his family. Sofyan remembers a military officer going around the house kicking students awake, and shouting "Wake up, wake up, you've won!"

Sukarno had divided the world into OLDFOS or Old Established Forces, and NEFOS, New Emerging Forces. But the student movement, with support from the middle class and the military, was consigning the aging and erratic revolutionary to an old order. The attack on the Chinese mission was one of the final blows before Sukarno succumbed to the New Order.

Semar, the wise clown in *wayang* plays, seemed to be Lt. Gen.

Suharto's muse and *Supersemar*, an abbreviation for *Surat Perintah Sebelas Maret* (Order of March 11th) gave him all the authority he needed. But Sukarno was the one trying to have the last laugh, clinging to power, making his rabble-rousing speeches, looking to the masses for support against the army and the Jakarta middle class. With the anti-Sukarno student movement threatening to renew their street campaign, Suharto finally agreed in March 1967 to ask the People's Assembly to strip the "President for Life" of all powers. The parliament did his bidding as it would continue to do for the next 32 years. Suharto was appointed "Acting President" and Sukarno, his health broken, was put under house arrest in Jakarta and died in disgrace three years later. Suharto took his time easing Sukarno out of power, Jusuf says, because his Javanese soul could not abide an abrupt and unpleasant departure for the ruler. He would seek the same conditions for himself when his time came to step down three decades later.

Jusuf, his work done, prepared to go back to teaching law. But Murtopo had other plans. He wanted Jusuf to join his special operations, Opsus. "That's how I got involved in politics," Jusuf said. He had just turned 30.

His first task was to help build a political machine to support Suharto. That work was interrupted two years later when he was asked to help organize a plebiscite to ensure that Irian – the western half of the giant island of New Guinea – became Indonesia's newest province.

The U.N. had declared that the people of Irian should decide themselves whether to integrate into Indonesia. But it fell to Suharto's government to decide how. The "Act of Free Choice," it was decreed, should be conducted by a vote of about 1,000 leaders who would be chosen by the community under the supervision of the Indonesian military. Jusuf said they felt heavy pressure from Suharto to make the campaign a success. "Can you imagine how damaging that would have been to his credibility as president?" Jusuf recalls. "A young president losing Irian Jaya in 1969 that he won as commander in 1962?"

Murtopo worked in typically unconventional style, overcoming the lack of budget by appropriating some $17 million of unclaimed Malaysian funds which had been frozen in Indonesian accounts during Confrontation to finance the campaign. "It was mostly black money, smugglers' money," Jusuf recalls. "Ali asked Suharto to use that money, because we had no money then."

Jusuf used some of the money to send groups of students on a "peace corps" mission after the plebiscite to help improve conditions for 1.3 million tribesmen, some of whom were still living in the Neolithic Age. "We sent more than 200 students to Irian Jaya as a domestic peace corps to get the trust back from the Papuans after the military plundered them." The campaign was vintage Ali: "He sent tobacco, beer, food stuff, prefab houses, everything."

The Irianese delegates voted overwhelmingly for integration with Indonesia, a decision sanctioned by the U.S. and the U.N. but condemned by some foreign observers who were not allowed to witness the voting.

During such adventures, Jusuf was able to watch Murtopo up close as he overcame the limitations of his education. "He was smart, naturally smart," Jusuf said. "He had little education – second class of junior high. You could see he was smart, but you could also see the lacunas because of a limited educational background. Sometimes he would jump to something and the logic would be missing."

Jusuf, by contrast, was an educated man, able to discourse like a Harvard fellow at an Asia-Pacific panel in a bespoke suit, or chair a board meeting of *The Jakarta Post* in his trademark batik shirt. But both were men of action – operators from behind the scenes – and Jusuf would remain at Murtopo's side for more than one and a half decades.

Jusuf's friends call him "the Voice," both because of his prolific output of books, monograms and essays over the years and because he could be as blunt and exclamatory as a truck horn, and as passionate as a revolutionary. Longtime friend Fikri Jufri, his senior at Canisius High School, recalls that he could always hear Jusuf long before he spotted him in the school hallways.

Jusuf has not mellowed with age at 70, though now he has more time to indulge his tastes for classical music, traditional Indonesian paintings, fine wine and tennis. He still has "the Voice," but now it is finding expression through the memoirs he is writing.

Flushed with the plebiscite success, Jusuf turned his attention back to organizing an election. Suharto had been in power for two years and so far had there had been no democracy. But building a political machine for the New Order was going slowly. Murtopo had ensured the parliament would drag its feet over issuing an election law to give him time to reorder the political landscape, but after two years the tactic was wearing thin.

Murtopo and his team were summoned to the Presidential Palace. Suharto was furious. "We wanted to postpone elections, because we weren't ready," Jusuf recalls. "And Suharto said to us: 'I'm waiting for you? Until you're ready? You know what is going to happen? It will never happen. The people will hang me! And you will clap your hands. If I listen to you, there will never be elections!'"

Murtopo and Jusuf complained they still had no political party. "Use Golkar," Suharto said. Golkar, a Sukarno-era conglomeration of various civic groups, remained under the control of its founder, the army. Murtopo's group asked to put control of the party and the campaign in professional hands. Suharto agreed. "At that time, we could still bargain with Suharto," Jusuf said.

So Murtopo was given the task of organizing the election, appointing Jusuf to be Golkar's campaign manager. It was a daunting challenge, given the grassroots support of the long-established parties, particularly the Muslim ones. Suharto and Murtopo would deal with that in the years to come by manipulating mergers of existing parties. Non-Islamic parties--Sukarno's old PNI, a Catholic party and a socialist one – were eventually melded into the Indonesian Democratic Party (PDI). Islamic parties were corralled into the secular-sounding United Development Party.

The armed forces, embedded in the countryside through its "*dwifungsi*" (dual function) military and home affairs mission, ensured a good turnout for Golkar in the 1971 elections. It won with 63 percent of the vote, an astounding result even to Murtopo's group.

For Jusuf the 1971 election was not just a political campaign: It also launched his career as a newspaperman. Murtopo, aware of the need to spread Golkar's message, gave Jusuf 50 million rupiah (about US$130,000 at the time) and told him to start a party newspaper. He wanted it published on March 11 (*Supersemar* day) – three days before the election. "In three days I worked like mad to get 10-11 people to put out a paper of eight pages," Jusuf recalled. At its peak, *Suara Karya* had a circulation of 150,000, almost all of it to civil servants who were required to subscribe to the rag.

By the mid-1970s, Suharto's New Order had taken root, with his assistants Murtopo and Sudjono Humardhani the key players alongside him. "Humardhani and Ali were among the six or seven personal assistants to Suharto in the beginning. And in the end there were these two," Jusuf said.

Sofyan went to work for Humardhani, who in addition to being the president's chief financial advisor was also his channel to the Javanese spiritual world. "He was the only one who could see Suharto in his bedroom besides madam," Sofyan recalls. Suharto would dispatch Humardhani to various mystic priests in Java. They would go to sacred spots, a cave or a special lake. The mystic would go into a trance, and tell the future. "Sudjono would make notes and report back to Suharto," says Sofyan with a shrug.

For Jusuf himself there was plenty of work: His next project after the election was setting up a an institution to provide long-term strategic planning for the government, backed by Murtopo and Humardhani. Thus was born the Centre for Strategic and International Studies (CSIS), which remains today Indonesia's leading think-tank.

Suharto embraced a group of economists who became known as his "Berkeley Mafia" technocrats, whose policies succeeded in curbing inflation, stabilizing the currency and attracting aid and investment. Along with the best and brightest of the student movement co-opted into New Order policy-making, Suharto presided over a period of relative calm. It was not to last.

Some of the same students who had helped Suharto come to power now began voicing their opposition to it, chiefly over corruption and Indonesia's new strategy of development that emphasized big projects, foreign investment and aid. Indonesia cultivated ties with Japan for access to aid through the Asian Development Bank and investment. For its critics, Japan appeared to be reinventing its World War II "Co-Prosperity Sphere" in Asia, this time not at the end of a gun barrel but through aid and investment.

There was criticism, too, of Suharto's wife *Ibu* Tien, who had become known as "Madam Tien Percent" (*tien* being the Dutch word for 10) over rumors she was getting kickbacks from big state projects on behalf of the first family.

Things came to a head in late 1973 when a rice crisis pushed many Indonesians back into hard times. Criticism grew: In November of that year, several prominent individuals signed a statement critical of the power of foreign investments in Indonesia. Earlier, former Vice President Hatta and his Anti-Corruption Commission gave a critical assessment on high-level corruption.

Simmering resentments boiled over when Japanese Prime Minister Kakuei Tanaka arrived for a state visit in mid-January 1974. Tens of thousands of student demonstrators roamed the streets of Jakarta looting and setting fire to Japanese cars. Eleven were killed. Tanaka was flown by helicopter from the Presidential Palace to Halim Airport rather than risk a car journey through town.

Ali Murtopo was, as ever, at the heart of things. Only this time he was not alone in trying to control events. The crisis, which was later known by a New Order acronym of *Malari* for "the 15th January Disaster", arose out of a power struggle between Murtopo and Gen. Soemitro, the powerful head of the security command called Kopkamtib, and deputy commander of the Armed Forces.

Whoever started the rivalry, by late 1973 it was showing signs of getting out of control. "I was next to Ali," recalls Jusuf. "That was how I followed all this so closely. The offices of CSIS were next to Murtopo's. I was always there to help him." Things might have been resolved behind closed doors. Jusuf recalls, "but the straw that broke the camel's back was this problem with the students." Murtopo, Jusuf says, felt that Soemitro was egging the students on. "Soemitro went to the students, in ITB [the Bandung Institute of Technology],

University of Indonesia, everywhere, and invited them to criticize Suharto's government. So then of course, they got excited."

Murtopo returned from a trip to Australia and New Zealand in October 1973 to find that he and Humardhani had become the targets of student anger. The two men, Jusuf recalls, had become the butt of protests against a development strategy that called for big capital-intensive projects built with foreign aid and investment. "They felt these two were the compradors of the Japanese interest," Jusuf said.

Murtopo, who had no firm support within the military, felt increasingly vulnerable. By December of 1973, with student criticism at its height, Soemitro, who was in charge of security as the armed forces deputy commander, withdrew the detachment of soldiers guarding Murtopo's house, Jusuf said. Murtopo complained to Suharto, who had until then largely remained above the fray. Suharto called a meeting of all of his top generals at Merdeka Palace. There he ordered them to put aside their differences.

"He tried to patch things up between the two," Jusuf said. "He called all his Javanese generals together. Suharto said, 'let me be very frank with you. If there is anybody who would like to take over from me, let's organize it in a constitutional way,'" Murtopo told Jusuf afterward.

Soemitro denied that was ever his intention and broke down in tears. "My only weakness is women," Soemitro told the meeting, according to Murtopo. That was Saturday, Dec. 29. The following Monday the two rivals held a press conference to say there was no problem between them, contrary to rumor. "He and Soemitro were then forced to work together to calm the situation down," Jusuf said.

But by then the student movement had taken on a momentum of its own and the problem was now how to defuse it, Jusuf said. "It's not like flicking a switch. You need time, three to six months to whip them up, and another three months to calm them down.

"It was dangerous. There were troop movements," Jusuf said.

In the end, the students rampaged and the army stayed in the barracks. Both Murtopo and Soemitro were badly damaged – Soemitro forced to resign, and the system of special assistants disbanded.

The Wanandi brothers did not emerge unscathed. Jusuf spent those fraught days in January with Murtopo trying to understand and manage the military maneuvering and power plays behind the crisis. The protesters had targeted the Wanandi brothers because of their association with Suharto's "financial generals." People carried signs that read: "Hang the Wanandi brothers."

For Sofyan it was a defining time. "I felt embarrassed because so many of my student friends were attacking us as non-pribumi (Chinese). That is when I saw how unfair the whole political situation was. Because you're so idealistic. It was something that hurt me so deeply. And that's when I decided to move from politics to business. I could see we were the easiest target…because we were Catholic, Chinese and not from Java." After that, Sofyan embraced both the New Order and his own ethnicity, becoming a spokesman for an informal group of several hundred Chinese-Indonesian businesses that Suharto called upon from time to time to contribute to various causes – including election funds for Golkar. Sofyan's chummy relationship with Suharto, however, would change drastically in the 1990s.

By the time Jusuf sat in his office in 1982, Ali Murtopo was not the man he was. He was information minister – a fancier title but wielding less power than before. His health had declined and Suharto wanted him to take it easy, maybe take a leadership position in his Supreme Advisory Council of New Order heroes, acolytes and cronies. But he was still a player, illustrated by the steady stream in and out of his office.

The New Order was in solid economic health – approaching self-sufficiency in rice, while rocketing oil prices after the second Arab oil embargo in 1979 had filled Indonesia's coffers – and was able to crush what little political opposition it faced. The military now occupied East Timor (see box story); another eruption of student agitation in the late 1970s had led to a permanent ban on political activities on campus; the open opposition of a group of retired generals and prominent civilians called "the Petition of 50" had been extinguished by making them all virtual non-persons.

The latest election, in May 1982, had gone better than expected:

Golkar had won almost two-thirds of the vote, despite riots in Jakarta. Security forces had opened fire, killing seven protesters. *Tempo* magazine, the country's most respected weekly, was closed for two months for reporting on the incident.

Murtopo, however, was unhappy. He was particularly annoyed about what he deemed was unbalanced coverage of Indonesia by Western wire services and newspapers. And there was no worthwhile English-language publication for foreigners to read Indonesia's side of events. Indonesia was the largest and potentially richest country in Southeast Asia but had two embarrassingly bad English-language dailies that were more the object of ridicule than a serious source of news.

Jusuf had an answer. "I asked him: 'Why don't you give us a chance to produce something decent in English?'" Jusuf recalled. "Because it's such a shame that we as the biggest ASEAN country, and who are supposed to be the leader of the region, cannot even produce a decent paper in English.' That was the emphasis."

But setting up the *Post* would not be as simple as setting up *Suara Karya*, the mouthpiece of Golkar, which had taken him just three days. A new English-language newspaper had to have credibility from the start, not to mention journalistic talent and resources. So Jusuf was about to pitch an idea he knew would appeal to Murtopo.

He proposed that the new newspaper be collectively owned and operated by the largest media groups in Indonesia, and bitter rivals to boot: Golkar's *Suara Karya*; the Catholic-affiliated morning newspaper *Kompas*; its biggest competitor, the afternoon daily and Protestant *Sinar Harapan* (Ray of Hope); and the secular weekly magazine, *Tempo*.

Murtopo, the unorthodox thinker and master political puppeteer, loved the idea. Giving *The Jakarta Post* a license to publish would be one of his last official acts as a cabinet minister.

Now it fell to Jusuf to bring the elements together. He had to use his entire suite of skills to put together the unlikely and unwieldy group he hoped would publish the *Post*.

He went first to see Jacob Oetama, the Javanese Catholic co-

Operation Komodo

The prospect of having "another Cuba" at Indonesia's backdoor was a source of growing alarm to the staunchly anti-communist Suharto and his cohort of generals in 1974. That year a leftist military coup in Portugal had led to a policy of rapid decolonization in Portugal's Asian and African territories, including East Timor, which faced the prospect of independence or integration with neighboring Indonesia. Jakarta feared an independent and left-leaning East Timor at its doorstep could serve as inspiration to other separatist movements in the far-flung Indonesian archipelago.

Since East Timor lies near key shipping lanes, the United States, Indonesia and Australia were also concerned the territory could turn into a Soviet satellite – a Cuba in Asia – at a time when America was pulling out of Vietnam.

So in 1974, Suharto took Australia's Labor Prime Minister Gough Whitlam to his cave to talk about it. They flew to Wonosobo in Central Java and proceeded to the Indonesian president's favorite meditation spot, the Cave of Semar on the eerie volcanic plateau, said to be at the exact physical center of Java. Whitlam told Suharto just what he wanted to hear: that an independent East Timor would be an unviable state and a potential threat to the stability of the region.

Thus was born *Operasi Komodo*, named after the large lizard that occupies a nearby island of the same name. Another of Ali Murtopo's brainstorms, this latest in his series of "opsus" projects aimed to find a solution to the East Timor problem, by diplomacy – or other means.

After his *tête-à-tête* with Gough Whitlam, Suharto sent Murtopo to Lisbon in September and London in November 1974 to talk to the junta. "It was a very uncertain regime and very leftist," said Jusuf Wanandi, then executive director of the Centre for Strategic and International Studies, who worked with Murtopo on the diplomatic side of the operation. "We asked them to give the people of East Timor a chance to know Indonesia. And so Ali asked for a transition period for them to learn about governance. Ali and the Portuguese agreed to a 7-to-8 year transition period of getting to know each other before a plebiscite. Because they were not trained! There were only 12 (university) graduates when we

took over." Follow-up meetings in Rome between the foreign ministers
of the two countries in March 1975 confirmed the transition agreement,
Jusuf said.

But things were unfolding differently in East Timor as three parties
struggled for political supremacy: the UDT representing civil servants,
the leftist Fretilin with support in the countryside, and the pro-Indonesia
Apodeti party. Jakarta accused the Portuguese junta of arming the
Fretilin. With diplomacy floundering, *Operasi Komodo* turned to covert
operations.

Indonesian military intelligence began trying to sow divisions
among the pro-independence parties, while promoting support for the
pro-Indonesian Apodeti party. Indonesian military officials told UDT
leaders Jakarta would never allow a Fretilin-led administration in an
independent East Timor. That, and the threat of Fretilin to take over,
persuaded the UDT to attempt to seize power in August 1975, but the
better-armed and organized Fretlin gained the upper hand instead.

Indonesia sought to portray the tussle for power between Apodeti,
UDT and Fretilin as a civil war, while making secret preparations for an
invasion. In October 1975, in Balibo, a mountain outpost on the border
between East and West Timor, Indonesian Special Forces, conducting
covert operations under *Operasi Komodo* in East Timor, killed five
reporters working for Australian television networks – two Australians,
a New Zealander and two Britons.

Jakarta has always insisted they were caught in the crossfire during
a confrontation with Fretilin fighters at Balibo, just over the Indonesian
border that divides the island into East and West Timor. But in
November, 2007, an Australian coroner in New South Wales ruled the
five had been captured and then killed by Indonesian commandos to
stop them from reporting on the clandestine operations prior to the
actual invasion in December. The coroner, Dorelle Pinch, also said there
was strong circumstantial evidence that the orders to kill the newsmen
came ultimately from the commander who was in charge of planning
and leading the invasion, Maj. Gen. Leonardus Benyamin Murdani,
an Indonesian military hero who died in 2004 at the age of 74. Jusuf
said he has always doubted that the Roman Catholic Murdani, whom

he was close to for four decades, was in any position to give an order like that as he had already relinquished operational control to military headquarters.

The deaths of the Balibo five – Greg Shackleton, Tony Steward, Gary Cunningham, Brian Peters and Malcolm Rennie – had been a long-running source of tension between Australia and Indonesia, with their relatives accusing both countries of a cover-up.

Indonesia's invasion plans were now a poorly kept secret. On November 28, 1975, Fretilin made a unilateral declaration of independence of the Democratic Republic of East Timor (Republica Democratica de Timor-Leste in Portuguese), which almost no country recognized. Indonesia's response was to have UDT, Apodeti, and other leaders of smaller parties sign a declaration calling for integration with Indonesia. Known as the Balibo Declaration, it was drafted by Indonesian intelligence and signed in Bali, not Balibo. Fretilin leader Xanana Gusmao, now East Timor's prime minister, famously described it as the "Bali *bohong* Declaration," a pun on the Indonesian word for lie.

Even up until then, Jakarta believed Indonesian objectives could be achieved with diplomatic pressure, Jusuf Wanandi said. Indonesia was poised to invade East Timor when U.S. President Gerald Ford and Secretary of State Henry Kissinger made a brief visit to Jakarta on December 6. "Kissinger talked to Benny (Murdani), who said we have to go in," Jusuf recalled. "'Just make sure you do it after we leave. And if you feel you have to do it, do it quickly and neatly,'" Jusuf quoted Kissinger as saying. "Well, as we all know, it wasn't quick and it wasn't neat."

Neither Kissinger nor Ford ever acknowledged giving the green light for an invasion. But no sooner were they "wheels up" flying out of Jakarta than the invasion began. Suharto never explicitly ordered the invasion, Jusuf says (just as he never explicitly ordered a massacre of communists after the abortive coup). "He simply indicated in a Javanese way that the job should be done, but that he didn't wish to know about it."[+]

In the weeks after the invasion, a series of U.N. resolutions, supported by the United States, called for a quick withdrawal of Indonesian forces. Indonesia may have hoped that would be the case, but instead it became mired in a low-level conflict for 24 years in East Timor – its own Vietnam-like quagmire. Some estimates put the number of those killed in the conflict or dead from starvation and related diseases during the occupation at up to 250,000 people. USAID in 1979 estimated that 300,000 East Timorese – nearly half the population – had been uprooted and moved into camps controlled by the Indonesian armed forces. In 1999, with Indonesia wounded by financial crisis and undergoing its own wrenching transition to democracy, East Timor voted to break free of Indonesian rule and gained full independence.

† *Suharto: A Political Biography*, by Robert Edward Elson, p. 213

founder of *Kompas.* By then, the daily had the largest circulation of any newspaper in Indonesia, building a reputation for comprehensive and credible reporting – and long-winded, intellectual writing. Its co-founding publisher, PK Ojong, was an activist with the Catholic Party and a leading light of the non-communist left. The launch of *Kompas* three months before the 1965 coup was quietly encouraged by the military, which saw in it an ally in the battle against Sukarno for hearts and minds.

That did not mean that *Kompas* had an easy ride. Jacob, the son of an elementary school teacher, joined Ojong in setting up Kompas after getting a journalism degree from Gadjah Mada University in Yogyakarta in 1962 at the age of 31 and became chief editor at *Kompas* from the start.

Now 76, his bespectacled face creased with an ever-present smile, gray-streaked hair worn in long, bohemian fashion, Jacob recalls the paper's beginnings. Wearing sandals and a simple shirt, he looks like the parish priest he once studied at a Jesuit seminary to be. "It was very logical that the military supported us because we had more or less things in common," he recalls. "We had a common goal: anti-communism."

The early years of *Kompas* were slow. The newspaper professed a quaint Fabian socialism that was in vogue in the first half of the last century in the Dutch Catholic church. Jacob and Ojong were close to Prof. Widjojo Nitisastro, guru to the "Berkeley Mafia" economists. Jacob today speaks of *Kompas'* intellectual underpinnings as one of "transcendental humanism," a kind of spirituality rooted in human beings instead of the divine. "We believed in transcendental humanism. We cared for people, stood for good business with very strong ethics, and family values."

The paper attracted a modest readership and plenty of teething problems. It started with a circulation of around 5,000. Part of the problem was logistics. "Those days, people gave us the nickname: '*kom pas morgen*', or 'coming only tomorrow' in Dutch, because we were so late with the paper all the time," Jacob recalls. "We were doing everything really from scratch."

Other journalists used to kid that the name Kompas actually was derived from *komplotan pastor* or "plot of pastors" because so many seminarians have worked at the newspaper over the years.

Jacob says *Kompas'* greatest asset has been its integrity. "Editorially we won the credibility of the readers because we tried to be professional with ethics, balance, commitment and dedication." That might not seem so unusual in the Western press, where balance and objectivity have long been bywords. But Indonesian journalism has a history of partisanship, first as the "battling press" against the Dutch colonial masters, then as mouthpieces for political parties in Sukarno's regime. "Journalism has always been associated in this country with the fight for freedom," Jacob says. "It started with political parties having their own magazines. And journalists were involved in the freedom struggle, people like Adam Malik, Mochtar Lubis, Rosihan Anwar."[3]

Kompas' style was perhaps its saving grace. "I suppose the newspaper reflects my style to some extent," Jacob muses. "I have the tendency to write indirectly. The Javanese way is indirect, not straightforward and businesslike." This meant *Kompas* could leave readers to draw their own conclusions and avoid the ire of officialdom. "We tried to survive and to know oneself and left it to the reader to read between the lines."

The tactic did not always work. Jacob faced his biggest crisis when *Kompas* was temporarily banned in 1978 for reporting on campus protests at ITB demanding that Suharto not be a candidate for the next presidential term. "They never gave us a reason," he said of the officials. "We just got a phone call one day and they told us to stop publishing."

The government offered to allow *Kompas* to publish again, but only on three conditions: that the paper not print stories that stirred up trouble among ethnic or religious groups; that it not oppose the military's "dual function" role giving it a civic as well as a military mission; and, finally, that it not "disturb" the family of the president.

"Number three was difficult," Jacob says. "My consideration was

---

3 Adam Malik, a former vice president, started the state Antara News Agency; Mochtar Lubis, a crusading journalist and humanist philosopher, was jailed under both Sukarno and Suharto; Rosihan Anwar was also a crusading journalist and author, whose newspaper *Pedoman*, was twice forcibly closed, under Sukarno in 1961 and Suharto in 1974.

that everything changes, but the frame of change is more complex in developing countries than in industrialized ones. But of course there was a conscience problem. We struggled whether this was proper or not; whether it was in our principles." For Jacob it was not about politics or business, since he had no political ambitions and *Kompas* was more than enough for his modest business goals. For him, it was about keeping his employees on the payroll and living on to fight another day as a journalist. He agreed to the terms.

So when Jusuf approached him four years later about helping set up *The Jakarta Post*, participating for Jacob was more an act of civic duty than a business opportunity. *Kompas* agreed to run the business side of the operation, including the printing, circulation and advertising sales. In return it took 25 percent of the shares. "I met Ali Murtopo once or twice for this business, but Jusuf was the one pulling it together," Jacob says. "We thought it was a good opportunity for Indonesia to have a newspaper in English, but it has never been a significant part of our business."

Jusuf then visited Fikri Jufri, one of the founders of *Tempo,* which anteed up for a 15 percent stake. The magazine also agreed to donate a managing editor who would put together the staff and operations and run the newsroom.

A key piece to the ownership puzzle was Harmoko, owner of the mass tabloid *Pos Kota* and chairman of the Indonesian Journalists Association (PWI). He was brought in because a letter of recommendation from the association – one of the many groups that made up Golkar – was a requirement for getting a license. What would otherwise be a bureaucratic and political headache was resolved in a few minutes: Harmoko, who was about to replace Murtopo as information minister in Suharto's new cabinet, sat down at a typewriter in Jusuf's office and wrote up the letter of recommendation on the spot. He then phoned the ministry of information and hounded a cowed official to expedite the license, Jusuf recalls. For his work Harmoko got a 5 percent stake in the newspaper, whose initial capitalization was a mere 500 million rupiah ($700,000 at the time.)

Jusuf was keen to have Sabam Siagian at the helm of *The Jakarta Post* and threw hints his way about taking the job. But Sabam, then Deputy Editor at *Sinar Harapan*, kept giving evasive answers. "I had the uneasy feeling that he wanted me to be involved in what I then considered to be a dubious experiment," Sabam said. On the other hand, the job did offer a face-saving way out of an uncomfortable situation he faced at *Sinar Harapan*, where the publisher H.G. Rorimpandey appeared to be easing him out the door in a power tussle at the top of the newspaper.

"As I was agonizing between plunging myself into a new adventure and remaining in an undefined situation, I read in the *Straits Times* of Singapore that a new English-language newspaper was soon to be published in Jakarta, with the 'temperamental' Sabam Siagian as chief editor," Sabam recalls. "It was clearly a case of forcing my hand to take a decision, but I did not react."

His old friend Fikri Jufri alternately cajoled and kibitzed Sabam to take the job. "He was saying I was too chicken to take the job," Sabam chuckled. "He told me I was leading too easy a life, writing a few editorials a week while listening to Beethoven symphonies and ordering flowers whenever the flower vendor happened to pass by."

He was ultimately persuaded when he realized that all the main publishing groups had committed resources to the proposition, and that the government, through Wanandi's patron Ali Murtopo, had given its approval. Failure was not an option.

Sabam had one condition, however: *Sinar Harapan* must be made a shareholding partner. "Not that I loved *Sinar Harapan* that much, but I wanted to avoid the impression that I was soliciting for a job. I could sense that the publisher wouldn't cry if I left. But at the same time, he realized I was a public relations asset." Sabam also realized that with *Sinar* as a key shareholder his own position in the new company would be considerably strengthened.

But making *Sinar Harapan* a shareholder meant the other partners would have to agree to reduce their stakes and let a competing publishing house join the group – not an easy sell.

The final meeting in March 1983 to hammer out the ownership and licensing agreement, held at Wanandi's office at CSIS, "was a setting that was politically loaded," Sabam recalled. The newspaper was due to come out in a month, the newsroom was already putting out practice editions, but the publishing company had yet to be legally formed and the ownership group was still negotiating the shareholding structure. "You're talking about the heyday of Ali Murtopo, the Wanandi brothers, Harmoko, who was soon to join the Cabinet," Sabam said. The three existing shareholders agreed to give *Sinar Harapan* a 10-percent stake, but Rorimpandey suddenly threw a spanner into the machinery. "Rorimpandey said thank you for the opportunity, but if and when I take part in a joint enterprise it's never for less than 20 percent and 10 percent was too small for him," Sabam recalled. They finessed that in the end, since everyone realized that Rorimpandey was making a point more than he was driving a deal. "After all, releasing me from *Sinar Harapan* to become the chief editor of *The Jakarta Post* was a graceful solution," Sabam says.

Finally there was the matter of whose name would appear as publisher. Mohammad Chudori, a former general manager at the national news agency *Antara*, was a respected name in the business with the added benefit that he was a Muslim in a Christian-dominated ownership group.

All that remained was to choose a managing editor to run the newsroom. "Knowing Sabam was a big man, we needed a strong managing editor," Jusuf said. *Tempo* proposed Amir Daud, who had worked with the legendary Rosihan Anwar at *Pedoman* before becoming national editor at *Tempo*, and who had a formidable reputation himself. Amir was duly appointed. It would prove to be a combustible mix in the newsroom.

That four rival media companies had managed to agree to jointly publish an English language daily, whose commercial justification was doubtful at best, was a unique event in Indonesia, if not the world. "It was a strange baby, this English-language newspaper. At the same time it had the backing of Harmoko and Murtopo – that was very important when you reconstruct the political structure of those years. But those initial years? An eight-page, English-language newspaper? And so little guidance," Sabam said of his mandate from the ownership group.

On the other hand, there would be no end of guidance from the government and the military for what news "a free and responsible press" could cover.

᭬

CHAPTER TWO
GROWING PAINS

After my chance meeting with Bambang Harymurti in Bandung, I went to see Amir Daud at *Tempo* magazine, where he was national editor. He seemed happy to see me. *The Jakarta Post* was looking for Americans: The style (and spelling) of the newspaper would be American. Amir was particularly looking for a trainer/editor, and he hadn't hired anybody yet. So my timing was excellent.

Amir was the first person I had met who seemed at all impressed with my Master's degree in journalism – that and 50 cents would get you a cup of coffee in America in those days. But Indonesians had great respect for degrees, which were usually listed in a long series of abbreviations on their business cards. My degree and erstwhile teaching experience in Bandung qualified me in his eyes to help lead the training seminars we would run in the weeks before the first issue.

I was sent almost immediately to Singapore and came back with a bona fide work permit. That was my first indication of how well-connected the new newspaper was. It usually took days of hanging around the Indonesian embassy in Singapore to wrangle a three-month visitor's pass, staying in cheap hostels on Bencoolen Street and having the irksome duty of defending the Reagan Administration from the sneering criticism of European backpackers, who didn't like the fact their countries were hosting U.S. tactical nukes aimed at the "Evil Empire." This time, with Jusuf Wanandi as my sponsor, I was ushered straight into the consul's office, giving my best Mr. Bean smirk to the Eurotrash waiting in line, and was given a rare and highly prized multiple-entry work permit. Indonesia usually kept foreigners on a much shorter leash.

When I returned to Jakarta, Amir explained the newspaper would not be doing much reporting of its own in the beginning, but translating and polishing stories from Indonesian language dailies. My role, and that of other editors, would be to present the news in a readable and attractive way. So forget about writing news stories for this Indonesian daily, he said with a wry grin. I could do the odd lifestyle piece or film review, but foreigners would not be allowed to cover news events for an Indonesian daily.

Amir, who died in 2004, was a highly respected journalist, with a reputation for being a stickler for the facts. He was pedantic and prescriptive, an old school editor. It was his way or the highway. He had begun his career as a clerk for *Antara,* the national news agency founded by former vice president and independence hero Adam Malik. He made his name as a senior journalist with *Pedoman* under the legendary chief editor Rosihan Anwar, a newspaper that was considered one of the leading examples of the *pers perjuangan* or "battling press" that first took up the struggle for independence and then fought against authoritarianism afterward.

Short and compact, from Padang in West Sumatra, he was fond of making fun of the indirect, evasive and circumlocutory speaking and writing style of the Javanese, the dominant ethnic group in multicultural Indonesia. Arms folded on the desk, he would peer over reading glasses at the end of his nose and pour unholy scorn upon an editor who had let through a lead first paragraph that was badly constructed or poorly sourced. But during the training session, he was avuncular and retiring, content to let me or my new counterpart, Australian Lionel Northrop, take the lead.

The *Western Australian,* a Perth-based newspaper, had loaned Northrop, one of its senior desk editors, to the cause in a deal that Jusuf Wanandi had arranged. It was understood to be part of an arrangement that would pave the way for Australian journalists to be accredited in Indonesia again, after ties had been strained over the October 1975 killings of the "Balibo Five" in East Timor.

The *Jakarta Post* newsroom could be generously described as modest. Housed in a long, one-story warehouse across from *Kompas,* it was, in fact, *Kompas'* old laundry room. It had no air-conditioning. A phone system had yet to be installed. We did not have word processors, let alone computer workstations. Instead, we practiced writing leads, stories, headlines and photo captions with Olympia manual typewriters on old second-hand desks from *Kompas.*

Our group of grizzled veterans and fresh-faced university graduates talked about what kind of newspaper we would create at these training sessions and started to develop a sense of collegiality and excitement that we could be breaking ground with a newspaper that had a different look – one that perhaps could push the envelope in testing the boundaries of censorship.

Like *Kompas,* whose composing room and printing press it would be using, *The Jakarta Post* would be a morning newspaper. Mohammad Chudori, the newly named publisher, dropped by to show proposed mastheads, with different fonts, and we offered our opinions. I suggested we add a slogan to the masthead. That got kicked that around the table, and we came up with this: "The Journal of Indonesia Today". It was the slogan of the paper for most of the past quarter-century, until 2002 when it disappeared from the masthead.

After our seminars on news and news writing, Lionel took over to teach us how to design newspaper pages. He gave us pica poles, a kind of ruler to measure copy length and calculate fonts, and photo wheels to size photos for layouts. He talked points, picas and percentages; the comparative advantages of modular page designs – pictures and headlines leveled off across the page.

And then one day, Northrop realized we were all hopelessly lost in this newspaper design arcana. So he came up with the idea of giving us page layout sheets the same size as the broadsheet newspaper page. We used our pica poles only as straight edges to draw lines on the page to make a layout that was exact to scale. He gave us a simple arithmetic formula for calculating how many column inches a typewritten story would occupy. And he gave us the newspapering-for-dummies technique for sizing a photo that even a kindergarten kid could employ (and enjoy). So with our scissors and glue, colored pencils and big, big layout sheets, we did, in fact, look like big kids in an elementary school art class.

Endy Bayuni, now chief editor of the *Post*, recalled those early days. "I remember when we joined," he said. "Every single reporter and editor was given a pica pole. They were like newspaper totems." It's true. I've kept mine in a desk drawer at home all these years. No-one uses them anymore in the era of electronic pagination; they are as anachronistic as linotype. "My best memory of those days?" Endy continued. "Lionel always had his cold beer in our little newsroom fridge to relieve all those tensions of botched deadlines and so forth. And one day he opened the fridge, saw it was gone, and he bellowed out in a voice we could hear all over the newsroom: 'Who took my fuckin' beer?'"

I remember that, too. Everybody's head swiveled around to look at me. I still don't know why.

One day toward the end of the training session, a distinguished-looking gentleman with a leonine head of silvery hair and dressed in an immaculate safari suit strode into the newsroom, a smoking pipe jutting from his mouth, trailed by a driver carrying his briefcase. He looked neither left nor right, and disappeared into a modest office behind a partition in the ersatz laundry room and closed the door.

Amir leaned into me at our big seminar table in the newsroom and said: "That is our new chief editor, Mr. Sabam Siagian," he said. "*Sombong, dia* (he's arrogant)," he added with a chuckle.

In fact Sabam – alone in the office, his reporters and editors out *there* and well into planning and practicing for publication without him – was feeling a bit daunted, dubious and dismayed, despite his deliberately staged grand entrance.

He had been deputy chief editor at *Sinar Harapan* (Ray of Hope), a feisty afternoon daily that was owned by about 20 of the leading Protestant families in the country, including Sabam's, whose father was a pastor in the Indonesian Dutch Reform church. *Sinar Harapan* had been already banned once before and would be closed down permanently in1986 for its aggressive reporting. Now he was in the lair of rival *Kompas*, a staid morning daily that never strayed much beyond the press limitations of the New Order.

"There were several big psychological blocks," Sabam recalled in an interview a quarter-century later at the rebuilt offices of *The Jakarta Post,* staring out of a window at the massive *Kompas* compound across the street. "One was working for a morning newspaper, meaning your working hours are your evening hours. Secondly, this compound: To come over here amidst the bastion of the Catholic *Kompas*, which at *Sinar Harapan* we considered our main competition. But thirdly, and more important, Amir Daud had already set up everything. Amir was working as if there was no chief editor! Instinctively, I realized it wouldn't last long. But that was not an easy situation, far from it."

Sabam was considered ideal for the job of chief editor for any number of reasons. He had spent more than a decade as a journalist in New York, including a stint with the Indonesian mission to the United Nations. He and his family were part of the Jakarta establishment. He was smooth, debonair, well-educated. And like others in this new venture, he had cut his teeth in the student movement against Sukarno.

Sabam was born in 1932 in Jakarta, then known as Batavia under Dutch colonial rule. His father was among the first wave of Bataks from North Sumatra who came to Jakarta for higher education around World War I, and became pastor of a Dutch Reform church in Batavia.

"We went to Dutch school, and during the Japanese occupation, I was taught in Japanese. At the end of Japanese occupation, I could read and write 800 *kanjis* (characters)," Sabam recalled. He won an essay contest at 17 sponsored by the old *New York Herald Tribune*, before enrolling in the University of Indonesia's prestigious faculty of law, thinking of the foreign service as a possible career. "The faculty of law in the 1950s still had Dutch professors and law books in the Dutch language. But I was simply not interested in law. What attracted me was the name Faculty of Law and Social Science." He got involved in student politics and in 1956, at the age of 24, became editor of a monthly student Christian magazine. "Looking back, although I didn't want to admit it at that time, journalism was already in my blood."

But Sabam's journey into journalism took a meandering course. He received a church scholarship to study at Vanderbilt University in Tennessee, but then ended up giving Indonesian language lessons at Yale University, where he took courses on, among others, the history of political radicalism.

They were hard years, too. He and his college sweetheart Stella Maris took the subway to City Hall in New York on a Wednesday in 1962 because that was the day of the week when marriage licenses were cheapest. "Even in my hardship years in New York, I faithfully read *The New York Times*. I couldn't afford a dime (for the paper), but I fished around in the wastebaskets of the subway. People tended to read the sports and throw away the meaty stuff. So that was especially during the days when James Reston had his column. He was my editor model."

When Indonesia rejoined the United Nations in 1966 following the end of Confrontation, Sabam was hired by the Indonesian mission in New York to write speeches and excerpt and translate U.S. newspapers. "That was my informal grounding as a journalist, to be in New York and read *The New York Times* every day."

Radio Australia hired him as a stringer for their Indonesian language program during the turbulent late 1960s in America. "Those were marvelous years. Going to their building in midtown Manhattan next to Radio City after work for their evening transmission at 9 p.m. It was hard, but it was thorough grounding for me. To type out a two-to-three-minute news item was an agonizing job, because the Indonesian language tends to be wordy. Sometimes my soul was more in that than in my work for the Indonesian mission."

By 1972, Sabam and Stella had two sons, 8 and 6, going to school, and times had changed, both in New York and back home in Indonesia. "We found bringing up children in New York was going to be a challenge: crime, drugs in the schools. And should we live forever in New York, when exciting things were happening in Indonesia? It was the beginning of the New Order. Things were becoming 'normal.'"

When Sabam got back to Jakarta in 1973, *Sinar Harapan* was

getting ready to publish again after being banned for leaking the draft state budget.[1] The government agreed to lift the ban if the newspaper reorganized and shifted out editors who were prone to challenging the government. Sabam was asked to become deputy chief editor.

Sinar Harapan had been started by the Protestant establishment in 1962 at the height of Sukarno's "Guided Democracy," with tacit support from the military, which was looking to counter the strong leftist newspapers of the time. Catholic *Kompas* began publication in 1965 with the same aim. But unlike *Kompas,* the afternoon *Sinar Harapan* under Managing Editor Aristides Katoppo had a tendency to squirm against the strait jacket the New Order government imposed on the press. Katoppo was sent for an extended sabbatical in the United States and the more diplomatic Sabam was brought in.

"My late father, who was a shareholder in the company and realized it was important that *Sinar Harapan* should continue to be published given its distinct background – strongly imbued with the social consciousness of the Christian Protestant community in Indonesia – persuaded me to work there, even if only for a few years," Sabam recalls. "He knew that I had other plans, but as I was to find out, being involved in the newspaper business is like sipping quality wine: You never know when to stop."

Sabam got a baptism of fire not long after joining the newspaper when the Malari riots of 1974 erupted not far from *Sinar's* office. He drove home that night in the little, yellow Fiat he had bought in New York, past burning Japanese-made cars that made central Jakarta seem like a war zone. "And somewhere I was stopped. They saw the yellow car. 'Ah, *mobil Jepang*! (Japanese car); one said. Well, the best defense is attack, so I jumped out and said 'Look at the brand: Piat!,' giving the word its Indonesian pronunciation."

When Aristides Katoppo returned to Jakarta, Sabam went for an extended study himself: a Nieman Foundation fellowship for journalists at Harvard in 1979. He returned home to discover

---

1 The national budget, like most acts of government in the New Order, was considered a state secret until it was officially released.

he had been relieved of his position as deputy chief editor. "I was given the lofty title of senior editorial writer and could cover major international events while producing a few editorials a week." It also gave him time to attend CSIS seminars organized by Jusuf Wanandi, who was already sizing him up to head the new English-language newspaper.

Even as the shareholders were cobbling together the new publishing company (PT Bina Media Tenggara), a group of newly hired editors were putting together practice editions of the newspaper every day in the month before the first issue. We cut and pasted stories together, wrote headlines, chose pictures, designed a layout and took it all across the street to the *Kompas* plant where the pages were composed. The exercise stopped just short of running the presses. The practice editions featured Suharto and his new cabinet, which included, as expected, Harmoko as the new information minister. Suharto himself was elected without opposition (again) to a fourth term as president by the MPR, an assembly that included elected legislators, Suharto-appointees and army officers.

It was the height of the Cold War, and the anti-communist New Order, though not aligned with America, was certainly friendly toward it. U.S. oil companies were exploring throughout the archipelago and American foreign investment was being assiduously courted again. It was one reason *The Jakarta Post* adopted an American style of journalism.

It was a time when America was recovering from its post-Vietnam War malaise and reasserting its place in the world: U.S. President Ronald Reagan had just called the Soviet Union an Evil Empire and, a few weeks later, had unveiled a Strategic Defense Initiative that featured technology to intercept enemy missiles. The media dubbed the plan "Star Wars." That made the front page of one of our dummy editions. The U.S. embassy in Beirut was bombed, killing 63 people.

Nuclear holocaust was on the minds of many. Soviet leader Yuri Andropov invited a schoolgirl in Maine, Samantha Smith, to visit Moscow after reading her letter expressing fears about nuclear war. Astronauts on the space shuttle Challenger performed the first space walk, the Irish band U2 released its breakthrough "War" album and IBM released its PC XT. The British film *Gandhi* won eight Oscars.

On April 25, 1983 *The Jakarta Post* published its first eight-page edition. The newspaper, aiming to appeal to foreigners and well-educated Indonesians, was designed to look different to the other Indonesian dailies. It had eight comic strips on a lifestyle page, for instance. Photos and graphics were used extensively. The type font for text and headlines was larger. The front page featured a "Where To Look" index and a "This Odd World" box for "brights," or short off-beat stories. Stories did not jump from one page to another so they had to be tightly edited.

The newspaper had almost no original reporting in the beginning. Amir's shrewd idea was to have his page editors pull together Indonesian stories using bits from various local newspapers and wire services, with a Western-style news lead at the top. The whole story, as a result, was usually greater than the sum of its parts. He also was a little wary of turning loose his bright young reporters on to the minefields of New Order journalism, when editors could be raked over the coals by the press overlords in the military and information ministry.

Given the penchant for many Indonesian language newspapers to bury the lead in the 19th paragraph after a long and torturous introduction, the *Post* version was often far better than the original. "Those days, most of the time we were rewriting the newspapers, enriching the story," says Vincent Lingga, the first business editor and later managing editor of the paper. "It was like fried rice, but the foreigners were hungry for it and they ate it up."

Foreign wire services were picking up the *Post*'s version of stories that had run a day or two before in the Indonesian language press. Still, most of the stories in the newspaper those first few months were from wire service copy. It was a struggle for the eight page editors just to get anything out the door on deadline.

The opinion page was also meant to be distinctive. And while early editorials were often tentative, it wasn't long before they began to be quoted by the foreign press. That was probably because it was easy to see their point. Unlike opinion in the Indonesian press at the time, which tended to sprawl across half a broadsheet page, Jakarta Post editorials were usually no more than eight paragraphs. "Our editorials from the beginning tended to be short – not too many jabs, just one big punch," Lingga said. "That was our competitive edge in getting new subscribers. And until now that is our main advantage."

The Jakarta Post was meant to compete with the likes of Singapore's Straits Times, Malaysia's New Straits Times, Thailand's Bangkok Post and the Philippines Inquirer for regional prestige. But unlike many of its neighbors, Indonesia did not have a historical link to an English-speaking country. Singapore and Malaysia had Britain, while the Philippines had the United States, but Indonesia had been a colony of the Netherlands and the Dutch language had been used as the official medium of communication. Even until the late 1950s some schools continued to use Dutch.

Lionel Northrop returned to Australia a couple of months after the Post began publishing, and for a while I was the only foreigner employed, with responsibility for the front page and coordinating world news. But I would be followed by a stream of other foreigners in the months and years to come. "It was the first time an English language newspaper had ever employed a native speaker from the very beginning," Lingga noted. A cross-cultural learning curve had to be traversed.

We were working 12-15-hour days and I was drinking kopi tubruk by the gallon. This traditional Indonesia style of coffee involves pouring heaps of grainy coffee powder into tall glass, adding hot water and copious amounts of sugar, and capping the glass with a metal lid. I had never had a beverage with a metal lid before. They can be quite useful, as I found out one time when I neglected to cap my drink and felt a fly swimming frantically in my mouthful of coffee, before, with a shout of horror, I expelled it over my finished layout.

The windows were often open – we had no air-conditioning in the old laundry room – letting in the Jakarta symphony of kaki lima (street vendors) with their distinctive cries, toots and whistles, blaring car horns and bird songs. Inside was the clattering of typewriters and telex machines. During the rainy season, we had to roll up the layout sheets, story copy tucked inside, and race across the road splashing through puddles and arriving drenched and bedraggled at the *Kompas* composing room. But at least our precious layouts were dry.

From the first days of publication, the *Post* began carrying small items about bullet-riddled bodies with tattoos marking them as criminals turning up in rivers and canals around the country, their hands tied with fishing line, and execution-style wounds to the head. The media soon began referring to these as "mysterious shootings." Most folks assumed this was the work of the military, though Armed Forces chief Benny Murdani initially insisted the killings were the result of "inter-gang warfare."

The *Post* ran a small story on page 2 from the Legal Aid Institute, or LBH, on April 30 – something the Indonesian language press dared not do because LBH was one of the few open supporters of human rights in the New Order – expressing concern. "An impression has been created that the current efforts are aimed at eradicating criminals – not crime," LBH said in a press release. Thus began a practice that lasted throughout Suharto's regime of burying sensitive items on the City Page, which readers soon learned to look for.

In June, Armed Forces Commander Gen. Murdani, finally acknowledged that the "mysterious shootings" were, in fact, an anti-crime campaign, and the killings the work of avenging "angels." Indeed, the shootings were commonly referred to as Petrus, an acronym from *penembakan misterius,* or mysterious shootings. Petrus is also St. Peter in Indonesian. Ali Murtopo, who had been shuffled off as the vice-chairman of Suharto's Supreme Advisory Council, said the government ordered the campaign because "conventional methods to combat crime have proved inappropriate in Indonesia."

The exact number killed was never made official, though most estimates put it at around 3,000 by the end of 1983. Because some of the victims were killed soon after release from prison, *Tempo* magazine reported, some inmates became so fearful they pleaded to stay in jail. Others committed crimes the moment they got out so they could be re-arrested. In his 1989 autobiography, Suharto took the credit for a campaign that had popular support among a public fed up with rampant crime in the streets. He said he personally gave orders to "shoot to kill" because "we needed to have our own treatment, firm measures," adding it was "for the purpose of shock therapy."

The *Post* newsroom seemed remarkably unperturbed by the campaign. Amir explained that while many Indonesians were a little uneasy about the methods, they heartily approved of the results. A *Tempo* poll found that nearly two thirds of the respondents approved of the mysterious shootings, though only if the victims had been convicted of a crime.

Sabam, Lingga and I were writing most of the editorials in the beginning, and it fell to me to write the *Post*'s view of the mysterious killings. We peddled the government line: "The fact is there is nothing very mysterious about these killings," the editorial said. "The government has been conducting a crackdown on crime in the wake of an alarming increase in criminal activity in the country, amounting to virtual terrorism. A consequence of that crackdown is a frenzy among criminal gangs, not unlike ants running *amok* when the ant hill has been destroyed."

But the truth was far different, as so often was the case in the opaque political world of Suharto's Indonesia. Jusuf Wanandi, in an interview a quarter-century later, told me the campaign originated because the military wanted to exterminate part of Murtopo's Zoo – the thugs hired in the 1982 election campaign to disrupt opposition rallies. "It started with the general elections before when Golkar used these gangsters in the election campaign. On the other side there were Muslim extremists, leftist elements, unions, the PDI. We were the bureaucrats, intellectuals. How could Golkar fight on the streets? So we used these gangsters to fight their street fighters. And they had, of course, gangsters on their side, too."

Trouble started after the elections when Golkar's gangsters began to feel empowered. They set up protection rackets and extortion rings and started shaking down the middle class, Wanandi said. "The Yogyakarta commander got mad. And that's how it started. And then Benny did it throughout the country. He let the Special Forces do it,"

Jusuf said. "The people supported it because the law was not working for them. The police were not responsive."

Nevertheless, the message was clear to both the public and any putative enemies within or without: The New Order, born in a bloodbath, would not blink an eye at utilizing terror as a weapon.

Amir and I had become close. After we put the paper to bed, he would drive me to my house in the leafy, old money Menteng area of the city, where Suharto also lived. My modest little house, behind the *dangdut* bars of Blora and next to the railroad tracks where the transvestites known as *banci* plied their trade, was across from one of the most famous *soto* (soup) stalls in the capital. Amir introduced me to the torpedo special there: soup à la goat testicles.

But he was becoming more distant from the other page editors in the newsroom, who chafed under his critical regime. Unlike many Indonesian newsrooms, the *Post* had a daily "budget" meeting among page editors to decide what would go into the next morning's edition, and to go through that day's newspaper to point out the good, bad and ugly.

The editors sat around an octagonal table at the back of the newsroom going through the misspellings, inaccuracies, weird syntax, bumping headlines, and other sins of newspapering. The scrutiny was not popular, particularly among the more senior journalists who were unused to open criticism, which is frowned upon in Indonesian society. Over time, the perception grew that Amir was playing favorites; that he was aloof and hyper-critical. The silence around the table could sometimes be deafening and it was often left to me to lead the post-mortem part of discussion.

The newspaper itself was proving to be a hit among readers, and while ads were scarce, circulation was steadily growing. But the 12-to-15 hour days were wearing on people. Tempers frayed and resentments grew. "At that time things were hard," Lingga recalled. "There was little advertising. We were working very hard and the perception was that the managing editor was giving preferential treatment. And there was, of course, a problem between the chief editor and managing editor."

The junior reporters were mostly unaware of the tensions that were brewing. Harry Bhaskara, who joined in early 1984 and who would become a managing editor in the 1990s, recalled it being a happy time for the new recruits. "The best newsroom climate was those early years, because we were all comrades and there was the feeling of struggling to make a good paper, of being part of a solid team, of togetherness," Bhaskara said. "We sat at a very long table, the reporters' table, in front of typewriters. The working spirit was very high. We worked from morning till after midnight. Amir made the newcomers stay behind at night as proofreaders in the composing room till the paper was taken to the press as part of our training. I remember my motorcycle breaking down at 3:30 a.m. on the way back from work one night in a bad part of town, and I was so afraid I would be robbed."

He remembered his first story was a translation of an item about graveyards. He thought it was a writing test during training, but editors were so desperate to fill the newspaper with Indonesian stories they often used candidates' test stories to fill the pages in those early days.

Like other reporters, Harry chafed under the chore of translating instead of reporting stories. "We were reporters, but we couldn't go out and report, because what we did every day was rewriting and translating. Management was afraid there wouldn't be enough stories to go into the newspaper if the reporters were out." This wasn't exactly true: I remember the editors did encourage reporters to write by-liners – stories that carried their own work and their name – during their off-time.

As the *Post* approached its second anniversary, tensions were growing in the newsroom, tempers shortened by trying to put out a broadsheet newspaper of eight pages with no ads. Factions began to form. "Those days you wrote and edited stories, sized and cropped the photos, wrote the headlines. And then you went across the road to *Kompas* to supervise the cutting and pasting of the layout in the camera room," Endy Bayuni remembers. "We'd come in at 8 a.m. and leave at 2 a.m. The tension was always about deadlines. In 1983, you had different editorial cultures. You had people from newspapers, magazines, the wires, from Time, from *Antara*," Endy continues. "You had the conflict of personalities, particularly between Sabam and Amir, but with other personalities as well, who all had their own way of doing things."

Nearly two years after the launch the newsroom presented management with a petition of grievances, signed by almost all the reporters and editors. In Indonesia, once a consensus is formed, nobody wants to be outside the pale.

I was not asked to sign. For one thing, I was the foreigner. For another I was one of the grievances: Amir had given the "language consultant" too much responsibility, and I was rude and "insensitive" to Indonesian ways and culture. This was undoubtedly true. I once made a basketball shot out of crumpled piece of paper that accidentally banked off a colleague's head before landing in a wastebasket. Touching someone's head is a cardinal sin in Indonesia.

"We started making our little cliques and it was energy-sapping," recalled Debra Yatim, then the city editor and now one of Indonesia's leading advocacy journalists. "The newsroom appeared divided between the Amir camp and the Sabam one, with Chudori maneuvering between. Now in my old age, I see that it was a microcosm of what Indonesia was all about," she said. "We had these conflicts, with no mechanism to resolve them. We could only threaten."

Management responded by sending in the board of commissioners to address the staff: Chairman Eric Samola from *Tempo*, Sofyan Wanandi, and Raymond Toruan from *Kompas*. The late Samola, a Christian from northern Sulawesi, was *Tempo*'s publisher. He was also a Golkar executive and represented a wealthy Chinese developer called Ciputra (Tjie Tjin Hoan), who owned part of *Tempo* at the time through a foundation.

Samola spoke quietly, almost monotonously, telling a hushed newsroom it was "not good for people to be unhappy." It didn't make sense for unhappy people to stick around and make other people unhappy, he pointed out, his hand tapping the desk in front of him like a metronome. In chilling words still remembered a quarter-century later, he told the assembly of English-speaking journalists

Night of Terror

I was sitting at home having a beer on the eve of Halloween, 1984, enjoying a rare night off from the *Post,* when a colleague rang up to say the neighborhood around Jakarta International School had come under heavy artillery fire for some odd reason.

I raced to the Pondok Indah (Beautiful Hut) neighborhood of South Jakarta with my roommate, John Hail of UPI, flashing my Florida driver's license at the security checkpoints hastily erected around the neighborhood, lacking the requisite reporting credentials as a "language consultant" for *The Jakarta Post.* Stunned residents had gathered along a security perimeter around the neighborhood as rockets, mortars and tracers – all without live warheads, thank goodness – rained down on their expensive homes.

Tons of projectiles screeched, whistled and roared into the night, turning the sky a roiling orange hue, as metal thudded into roofs, yards and roads. The barrage went on through the night, killing 15 people and injuring 26. At least 800 homes were damaged or destroyed. President Suharto, accompanied by Armed Forces Commander Benny Murdani, made a rare unscheduled visit to the neighborhood, talking to shell-shocked residents.

The official explanation was that an accidental fire at the ammunition dump set off all the munitions stored there. No group claimed responsibility, but the incident remains one of those mysteries of the New Order that has never been satisfactorily explained.

Beata Mirecka-Jakubowska years later created a website to record the impressions of her expat neighbors, entitled "The Night the Sky Fell Down". Their bewilderment to this day about what happened underscores the opacities and mysteries of the New Order political culture. Jakarta International School math teacher Liz Stamp said she watched the flames at the arsenal reaching into the sky. "Then the whistling and whizzing started and we suddenly realized that the objects causing the strange loud, squeaky, whining, whirling sounds were passing right over our heads. We could not quite see them, but they were certainly zooming past us in the darkness of the night, illuminated by the deep and powerful glow of what was, by now, a huge blazing inferno."

Hardly anyone realized what was happening. Smith, who had lived through civil unrest in El Salvador, went indoors, filled a bath full of water and opened all the windows. "We still did not know what the problem was, but it was getting a lot worse. "Inside the house, I was scared stiff, making sure that we had candles everywhere, although the electricity and the phone were all working perfectly. I was sure that these shells that were flying past were going to finish us off."

Laura Schuster, an elementary school teacher, said she grabbed cans of tuna fish, water, bread, bananas and her passport and ducked into a room furthest from the inferno. "Many people were seen aimlessly walking with mattresses on heads – traveling to who knows, wherever they perceived might be safer haven. It wasn't until a few days later that we discovered what had happened and even then it was all rather grey. Not having been in Indonesia for any length of time, I had no history to compare it with and figured this was one of the 'experiences' I was told about when moving to an international scene."

Gene Magill, a high school social studies teacher, writes on the Web site that he had just gone to bed when he heard loud noises from the room above. "I went upstairs to see what was going on, and my housemate, Jim Herbert, walked out of his room and asked 'What are you doing down there?' Outside, they could see a large fireball in the sky in the general direction of the school. Jim exclaimed, 'I must have left some chemicals out.' We both thought the school was on fire. We soon found the truth as refugees from Cilandak came knocking on our door to escape the inferno."

In an editorial the next day *Kompas* seemed grateful for the half-baked official explanations and even that the authorities had allowed anything to be printed about the frightening incident. However, a posh suburb being turned into a war zone could hardly be covered up.

they were like "screws in a chair," easily replaceable. "That really hurt many people," Lingga said. "People thought they were just basic material in a manufacturer process."

It was, in fact, a shot fired by a representative of an emergent "industrial press" at journalists who saw themselves and their petition as being in the tradition of a "battling press," in which journalism was part of the national struggle against the Dutch colonial masters and, later, Sukarno's authoritarianism.

The problem with Samola's argument was that English-language journalists were few and far between in Indonesia and those willing to work 12 hours a day for peanuts were rare indeed, Debra notes. "He was describing us as blue-collar workers, and said in effect, that if you leave, 1,000 other people will replace you. And that was unfair, because it's just not true that you could find good, English-language journalists then," she said. "What we badly needed was leadership, and we didn't get leadership."

But Samola's speech was effective. Taking a page from Suharto's book, he had managed to deflect the threat against management and get the opposing factions to lose. The staff was cowed but Amir had lost face. Amir agreed to make some changes in the newsroom. But less than a year later, he found a graceful exit as the editor-in-chief of a new newspaper, *Bisnis Indonesia,* and took a few loyalists from the *Post* with him.

Sabam realized he, too, had not emerged entirely unscathed and needed to step up. "It was a wake-up call, but when it happened I called a meeting of the senior page editors in my office. I said, 'Look here, this is the situation: Shall we continue to have a newspaper?' I was seeking support from them, because suddenly it was on my shoulders. The challenge makes you come alive. Now it was up to me. I'm the chief now. But then it was not knowing how to shape the newspaper."

Part of the problem, he suggested, was establishing a corporate culture with a group of English-literate Indonesian journalists, few of whom had a background with any of the publications that owned the paper. "This coalition of competing publishing houses was not quite reflected in the newsroom," Sabam said. "And how do you homogenize characters with different backgrounds and histories? On the one hand, Amir Daud's dictat was necessary to bind together this heterogeneous group. But on the other hand, when it was too much, it become counter-productive. Since I came from a newspaper culture in which newsroom revolts were not unusual – beer bottles were thrown – I sort of expected it. It was a collision course. At the end, Amir's presence was reduced and my position was reinforced."

For young Endy Bayuni, who had been identified as a rising star and was being trained as front page editor, it was all a bit disillusioning. When an offer came to join a foreign news agency, he jumped before the newsroom insurrection came to a head. "The tension was building. It was one of the reasons I decided to leave – that and because there was an offer from Reuters. My last day, I was at the editorial meeting and Sabam's parting words were: 'We wish you well, and bear in mind you can always come back.' And (the Reuters bureau chief) said the same thing: 'If you want to be a newspaper editor, this is good training, constant deadlines, and you're exposed to various disciplines. Seven years later, I did come back to *The Jakarta Post* and I did end up becoming chief editor."

But a pattern had been set.

Over the years, *The Jakarta Post* would become an incubator of talent for foreign news organizations, international agencies, and later, during the boom times of the 1990s, for banks and brokerages looking for bilingual staff that understood politics and markets.

Tensions were growing outside the newsroom as well. It seemed innocuous enough, at least to me, when Suharto's government introduced a bill in the national assembly in May 1984 requiring all organizations, including Muslim ones, to adopt *Pancasila* – the five principles that, like Humpty Dumpty's view on words in Alice in Wonderland ("When I use a word it means just what I choose it to mean,") meant whatever the strongman president wanted them to mean.

The Muslim PPP party, one of the three officially sanctioned parties, adopted Pancasila as its sole ideology that August after a stormy debate at its first congress in 11 years. Around the same time hard-line Islamic preachers were giving anti-Chinese, anti-Christian and anti-government sermons in poor areas of Jakarta, including the port area of Tanjung Priok.

A flashpoint came when a police officer entered a mosque in his boots and ordered that anti-government slogans painted on the wall be removed. When he was ignored, he soaked paper in drain water to wipe them out. That triggered demonstrations and arrests climaxing on September 12 when troops fired on demonstrators killing or injuring scores of people. Soon after the massacre, army trucks arrived to take away the bodies, while the injured were taken to an army hospital. The exact number of victims has never been clear, though the Al Araf Mosque put the number at 63 dead and more than 100 seriously wounded.

Gen. Murdani summoned editors of Jakarta newspapers the next day for a briefing. He said 15 soldiers came under attack by a mob of 1,500 people, brandishing sickles, crowbars and gasoline cans who demanded the release of those arrested. Troops fired warning shots in the air, then at the feet of the crowd, "unavoidably causing casualties," Murdani said. He put the toll at nine dead and more than 50 injured. The incident was a pivotal point for Indonesia. With communism all but obliterated after 1965, the radical right had now supplanted the left as the chief internal security threat.

In October, a series of mysterious fires and bombings rocked Jakarta. Bombs blasted two offices of Bank Central Asia, owned by Liem Sioe Liong, reputedly the richest man in Indonesia and close to Suharto since the 1950s. Two people were killed and 16 injured. On Oct. 30, ammunition from the Marines depot in a posh neighborhood not far from the Jakarta International School exploded in spectacular fashion, killing 15. But the January 1985 bomb that destroyed nine *stupas* atop the world-renowned 9th century Buddhist temple of Borobudur in Central Java was the last straw.

The Jakarta Post, in an editorial, expressed the outrage many Indonesians felt: "Terrorist acts have no place in Indonesia and anyone who resorts to such base tactics will suffer the terrible retribution of the Indonesian people who are shocked and revolted by the Borobudur bombings," the *Post* thundered. "Those responsible will soon regret that they could have been so gravely mistaken as to believe they could insult the people of Indonesia and get away with it."

The military, which had been carefully trying to characterize the attacks as the work of a few madmen, now began linking them to the Shi'ite followers of Iran's Ayatollah Khomeini, although most Indonesians are Sunni Muslims. Suharto responded with an unprecedented sweep against the Islamic opposition.

Through the crafty Murtopo, the New Order had once cultivated Islamic radicals. They included Komando Jihad, a 1970s incarnation of Darul Islam, a Sukarno-era movement aiming to turn Indonesia into an Islamic state. Murtopo used them first to help exterminate atheistic communism after the botched 1965 coup and then to mobilize votes in the 1971 and 1977 elections. But like the U.S. support for Osama bin Laden and Saddam Hussein in the 1980s, this was a tactic that would have severe blowback for Indonesia in the new millennium.

The courtship ended when an outfit called the Islamic Revolutionary Council linked to Komando Jihad hijacked a Garuda airliner to Bangkok. Elite forces led by Murdani stormed the plane on the tarmac and killed all the hijackers. The 1979 Islamic revolution in Iran and the rise of the Ayatollah Khomeini had a galvanizing effect on Muslims everywhere. The Sunni Muslim Brotherhood in Egypt, emerging around the same time and emphasizing a pan-Islamic solidarity that went beyond national boundaries, also had a profound effect on a second-generation of Muslim radicals in Indonesia, the world's most populous Muslim country.

Among them was Abu Bakar Bashir, who was arrested in November 1978 after a series of incendiary sermons on his small radio station in Solo lambasting the New Order. At his 1982 trial on subversion charges, Bashir was sentenced to nine years in prison, though it was reduced to time served on appeal.

Dozens of prominent figures were arrested in Suharto's mid-1980s crackdown against the Islamic opposition. The wearing of Islamic headscarves was banned in schools. Bashir's *pesantren* was closed down. Feeling the heat come down on them, Bashir, and his cohort, Abdullah Achmad bin Sungkar, fled in May 1985 across the Malacca Strait in a speedboat to neighboring Malaysia, where they built what was to become one of Asia's most dangerous terrorist networks, Jemaah Islamiyah.[2]

In May, former cabinet minister Mohammad Sanusi, then 64, was sentenced to 19 years in jail for subversion in connection with the bombings in Jakarta's Chinatown, the climax of four months of highly publicized trials against Muslim militants. Sanusi's motivation, according to the court, was to bring down Suharto's government by spreading terror. The court also found him guilty of financing the publication of a "subversive pamphlet" challenging the government's version of what happened in the Tanjung Priok harbor riots. Suharto, the smiling general, was showing an iron fist to any sign of real opposition by the mid-1980s and his government expected the press to toe the line as well.

Covering these stories was always problematic.

Nan Achnas, now one of Indonesia's leading film-makers, was a newly graduated cub reporter with the *Post* at the time and recalls that her first assignment was to cover a demonstration by schools protesting the ban on headscarves. "Suddenly there was call from (the government) because the story was about a demo and it was about *jilbab* (headscarves), a religiously sensitive issue. So my story was killed. That was my first disillusionment with journalism."

Nan, an Indonesian who grew up in Malaysia and Singapore, left less than two years later to pursue her career in film.

Despite the tensions within and without an ethos had formed in the newsroom. People made sacrifices for the paper, and no task was too big or small for anyone.

Sabam recalled the night of January 28, 1986. He, the night editor and a junior reporter were checking the composing room layouts for the usual sins: typos in the headlines, misplaced photo captions, chunks of white space to be filled with short items and the like. The

2   *The Second Front*, Ken Conboy, pp 12-20

only person left in the newsroom was the office boy, Suyoto, who knew that when bells started ringing on the wire service telex printers, something urgent was coming in. And that night they were ringing hard. He tore the copy off the machine, and raced across the road to the Kompas layout room, shouting: "*Pak, ada ledakan!* (Sir, there's an explosion!)" The space shuttle Challenger had exploded shortly after take-off, killing all seven astronauts aboard. Sabam inserted a bulletin on the front page, and alerted the *Kompas* newsroom.

An explosion in Indonesia, however, might not make it into the paper at all in Suharto's Indonesia.

༄

CHAPTER THREE
CENSORSHIP GAMES

I had just come back from the *Kompas* composing room one night, around 11 p.m., when a call came from an Indonesian military spokesman. He wanted to know if we had heard about the bombing of an army barracks in Palembang, referring to the port city in South Sumatra that was once the capital of the Sriwijaya kingdom controlling much of what is now Malaysia and Indonesia.

Noooo, we hadn't heard that, I said, grabbing a pen and thinking about how to retool the front page to accommodate this late-breaking story.

"Good," he replied, pausing a little uncertainly over how to deal with the foreigner on the line. "It's only a rumor. It's not true and you must not print anything on it. Tell the editor."

Sifting rumor from fact, and deciding how far to go with controversial stories, were both art and science in Suharto's Indonesia. The barracks may well have been bombed in Palembang. Nobody would have been the wiser. Steering the Indonesian media away from sensitive stories was the job of factotums at the ministry of information and at armed forces headquarters. They were not always explicit or very clear about what not to print, and so editors indulged in a great deal of self-censorship under the New Order.

When it came to foreign media, censorship was cruder, because the stories could not be influenced before publication. A squadron of censors armed with black ink and possessed of dubious English-language abilities were tasked with going through foreign newspapers and magazines and identifying offending paragraphs, which were then blacked out. It wasn't just English-language material that attracted the censor: Chinese characters, banned because Suharto was convinced that Beijing had been behind the 1965 communist coup attempt, also had to be obliterated. A story about Hong Kong's subway system in the *Far Eastern Economic Review*, for instance, had printer's ink smeared all over a photo of an underground train sign featuring Chinese characters – perhaps on the grounds it could have been secret code sent to the underground communist movement.

Foreign wire services such as AP, UPI, Reuters and AFP escaped censorship because in that pre-Internet age, their stories were distributed only to Indonesian media, who were expected to deal "responsibly" with any naughty reporting.

While the *Post*'s ownership group did not push any ideological line for the newspaper, other than to produce a literate and credible publication that would do Indonesia proud on the international stage, the newsroom knew what the New Order taboo issues were: Don't question what happened in 1965; never criticize the military over human rights issues or the "dual function" mission giving it a prominent political role; stick to the official line on separatist movements and the civil war in East Timor; avoid stories involving peasant land rights disputes (especially if they involved the military); avoid stories that stir up tensions between religious, race and ethnic groups; and the biggest no-no of all – don't "disturb the president's family" or his cronies with impudent reporting about their rampant business activities.

But, as an English-language newspaper, *The Jakarta Post* did have a little more room to push the parameters of press freedom. Debra Yatim, one of the original group of *Jakarta Post* page editors, wrote a ditty about that for the 20th anniversary edition of the *Post*:

> *Sometimes in days of old*
> *You got away with certain élan*
> *Because you wrote in a language*
> *The powers didn't always understand*

At the afternoon "news budget" meeting, editors debated whether to put photos of South Korean demonstrations against the strongman government of Gen. Chun Doo Hwan on the front page or inside. And how to play the decline and fall of Marcos and the rise of "people power" in the Philippines? Street demonstrations against the Suharto regime were unthinkable then, and the government certainly didn't want to give people any ideas.

Information was a valuable commodity in Indonesia during those secretive times. Journalists were special, even if they were not particularly well paid. They knew what others did not, but had to be careful how they spent that particular currency. As far as the government was concerned, the country had seen factions, conflict and bloodletting in the name of democracy under Sukarno, and the press had a responsibility to help the New Order keep order. Survival journalism in Indonesia meant passing on a good story to fight another day.

Thus, when the late French president François Mitterrand came to Indonesia in 1986 and he and Suharto went to Bandung to address students who had studied in France, we were tempted to use an AFP story that described students chanting *"liberté! liberté!"* and waving antigovernment placards.

It caused ripples of excitement in the newsroom, but no Indonesian newspaper could report that story and certainly could not publish a photo of the two leaders against a background of antigovernment protesters. We knew that even before the man from the information ministry called. Instead, the *Post* had blanket coverage of "people power" protests in Manila that day. Our mantra was that of former vice president Adam Malik, who was fond of saying: "Everything is possible, and everything is impossible in Indonesia."

By 1986, Indonesia's economy was in the doldrums, with sluggish domestic demand, growing unemployment and a prolonged manufacturing recession ahead of a politically charged general election. Economic growth had fallen to 2 percent in 1985 from the 6-7 percent average rate of the New Order period. Crude oil prices in OPEC member Indonesia hovered around $13 a barrel in 1986, half what they were only six months earlier. Foreign investment had fallen to just $859 million in 1985, barely a third of the total in 1983. Trade monopolies and high import tariffs that protected woefully inefficient industries were discouraging investment. Western aid donors who funded the vast majority of development projects in the country were starting to ratchet up the pressure on Indonesia's crony economy, particularly on the trade monopolies they enjoyed.

In September 1986, the *Post* waded into this issue after the government surprised everybody with a drastic devaluation of the rupiah to boost export revenues and rescue the national budget. The *Post* editorial argued the case purely on its economic merits, saying that by raising the cost of imports, the devaluation gave "broader leeway for the government to remove import monopolies."

"All studies about Indonesia's manufacturing industries have concluded that those non-tariff import barriers have substantially increased the production costs of industrial goods, thereby making them uncompetitive on the international market…All in all, the bottom line of the restrictive import policy is negative for the development of an efficient and sound manufacturing sector," the editorial said.

The *Post*, like its parent owners *Kompas* and *Sinar Harapan*, had contacts with the technocrats running the economic ministries, and had begun hearing hints that the monopolies had come under review.

It was around that time that Suharto started executing communists again. The military-backed government also issued warnings about a communist comeback and purged suspected leftists from sensitive jobs, even though nobody would dare admit to being leftist after the party was wiped out in the 1965 counter-coup. Nothing like the old communist bogeyman to distract unemployed peasants with pitchforks from storming the palace in the midst of an economic downturn and months ahead of a general election. All the more so if they are grumbling about monopolies enjoyed by Chinese tycoons close to the president. In September 1986, Indonesia executed nine ageing communists convicted in the botched coup, prompting immediate protests in Australia and Europe that their deaths were cruel and inhumane after two decades behind bars.

Things would go from the sublime to the ridiculous in the months to come, when Suharto ordered that *Tai Chi,* the traditional Chinese exercise that had become popular in Indonesia, be given an Indonesian name, "Indonesian Therapeutic Exercise." The Chinese commands, chants and songs in the exercise would have to be translated into Indonesian. Air Force Lt.-Col. Parwandono hinted darkly to reporters that *Tai Chi* "could be exploited for certain purposes." A local columnist took the debate to its logical extreme, suggesting if Tai Chi was possibly subversive, what then to do about Chinese food?

Next to the Chinese, Australia was the favorite scapegoat. Ties were strained after *The Sydney Morning Herald* published a story in 1986 about the Suharto family businesses during U.S. President Ronald Reagan's visit to Bali. The army newspaper *Harian AB* called Australian press freedom a threat to Indonesia because opinions beamed across the archipelago could destabilize the country. *Harian* warned ominously of increasing communist influence within the Australian Labor party and said the communist faction in Labor supported Indonesian separatist movements.

It was against the fraught background of a faltering economy and foreign criticism that *Sinar Harapan,* Sabam Siagian's old newspaper, was deemed to have crossed the line on the most dangerous taboo: a story in October 1986 that touched on the First Cronies for which the newspaper paid the ultimate price. The newspaper had a front-page scoop that the government was planning to abolish the import monopolies and special licenses – many of them held by businessmen with close ties to Suharto. *Jakarta Post* reporters checked the story with various economic ministries and decided to run with a translation of *Sinar's* story.

"Suharto thought the technocrats were putting him under the gun by leaking it to the leading afternoon newspaper," Sabam recalled. "Liem Sioe Liong supposedly went to Jalan Cendana (Suharto's residence) in his slippers to bitterly complain because (the decree) would impact his import monopolies." *The Jakarta Post* received the dreaded phone call from the information ministry late that night just as the paper was being put to bed. "The managing editor said we're pulling the story," recalled Maggie Agusta, an American copy editor on what was then called the "check desk." "The information ministry said we just closed *Sinar Harapan* and if you use that story, you'll be closed too. That brought tears to my eyes, to have a newspaper die just like that. We soon learned that sensitive economic stuff was on the list of subjects unfit for publication.

Sinar would eventually be allowed to publish again but with some onerous conditions: reorganize the company, change the name of the newspaper, and get rid of the chief editor for failing to toe the (often obscure) line. Nothing could be more humiliating or obliterating than a name change, as ethnic Chinese discovered at the beginning of the New Order. For a newspaper its masthead was also its brand. "They said give us five names (for the new newspaper)," said Aristides Katoppo who was involved in the talks with the government. "I said *Sinar Harapan, Sinar Harapan, Sinar Harapan*…And the answer was no, no, no." They settled on *Suara Pembaruan* (Voice of Renewal.)

Aristides said a half-brother of President Suharto then offered to get the newspaper a license in exchange for a controlling stake. "This was simply piracy. I just wanted to negotiate the capitulation and go, and engage in guerrilla warfare after that."

But in the end it was Suharto himself who vetoed that deal. "So there was no deal with the half-brother," Aristides said. "Essentially, we were the same operation, except I would not be on the board of the new company. And the first decision of the new company was that henceforth all board meetings will be joint meetings between the old company and the new company."

Sinar had been warned a few weeks earlier by the information ministry about another taboo subject after an editorial suggesting the presidential term should be limited to two five-year periods. The two issues – Suharto's succession and the succession of licenses and monopolies that the President's family and friends were accumulating – had begun to crystallize in the minds of the urban middle class that had been supporters of the New Order.

Suharto had made the nation self-sufficient in rice, its main food staple. He had provided free education, established health centers

Epicurus

In the 1980s, *The Jakarta Post* introduced a new character on the entertainment scene in the Indonesian capital. His name was Epicurus. Invented by the foreign editors of the newspaper to review restaurants, his brand of curmudgeonly hedonism was embraced by the expatriate community at a time when the city's night life was beginning to take off. The real Epicurus (340-270 BC), considered to be the founder of Hedonism, was a gentle soul who believed the key to life was knowledge, friendship, temperance and virtue. Alas, he died a painful death from a bladder disease.

Here is a sample "Dinner Gong" restaurant review from 1985:

"Normally we don't patronize snake meat restaurants. We tend to share a widespread queasiness about things that slither stealthily through the weeds and bite one to death, unlike, say, chickens and fish, which have no teeth, and are otherwise defenseless against our more carnivorous instincts.

Still, the King Cobra restaurant, Jl. Kapten Tendean, No. 23, South Jakarta, caught our eye. It wasn't just the picture of the coiled cobra painted on the restaurant's window, but also the declarations affirming that snake meat was health food – good for what ails you.

On this particular night, the small restaurant was practically empty. Clean, though, and spanking new, having opened only nine months ago – about the same length, by the way, that a king cobra will fast after lunching on a rabbit or small pig.

The manager, *Ibu* Evani, could tell right away that we didn't know snake meat from monkey brains (another exotic food that tends to depress our appetite). She kindly recommended the king cobra soup (Rp 2,000), and the fried python (Rp 2,000.)

While *Ibu* was explaining to us the origins and wonders of eating poisonous serpent meat, not to mention its various innards, we dug into our snake fare, at first warily, and them with a bit more gumption.

Ibu Evani, herself, was not a bad advertisement for the healthful qualities of eating snake. After 10 children, she still looks trim and youthful at 51, and her youngest, a two-year-old, eats snake every day.

The king cobra soup wasn't bad at all, sort of like chicken soup, except the meat is unmistakably snake in appearance. The python was quite delicious, with a taste not unlike duck. Too bad it was fried in Blue Band margarine, a habit restaurants here should lose quickly, as it leaves food tasting like it was cooked with rancid fish heads.

We were most entertained when the gentleman from the city's garbage authority came in and sat down at our table for his weekly snake meat meal, washed down with a snake blood cocktail. We were invited back to the kitchen to watch his drink being prepared.

The back of the kitchen houses the snake pit, if you will: a row of aquariums with pythons and cobras tangled up and slithering over each other. We were most impressed with the way the cobra coiled up, raising its head, and spreading the skin of its neck into a broad hood, but we were thankful that a thick piece of glass stood between us.

Bad mistake for the cobra to raise its head like that, though. Our 18-year-old waitress fearlessly wielded her sick with a hook at the end, and lifted the squirming reptile onto a chopping block. Then in one deft movement, she grabbed it just below those lethal fangs with one hand, lopping its head off with a mean-looking meat cleaver with the other.

She then squeezed the blood from its still squirming body into a cup. It takes two cobras and a python to make a decent cup of snake blood, if you must know.

Our dinner companion tossed off the concoction in one draught, his face contorting slightly, as if he was drinking bitter medicine–or as if he was just thinking about the fact that he was drinking the blood of one of the most poisonous snakes on earth.

The restaurant features other cocktails made from *arak,* or rice wine, combined with snake innards. *Ibu* Evani gave us a complimentary cocktail made from a snake's penis. We didn't even know they had one. It was delicious.

Our dinner companion went back into the kitchen and emerged later explaining that he had already paid our bill and offering us a ride back to our office. He, too, had to get back to his night shift job as a garbage disposal supervisor. As he dropped us off, he thanked us for giving him company that night. It seems his father had died suddenly of a heart attack earlier that day and he just wanted to stop off at King Cobra for some snake's blood to lift his flagging spirits. He just didn't want to drink alone that night.

We were happy to give him our humble company, and wouldn't mind meeting him again there some time. Maybe it was just our imagination, but we did seem to be feel fairly peppy later that night. Certainly not sick. It might be worth your while too, if you're not fussy about vipers."

– Epicurus

in every village, installed a successful family planning program. He had brought stability and unity to the world's (then) fifth most populous country, and peace in the region. For that, parliament had anointed him "Father of Development." But he was in danger of undermining all he had achieved because corruption and nepotism were permeating every corner of the economy – and he was refusing to prepare a new generation of leaders.

The banning of *Sinar Harapan* sent a clear message to Indonesian journalists ahead of the April 1987 general election to avoid stories about succession and cronyism. But those issues had nevertheless taken root in the political consciousness of the country.

Despite the sensitivities and dangers about taking controversial positions on the opinion pages, the small band of foreigners that were manning the "check desk" at the *Post*, editing for language mostly, were also writing the occasional editorial – on safe (foreign news) topics. The check desk, an Amir Daud invention, brought in a diverse group of foreigners, most of them from America, who were either backpacking through Indonesia, on some sort of study-abroad university program, or looking for a life change. (In the early 1980s, the *Post* hired a middle-aged American who had lost his job as a television correspondent and was going through a divorce. He lasted a few months before reinventing himself as an advertising executive in Jakarta.)

Adam Schwarz, who would write a highly acclaimed book about Indonesia in the 1990s, *A Nation in Waiting*, was struck on his first day as a check editor in the humble newsroom by the noise of clattering typewriters, the smell of *kretek* (this was the 1980s: you could still smoke inside offices), and the oppressive heat and humidity in the non-air-conditioned room.

"As I glanced around, my eyes settled on Budi Sanusi, the sports editor and my soon-to-be-newsroom neighbor. Pounding his typewriter from a vantage point of about one inch above the keys, clenching a sparkling hand-rolled *kretek* between his lips and adorned in a navy-blue ski jacket, it took me some time to figure out what the first question should be. I settled on the weather: "Budi, why the coat?" I asked, perspiration soaking through my T-shirt. "Gets a little cold in the rainy season," he answered with the trace of a smile. I gathered pretty quickly that the coming year was going to be a lot more about what I didn't know than what I did.[1]

Indeed. Not long after I started at the *Post*, the page editor who sat across from me, Thayeb Sabil, came in one morning with angry red stripes on his neck and face. I didn't want to pry. But when he drifted over to Budi's desk, and the sports editor produced an aluminum coin, pulled down Sabil's shirt collar and began vigorously scraping his upper back, I had to ask.

Sabil, another future managing editor, explained he was taking prophylactic measures against "*masuk angin*" (literally, enter the wind.) This happens when the monsoon trade winds shift, dealing out flu and other ailments to the unprotected. Vigorous scraping brings the blood to the surface of the skin where it interacts with some sort of protective trace element in the aluminum coin, according to this folk wisdom. Budi's attire was also undoubtedly his way of warding off any malevolent "*angin.*"

Schwarz had arrived in Jakarta courtesy of the New York-based Henry Luce Foundation, which each year sent 15-20 Americans on a 10-month assignment to work in various capacities across Asia. He was the first such fellow to work at the *Post*. He recalls asking Sabam that first week of work, presumptuously as it turned out, if there was any news he might think about covering the following day. "Taking an unhurried inhale of his pipe, Sabam ventured that, yes, there would be news, but no I would not be covering it. Covering news was not something foreign journalists were meant to be doing. What you can do, he continued, is to write the editorial for tomorrow's paper."

Schwarz pointed out he had only just arrived in Indonesia and, in fact, had never written an editorial before. "I didn't say it had to be about Indonesia, and this is a good time to learn," Sabam told him. "And it would be good to have it done by 8 o'clock," he added. "I have a dinner to go to." Schwarz, with a degree in economics, and who had spent time in Buenos Aires, wrote a densely reasoned editorial

---

1 Schwarz wrote this account of his first day at the *Jakarta Post* in the April 25, 2003 20th anniversary edition of the newspaper.

about Argentina's debt crisis. Sabam was pleased. At a reception not long after, he met the then-coordinating economics minister, Ali Wardhana, who, after complimenting Sabam on the editorial, added: "I know you could never have written that."

Although the *Post* had a publisher in Mohamad Chudori, he was not empowered to do much: The *Post* had basically outsourced the business operations to *Kompas*. Raymond Toruan, representing *Kompas* on the board of directors, wrote the first business plan. It envisaged Indonesia's economy would continue to boom at the average 7 percent clip it had been growing at during the 1970s and early 1980s. More foreigners were arriving to do business with affluent and outward-looking Indonesians. Students who had studied abroad and had grown used to reading foreign newspapers wanted more international news. "So I made projections based on that and with the 500 million rupiah initial capitalization," Raymond said. "I figured we could make a profit in three years." But the United States had tipped into recession in 1982 and the rest of the world followed suit. "Within two years, we had spent everything. There were no ads, but circulation was going up steadily," Raymond recalls.

Circulation had doubled in the first five years to 17,480 in 1988 from 8,657 in 1983. *The Jakarta Post* had proven to be a hit with readers, but rare indeed were the display ads on pages crowded with stories and pictures. Page editors every day faced the daunting prospect of filling an entire broadsheet with editorial matter. They used wire service photos liberally to eat up space. But dispatched over poor telephone lines, the published photos tended to looked like black and white impressionist paintings. "In the early years, I didn't see how we could possibly stay alive," Maggie Agusta said. "I remember the first time we had an ad that bumped a story off the page. Everybody cheered. We were such a family then."

At a board meeting in 1985, Raymond asked for an interest-free loan. The owners reluctantly agreed to chip in another 700 million rupiah. "The mood was not good," Raymond recalls. "Everybody was feeling the crunch of the global recession." He said he resisted pressure both from the board and from ad agencies to give discounts for display ads, as many other newspapers were doing (*Kompas* being a notable exception.) "I told them what we had to provide was a very good newspaper, the best in the country. The people who read this paper are the *crème de la crème*. There's a price to pay for that audience. So, no discounts," Raymond says. "We created credibility both on the business side and the editorial side." By 1988, the *Post* was in the black, the loan had been repaid and the newspaper was running close to a full page of classified ads every day. The following year, the *Post* distributed its first dividend to shareholders. "It wasn't much, but there was a profit. We were no longer in the red," Raymond says.

The *Post* was looking for the elusive Indonesian educated middle class as a potential readership and saw signs it was emerging on the back of strong economic growth and a more sophisticated society that began to assert itself in the surprising 1987 election campaign.

Across the horizon, dust was billowing up on a hot day on an open field outside the cultural capital of Yogyakarta, largely obscuring the large crowd of people that was converging from all directions on the site of the first rally of the 1987 election campaign. A long caravan of pick-up trucks was also rolling in from all directions, packed with people brandishing the standard of the tiny Indonesian Democratic Party (PDI) and beating drums. Discernible through the roiling clouds of dust were the red party T-shirts that supporters were wearing, featuring a silhouette of man's head wearing a *peci* cap – the unmistakable visage of Sukarno. Indonesia's first president, whose ghost was even charismatic, had come back to haunt Indonesia's placid political landscape. I had my lead for Reuters, for whom I was now working, having left the *Post* a year earlier.

It was Ali Murtopo's idea to have a "floating mass" in Indonesian political life. That meant political assemblies and rallies were outlawed, except during election campaigns, when the masses could let off all that pent-up steam with boisterous rallies. These were occasionally accompanied by riots and mayhem as rival parties fielded their hired thugs against each other.

But no one expected this. PDI, the successor to Sukarno's

Indonesian Nationalist Party, was playing with fire by making the first president their standard bearer. And not only that, his daughter Megawati had agreed to abandon her life as suburban housewife to help lead the party.

Sukarno, who died in disgrace in 1970 under virtual house arrest over his connection to the PKI communist party and the murky events of 1965, remained controversial in Indonesia. The new airport at Cengkareng west of Jakarta was named Soekarno-Hatta – the latter was the country's first vice-president – because Suharto was uncomfortable giving his predecessor sole billing at the airport, which opened in 1985.

Yet, across the nation, young people who had only known Suharto as president started wearing that red Sukarno T-shirt and brandishing posters with his picture at rallies. The government later prohibited using the image of Sukarno in campaigns but the ban was widely ignored.

Stringent election rules, however, allowed little criticism of the government, and the 25-day campaign period was the shortest in the country's history. Foreign Minister Mochtar Kusumaatmadja raised eyebrows when he urged students at ITB in Bandung not to be afraid to demand their political rights and protest against justice. Mochtar was not invited to be part of the next cabinet. But his view had quite a bit of support among the Jakarta establishment and parts of the military, worried that key cognitive skills were not being developed among a young generation getting brainwashed on *Pancasila*. Politics had been banned on campus since the 1978 protests and students were generally apathetic and cynical. They joked about the general election being a "general selection" or "election of generals." An entire generation of university students, traditionally the keepers of the nation's conscience, had been depoliticized.

Instead they turned their attention to causes – Islam, the environment, ethnic grievances, human rights, poverty and labor issues. I visited the Bandung Institute of Technology (ITB) in 1987 during the election campaign and found students completely turned off by the politics of the New Order. ITB, whose most famous alumni was Sukarno and which was once a hotbed of political activism, "seems like a mellow religious community with a social conscience," I wrote at the time. The Salman mosque was the centre of activism, sponsoring "*Kharisma*" study groups whose mission was to practice orthodox Islam and "scientifically probe issues of economic and social justice."

This interest in Islam was not always welcomed by the Islamic leaders of the day. Abdurrahman Wahid, the leader of *Nahdlatul Ulama*, the nation's largest Muslim organization and a future president, told me at the time he was concerned about "shallow fundamentalism" taking root on campuses because young people felt that modern society had failed them. He said "undemocratic methods and economic policies that widen the gap between rich and poor are helping to drive youth into so-called fundamentalism."

Indeed, the mood of the electorate as the 1987 election campaign came to a close was not good, at least in Jakarta. When Golkar leader and soon-to-be vice president Gen. Sudharmono rhetorically asked a party rally if the people were satisfied with the country's development, he appeared stunned when the crowd shouted resoundingly: "No!"

"Neither are we," was his smart rejoinder.

At PDI's final election rally more than one million people marched down Jakarta's main boulevard, the likes of which had not been seen since the 1965-66 student demonstrations that helped push Sukarno from power. Film stars and celebrities joined bicycle rickshaw drivers and street vendors in the march. That parade could not have happened unless the armed forces, under the command of Benny Murdani, had allowed it.

But in the end it didn't matter how impressive the rallies were, or how dissatisfied the people. The Golkar man was the guy who delivered the fertilizer and rice seeds to the village headman, an ABRI soldier sat in the local council, and together they made sure the village voted the right way. Golkar garnered its biggest ever share of the vote, taking 73 percent, versus 65 percent in 1982. The "Father of Development" was set to be sworn in for a fifth five-year term.

Nevertheless, *The Jakarta Post* saw a watershed in an election "which has the interesting political implication that, at least in Jakarta, the growing middle class has cast its support for this party of commoners…This emerging middle class seems curious to see if PDI…will be sensitive and brave enough to fight for the issues that are important to this socio-economic group."

Already one of Asia's most enduring leaders, Suharto was installed for a fifth term in March 1988, and, as was the case at his last coronation by the rubber stamp parliament, he hinted that it could be his final term. Since he was about to turn 67, some people took him at his word.

Indonesia had known only two presidents and the transition between the charismatic Sukarno and the enigmatic Suharto was traumatic and violent. Suharto, father of six grown children, had never been opposed for the presidency. And the vice-presidency had never been contested either.

Suharto had outlived or outlasted most of those who helped him to power, jailing or muzzling several of his old comrades-in-arms and steadily reducing the ranks of retired officers in his cabinet. While military men had dominated his early cabinets, his long-time deputy in charge of the bureaucracy, Sudharmono, and Gen. Benny Murdani, due to retire as commander of the armed forces, were the only two left that were likely to be in the next cabinet.

Sudharmono, a military lawyer and Golkar chairman and widely despised in the ranks as not a true soldier, had been tapped to be vice president. But a faction in parliament, thought to have gotten a nod from Murdani, had put up another candidate. Such a break with precedent meant that a vote for the presidency could not be ruled out next time. Suharto was not amused, and in the event, Sudharmono was duly elected by consensus. But the armed forces commander had fired a shot across Suharto's ship of state.

Suharto was also coming under pressure from aid donors to reform an economy riddled with corruption, monopolies and crony contracts. Corruption was so endemic in customs and immigration that the customs service was outsourced to the Swiss firm Société Générale de Surveillance in 1985.

Economists estimated the amount of "black money" circulating in Indonesia was at least equal to the national budget. Foreign

National Editor Thayeb Sabil walks through the newsroom in 1983.
The Post had no computers then, only Olympia typewriters.

The Post's first managing editor, Amir Daud, chairs a daily afternoon meeting of senior editors in 1983.
To his left is chief editor Sabam Siagian, layout consultant Lionel Northrop, Debra Yatim, Hartoyo,
Thayeb Sabil, Bill Tarrant, Johan Akbar, Albert Saragih, Budi Sanusi and Abdullah Alamudi.

Former Indonesian President Sukarno (R) pins a medal on Gen. Suharto in early 1966. Suharto slowly edged the mercurial Sukarno from power after the abortive September 30, 1965 coup blamed on the communist party.

Prof. Widjojo Nitisastro was the main architect of President Soeharto's New Order economic system. He obtained his Ph.D degree at UC Berkeley. A number of young Indonesian economists who graduated from the University of Indonesia went for advance studies to the US, mostly to Berkeley,on fellowships provided by the Ford Foundation. A radical magazine, *Ramparts* dubbed the economists working for President Suharto headed by Prof. Widjojo as "the Berkeley Mafia".

Gen. Leonardus Benjamin Murdani, Armed Forces Commander
and later defense minister 1983-93.

Liem Sioe Liong, shown here in 1969, was considered Indonesia's richest man at
one point during the New Order. Many of his businesses were monopolies and
exclusive trade licenses due to his strong ties with the Suharto family.

Sabam Siagian, chief editor of *The Jakarta Post* from 1983-91, in a characteristic pose.

The Jakarta Post stages a family photo after launching on April 25, 1983.
Author Bill Tarrant is seated second from the left.

(top) Information Minister Harmoko holds a copy of the first edition of *The Jakarta Post* on April 25, 1983. Harmoko had a 5 percent stake in the newspaper, which he earned by helping the ownership group acquire the necessary publishing permits. To his left laughing is business manager Raymond Toruan, publisher Mohamad Chudori and chief editor Sabam Siagian.

The modest entryway to *The Jakarta Post* in 1983. The newspaper occupied what had been a laundry warehouse for the Kompas Gramedia complex across the street.

Security personnel sift through the rubble of a burnt-out building following riots in the Tanjung Priok harbor area in September 1984. Scores of people were killed and injured when police fired on a crowd who were protesting against a crackdown on hardline Islamic preaching at a local mosque.

The Jakarta Post/Soeryo Winoto

A resident of Jakarta's posh Pondok Indah neighborhood pick up the shambles after a terrifying ammunition dump explosion on 30 October 1984.

The Jakarta Post/Soeryo Winoto

Rockets and mortars rained down through the roofs of Pondok Indah neighborhood.

Ali Murtopo in this undated file photo. Murtopo, who died in
1984, was one of Suharto's main advisors in the early years of the
New Order. He and Jusuf Wanandi came up with the idea for
The Jakarta Post in 1982.

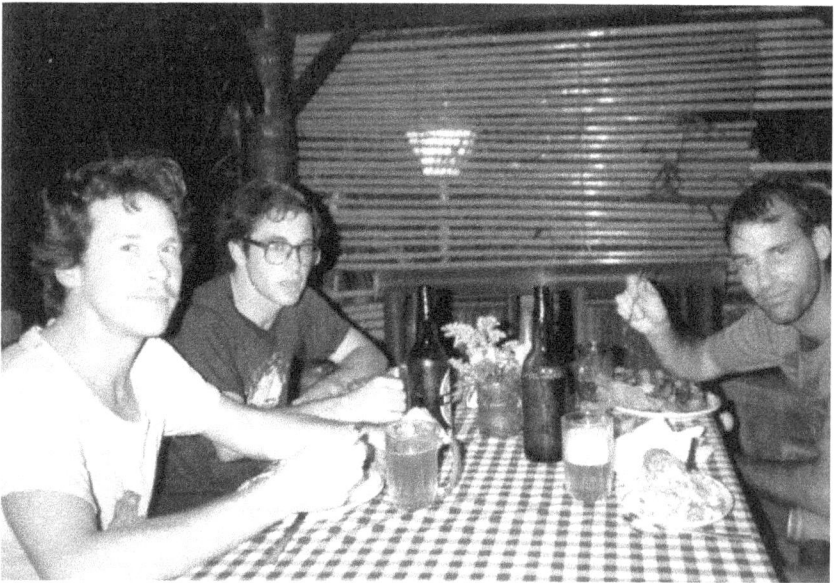

Author Bill Tarrant (right) with his brother Jim (left) and their brother-in-law Mike Carlton at a
Jakarta cafe in 1985.

Suharto raises a toast with French President François Mitterrand at a state banquet in Jakarta in September 1986. During the 1980s the West, happy to have an anti-communist bulwark in Southeast Asia during the Cold War turned a blind eye to human rights issues in Suharto's Indonesia.

The Indonesian Democratic Party (PDI) gathered more than one million people in Central Jakarta for the final campaign rally of the 1987 election. The stunning turnout, which the military did nothing to stop, marked a point when the urban middle class began to sour on Suharto's corrupt New Order.

The Jakarta Post

Post Managing Director Raymond Toruan (left), *Tempo* Deputy Editor and *Post* Board Member Fikri Jufri (center) and *Post* Chief Editor Sabam Siagian at a 1991 seminar.

The Jakarta Post/Arief Hidayat

Tempo chief editor Goenawan Mohamad talks to reporters after the magazine was banned in June 1994.

Sekretariat Negara

U.S. President Ronald Reagan with Suharto on a short visit to Bali in 29 April – 2 May 1986. Security throughout the island was tight with American marines patrolling Ngurah Rai International Airport.

The Jakarta Post/Alex Lumi

U.S. President Clinton chats with Suharto in November 1994. Clinton stitched up $40 billion worth of deals, most of it energy-related, during that visit, while dispensing mild criticism about Indonesia's approach to East Timor and human rights.

Lt. Gen Prabowo Subianto (R), shown here on March 31, 1998, helps a frail Abdul Haris Nasution, a former army chief commander who escaped assassination in the September 30, 1965 coup attempt.

Thousands of students occupied the grounds – and the roof – of Indonesia's national parliament in May 1998 in a student-led uprising that ousted the late former president Suharto from power.

Student protesters cool off in a reflecting pool in the compound of the national parliament in May 1998

Thousands of students and others gather in a festive atmosphere at the national parliament compound on May 12, 1998. The students vowed to stay there until Suharto stepped down, which he did 9 days later.

The Jakarta Post/Arief Suhardiman

People carry loot away from Chinese-owned stores in the Tanah Abang area of Jakarta on May 14, 1998. Hundreds of people were killed and scores of business destroyed in the riots a week before Suharto's resignation. Some saw a military hand in the mayhem.

The Jakarta Post/PJ Leo

Looters race out of a shop with pilfered goods in the May 14, 1998 riots.

Crowds burn a vehicle in the middle of a street in Jakarta's Chinatown district on May 14, 1998.

Parliament chairman and Information Minister Harmoko holds a press conference on May 16, 1998. Harmoko, once a *Jakarta Post* shareholder, called on Suharto to resign.

President Suharto announces his resignation on May 22, 1998. To his left is Vice President B.J. Habibie who would take over, Armed Forces Commander Gen. Wiranto and Suharto's oldest daughter, Siti Hardiyanti Rukmana.

Former Jakarta Governor Ali Sadikin (R) with democracy activist Sri Bintang Pamungkas in June 1998, weeks after Suharto quit the presidency. Sadikin, a former New Order General, was a member of the banned Petition of 50 group of dissidents.

residents used to joke that Indonesia's only real world-class industry was the pirated music cassette tape stores that had proliferated across the country, offering the latest pop, rock and jazz on top quality tapes – sometimes even before they had been released in the West – for about $1. Kickbacks or "commissions" were standard for all government contracts and Chinese businessmen were often asked to make donations to "good causes" with the money usually funneled to a spider's web of presidential foundations.

The Inter-Governmental Group on Indonesia (IGGI), linking 14 donor nations and four international lending agencies, had become one of the largest multilateral aid groups in the world, providing Indonesia $32 billion since it was set up after the 1965 coup was crushed. Nearly three-quarters of Indonesia's spending on development came from the group, much of it tied to exports from the lenders. In a confidential report the World Bank called on Jakarta to dismantle the trade and industrial monopolies that were throttling growth – the issue that got *Sinar Harapan* banned. It spotlighted industries with close links to Suharto's family as especially in need of reform: steel, plastics, food and beverages, among others.

But the donors were also concerned about keeping a good thing going. Indonesia straddled strategic sea lanes and was a pro-West bulwark against communism in a world that still had Cold War bipolar disorder. The country was a leading supplier of primary commodities and a major consumer of machinery and capital goods that provided jobs and income for the donor countries.

In editorials during the mid to late-1980s *The Jakarta Post* drew attention to the country's mounting indebtedness and urged the IGGI to reduce the quantum of soft loans in favor of grants. A June 1986 editorial predicted (wrongly, as it turned out) such a scheme "will enable the country to build up an adequate margin of protection against the kind of liquidity squeezes and debt service difficulties which many other Third World borrowers have encountered over the past few years."

Indonesia's worsening debt picture was a real cause of concern, however. Its external debt of $45.5 billion in 1988 was the sixth largest in the developing world, and had been rising sharply almost since the beginning of the New Order. The International Monetary Fund said the debt service ratio had risen to 39 percent of export earnings in 1986-87, compared with an acceptable maximum of 20 percent. In January 1988, the government budget revealed that 26 percent of projected income for 1988 would go toward servicing the debt.

Jakarta started to see capital flight after the 1987 election, with business fearing another devaluation was on the cards to deal with revenue shortfalls. The bout of market jitters ended after Suharto unveiled his new cabinet, which showed reformists had regained the upper hand. In October 1988 banking deregulation was instituted. Capital markets and foreign investment were opened up. And, on Dec. 25, the government gave business a Christmas present, announcing that most regulations on exports would be dropped.

That watershed liberalization package ignited a growth spurt that lasted well into the 1990s.

The *Post* worried about the proliferation of banks that followed the liberalization measures – 28 private national banks and eight new joint venture ones were set up within months. The fiercer competition, while bringing much needed market discipline to the industry, "has raised concern among many people, notably with regard to possible bank failures and the concentration of banks in the hands of a few business conglomerates," the editorial said.

But Western bankers, who would only be too happy to throw good money after bad at Indonesian businesses in the decade to come, were neither worried about the suddenly crowded banking business nor Indonesia's mounting external debt. "The debt position, while not easy, is under extremely good control and sound management," Chase Manhattan Chairman William Butcher told journalists after meeting Suharto in June 1987.

Jusuf Wanandi's job, as executive director of the Centre for Strategic and International Studies, was to provide long-range planning advice to the government as its "semi-official" think tank. And so after the April elections, he wrote Suharto a letter suggesting the president look to planning who would succeed him. Jusuf, dressed in his usual batik shirt, described over lunch at the American Club in Singapore that letter and its impact.

"I wrote: '*Pak,* you have been very successful and after 20 years society has changed so much because of your success. But that also means a challenge – to prepare a team of leaders to come and take over from you in the future. You cannot expect another hero to rise and take over such a complex society anymore."

That "hero" reference could well have intimated a widely held perception about Suharto and his beliefs about power. According to this theory, Suharto had greatness thrust upon him during the tumultuous events of 1965-66. He had the *wahyu,* the power in Javanese terms, or a divine mandate to rule. And over the next 30 years, he consciously projected the aura of an ancient Javanese king, with many of their same virtues – restraint, refinement, opaqueness, and a kind of double-dealing deviousness.

And what was Suharto's reaction to his suggestion that he should contemplate a more bucolic life at the Tapos ranch?

"He said, 'they want to get rid of me, huh?'"[2]

In Javanese mysticism, power comes from a higher source. What happens on earth is part of a matrix of mystical powers in which humans are not the agent of events but a medium for higher powers. Power for traditional Javanese kings was not something that could be transferred; it was indivisible, and to compromise it by naming a successor was dangerous.[3] "Suharto only knew one model of governance," Jusuf says, "namely the Javanese kingdom, where the King stayed in power until his death."

But what in retrospect really got the old man riled up was Jusuf's second point in the letter: his suggestion that Suharto give more empowerment to his coordinating ministers, "so that," in Jusuf's words, "you have the upper hand in the strategic vision of the country."

"He would like to deal with every project, because then he can decide to whom it was going, sons or daughters or friends. And so

---

2 Murdani, who was to join CSIS as chairman after leaving the government, is the source for Suharto's reaction to the memo.

3 See, for example, Benedict Anderson, "The Idea of Power in Javanese Culture."

when I asked him not to do that and to give it to the coordinating ministers it meant all these projects would not be dealt with by him. After that, he told the cabinet: 'don't involve yourself with CSIS anymore.' And no more memos, he told his aide de camp," Jusuf said, referring to the person who would receive and pass on CSIS papers to the president.

Up until then CSIS sent policy memos direct to the presidential office through his chief of staff. "That was the deal we had in 1971; CSIS would stay outside the government but give advice directly to the president. "He said to the cabinet: 'I don't want anything to do with them, and I don't want you to have anything to do with them.'"

"Then in March, at the presidential nominating convention, Benny's people in parliament decided to oppose Suharto's choice of Sudharmono," Jusuf continued. "This was all part of what he saw as Benny's conspiracy against him, and with the background that Benny was close to us (CSIS)," Jusuf said. "That was the problem with this leadership. Nothing was ever clear, transparent. It was all mysterious, conspiracy theories everywhere. Behind everything is a conspiracy."

In the New Order, conspiracy was interwoven with mystery and mysticism. Perhaps deliberately so, for it was deeply embedded in the culture of Indonesia's main island of Java.

Under a full moon, the vestige of a once mighty Hindu culture on Java gathered on Christmas day of 1987 on the sulphurous crater of mighty Mount Bromo in East Java to honor their ancestors. The *Tengger*, the Hindu community around Bromo, are descendants of the Majapahit kingdom which once ruled most of Indonesia, Soedjadi, a *dukun* or priest of the community, tells me at the sandy plateau at the crater's base – itself the top of an ancient extinct volcano – where his community has gathered.

Priests had been conducting prayers calling on the gods to bless the people, who were climbing to Bromo's smoking crater to throw offerings of food, flowers and live chickens into the steamy abyss. Cradling his grand-daughter inside a thick sarong against the damp air of the tropical highlands, Soedjadi tells the story of how his ancestors came to Bromo. When conflict broke out with newly arrived

Muslims at the end of the 14th century, most of the Majapahit court fled to Bali and founded a new Hindu kingdom there. But Princess Roro Anteng and her courtier husband Joko Seger led their followers across the narrow Bali strait to Bromo, the eerie-looking crater that bulges out of the high plateau of volcanic sand in East Java, about 40 kilometers south of Surabaya. The childless royal couple begged the fire god residing in Bromo for fertility. He granted their wish, but demanded the youngest-born child in return. Their 25th child was thrown into the crater. The *Tengger* believe the child's spirit must be honored by sacrificial offerings on the last full moon of the year.

Indonesia is a superstitious country in which ancient patterns of belief exist alongside modern religious practices. While 87 percent of Indonesia's 200 million people declare themselves to be Muslim, around 80 million or so are from the heartlands of Java where syncretic beliefs, melding Hinduism, Buddhism and animism hold sway.

Suharto meditated in sacred caves, and was also said to have bathed in water brought from a lake on the sacred Mount Lawu. He was a big fan of *wayang kulit*, his smile strangely similar to that of Semar, the divine and very wise clown in the shadow puppet theatre. An old story in Jakarta tells of Suharto calling a meeting with his ministers to deal with a thorny issue and presenting them with a *wayang* performance instead. At the end he said: "I trust my wishes are clear," as his guests looked at each other in bewilderment.

Suharto was sympathetic to practitioners of *"kejawen"* or as it was officially known, *"kepercayaan"* (belief). Indeed, most of Indonesia's six presidents have made visits to caves or mountaintops and ancient ruins and consulted with spiritual advisers before making important decisions.

A debate over the status of mystic beliefs in the world's most populous Muslim country nearly led to a vote in 1978 at the special session of the People's Consultative Assembly, held every five years to elect a president, vice president and set policy guidelines. Indonesia officially recognized five religions – Buddhism, Catholicism, Hinduism, Islam and Protestantism. Proposed new guidelines from the government would have allowed mystic beliefs, incorporated in the ancient rituals of "*kebatinan*" or "inner experience", to qualify as a religion (and get state funding from the ministry of religion). The teachings *of kejawen* and *kebatinan* already had their own weekly time slot on state-run television along with the five recognized religions. But in the end, even Suharto's tacit endorsement was not enough, and the guidelines never came to a vote.

With the Islamic opposition in jail or in exile, communism exterminated, and the "Petition of 50" effectively neutralized, political opposition was almost non-existent. The media devoted a lot of ink and broadcasting space to mystical matters in the 1980s. So much of politics and finance was off limits to the press that the paranormal became the stories that were meant to be read between the lines (or as Aristides famously put it, "between the lies").

In the mid-1980s, an expedition of "paranormal scientists" was mounted to hunt down the legendary *tuyul*, with a nod and wink from the presidential palace. *Tuyul* were little boy sprites, invisible to the naked eye, who if captured by a knowledgeable human (one versed in *kebatinan* rites), could be used to steal money from people's pockets.

The media, including *The Jakarta Post*, was full of stories about the *tuyul* phenomenon, who they were and why people believed in them. When the provenance of the New Order itself was shrouded in the conflicting conspiracy theories about what really happened on Sept. 30, 1965; when mysterious shootings and unexplained fires became hallmarks of the regime; when the president himself went off to meditate in a cave on a volcanic plateau and one of his top advisors was some sort of shaman; it should not seem at all unusual that naked little thieving sprites would become fodder for scientific expeditions in Suharto's Indonesia.

The Indonesian media, confined to reporting the government's agenda and views on politics, the economy and society, was only too happy to romp with paranormal scientists in something different for a change, especially if it could be parlayed into something of a metaphor about the state of the nation. *The Jakarta Post* played it safe and ran wire service copy – AP, AFP and Reuters – poking fun at the whole thing. Ali Murtopo must have been rolling over in his grave: *The Post* was meant to be the alternative to, not the medium for, foreign correspondents.

At the same time, given the rapid pace of modernization in Indonesia, and the strong ancient pull of *kebatinan* beliefs on Java, it was not surprising that people turned to the paranormal for explanations and to witch doctors for what ailed them. Suharto, for his part, had good political reasons to encourage discussion of ancient Javanese beliefs. While it was evident that his power stemmed from continued support of the army, he needed to cloak himself in the mantle of an ancient Javanese king to cement his credibility with Javanese heartlanders.

In the early 1980s Jusuf was running CSIS and helping to set up the *Institut Manajemen Prasetya Mulya* (IMPM) or the Noble Vow Management Institute along with his brother Sofyan. It was the first business school to offer a master's degree in business administration (MBA) and was aimed at cultivating a professional business class among "pribumi", (native Indonesians, as opposed to those with Chinese ancestry). The Prasetya Mulya Foundation was funded by some of the wealthiest Chinese-Indonesian business clans.

At the same time, Suharto – ever suspicious of the Chinese who dominated the economy – ordered the heads of the 300 largest conglomerates to take a 10-day course in *Pancasila*," said Sofyan, who like his brother favors Indonesian batik shirts as a gesture of patriotism.

Sofyan by then had become an unofficial spokesman for this group and their interlocutor with Suharto's administration, and was increasingly focused on building the Wanandi family's Gemala group. Though he was the newspaper's largest shareholder, he acknowledged giving *The Jakarta Post* little of his attention. "We didn't put our concentration or attention on *The Jakarta Post*. We just left it to the chief editor and the publisher. We didn't care how it developed. Now, we can't make that mistake anymore."

But by 1988, the *Post* had become commercially successful. Jusuf, now put beyond the pale of Suharto's inner circle, decided to take over the board chairmanship from his brother. "These two gentlemen,

Eric Samola and Sofyan, were too busy with other things, bigger businesses. This (the *Post*) was for them peanuts, so they weren't paying attention," Jusuf said.

By the end of the 1980s *The Jakarta Post* had built a reputation for being one of the most credible newspapers in the country, based on its straightforward, Western-style reporting and writing style with "inverted pyramid" story structures and strict rules on sourcing. "You cannot bullshit in English, like the Javanese way," Jusuf said.

But that straight-forward style, and the newspapers increasingly higher profile, was making it a target.

Sabam had come under pressure to be the chief editor of *Suara Pembaruan*, the new afternoon newspaper that replaced *Sinar Harapan*. "I had to do some soul searching about that. Not everybody over there was supportive of me, and by then I had gotten the feel of *The Jakarta Post*. I sensed the team was with me, and that something was beginning to happen with the newspaper. I wanted to be remembered that I had a part in shaping the development of *The Jakarta Post*."

He certainly did not want to be remembered as the editor who shut the paper down. But that was his fear in June 1988. A *Jakarta Post* reporter and a couple of other journalists had been invited in June 1988 to join the industry minister on a visit to the giant airplane factory in Bandung, the pride and joy of Research and Technology Minister B.J. Habibie. His deputy, Pusponegoro, led the group on a tour of the *Industri Pesawat Terbang Nusantara* (IPTN) plant, showing off a newly completed CN235 plane which was supposed to have been sold to Saudi Arabia – except that the Saudis apparently had objected to the interior design of the plane.

The reporters asked explicitly if the sale order had been cancelled. "Yes," the *Post* reporter quoted Pusponegoro as saying, "but don't make a fuss about it." The story appeared in Monday's edition on an inside page under the headline "Saudi Arabia cancels orders for CN-235 aircraft." The next day was a holiday so it was Wednesday when Sabam got a call from Habibie's office, asking to see him and the reporter, Riksa Abdullah.

"I knew Habibie," Sabam recalls. "I thought it was just going to be a chat. We entered his conference room with its long table filled with model airplanes, and all around the table were seated his staff and the director general of information, Janner Sinaga." The presence of Sinaga, Harmoko's attack dog, was definitely a bad sign. "Habibie's chair was empty, except for this sheepskin on it. When we were all seated, he came in and he was shaking. 'I thought you were my friend,' he shouted in English. He then repeated that in Dutch and finally in Indonesian. He slammed a file down on the table and said 'you know what this is? Your news has wrecked the market. This news item has been picked up by all the news agencies and if any of these orders get cancelled, I will sue!'

"And, as he shouted, he kept sliding, little by little, off the sheepskin to where his nose was almost touching one of the planes on the table," Sabam said. "It was all I could do to stop myself from laughing. I offered to print his counter-statement. But he replied: 'I talked to *Bapak* President and he said that for any media that do not support national development drastic action should be taken.' Well, that formula was a death sentence for a newspaper."

This appeared to be no idle threat, for Habibie was part of Suharto's intimate circle, a friend of the First Family since he was 12 and the technology minister since 1978. Sabam left Habibie's office and walked disconsolately down Jalan Thamrin, Jakarta's main boulevard, during rush hour. "I felt so lonely. Under my stewardship *The Jakarta Post* is to be closed down? That's when you start to think about who your friends are."

Sabam called on Murdani, who by then was the defense minister in Suharto's cabinet – in effect, a demotion. A Catholic Javanese who had fought in every military conflict in Indonesia after independence, Murdani was no longer the armed forces chief, probably the most powerful position in Suharto's Indonesia after the president himself. But the former intelligence officer knew Indonesia's corridors of power as well as anybody. Sabam had known him for years and didn't think twice about consulting him. "I explained the situation, and he dismissed it," Sabam said. "'What's the matter with you,' he said. 'You cannot handle Habibie?'

"No, but he saw *Bapak* President, I said."

"Then Murdani opened up a black notebook. He kept a notebook of the President's appointments. 'He lied. He didn't see the President,' Murdani said.

"What about my problem?" I asked.

"That's for you to worry about. I'm only telling you he lied."

Directors of the *Post*, including *Tempo* deputy editor Fikri Jufri, then contacted other cabinet ministers and senior military officers, seeking their intercession. In the end, Habibie neither sued nor caused the *Post* to close down.

As the 1980s came to a close Suharto was at the height of his heavenly mandate and all seemed well on his patch of earth. The economy was again posting 6-7 percent growth. His ambitious, if not avaricious, children would soon be trying to cash in.

The Jakarta Post was also heading toward its golden period.

꧁

CHAPTER FOUR
PUSHING UPWARD

On the morning of August 1, 1991, Susanto Pudjomartono was wandering around the sprawling complex of the Kompas Gramedia publishing empire looking for his newsroom. Finding *The Jakarta Post* offices was always a bit tricky anyway, tucked as it was behind a noisy *pasar*. He had driven up a narrow lane lined with food stalls; past the house with the aviary and chirping songbirds; past the Chinese temple with the dragon astride the roof, ablaze with candles and incense wafting into the street.

The new chief editor of *The Jakarta Post* eventually found his newsroom housed in temporary quarters on the *Kompas* compound, while a new office building for the newspaper was being built. Like his predecessor, Sabam Siagian, Susanto was also feeling a bit daunted about coming onto the hallowed ground of *Kompas Gramedia* from the weekly newsmagazine *Tempo*, where he had been managing editor. He was to be further discombobulated by the strikingly different editorial culture of the English-language morning newspaper

The Jakarta Post entered the 1990s as a reputable and financially-sound newspaper, unquestionably the best among the three English newspapers in the country. Sabam Siagian had left in 1991 to become Indonesia's ambassador to Australia; a position he would serve for the next four years at a time when Indonesia's occupation of East Timor was coming under greater critical scrutiny, particularly in the land Down Under. He had gone to university 40 years earlier with the idea of becoming a diplomat and now he has.

Under his watch, *The Jakarta Post* had become required reading in the foreign diplomatic corps; its opinion pages were influential and coverage of foreign affairs unrivalled in the Indonesian media. The ambassadorship was Sabam's reward for succeeding in making *The Jakarta Post* Indonesia's international face. "It had been a tradition in Indonesia to offer chief editors ambassadorships," Sabam said. They knew the issues of the country they represented and were presumably good networkers. But until Sabam's appointment it had been 20 years since an editor became an envoy. "Rosihan Anwar was offered the Vietnam ambassadorship in December 1968 – during the U.S. bombing of Hanoi. He refused and Suharto supposedly was so incensed by this that he declined to offer senior journalists ambassadorships again."

That first day on the job, Susanto went from desk to desk introducing himself to reporters and asking what they did. Translator, they kept saying. Translator. Translator. I'm a translator, too. He may have been lost on his way to his new job, but the *Post* was definitely, as he described it later, "lost in translation."

"I was shocked, not about the building. They were translating stories from yesterday for tomorrow's edition," he recalled. Later that day, during a discussion at the afternoon news budget meeting about an environmental issue, Susanto suggested a reporter interview Environment Minister Emil Salim. People gave him funny looks. "They said only the chief editor could interview a minister," Susanto said with a grimace. He was used to the enterprising and initiative editorial culture at *Tempo*, a feisty magazine the government had banned once already and would do so again for reporting that angered the authorities. "So at our first editorial meeting, I said we will stop that practice and all reporters must go to the field. I asked people for their ideas. They weren't used to that. They'd say 'just give your decisions, sir'. It took a while for people to get used to that. Then I was surprised that reporters were not reading the newspaper before coming to the office. Back then, TV news was not very important, so I asked all the reporters to read the newspaper before coming to work."

The new chief editor had come with his own agenda about taking *The Jakarta Post* to a new level. It was a credible newspaper, he felt, though a bit on the stodgy side, like its surrogate parent, *Kompas*. A chief editor in Indonesia had two options, in his opinion. One was to take the approach that much of the media practiced, and subscribe to "survival journalism" by adhering to the government creed of a "free and responsible press." Or he could push for more freedom – a much darker and dangerous path under Suharto, who was, if anything, becoming even more intolerant of criticism the longer he stayed in power. "Any newspaper that dared to take the latter approach," Susanto said, "had to be ready to be banned, or at least stamped as 'opposition' or an 'enemy of the state.'"

The change of editors marked a turning point for the newspaper. Under Sabam's leadership, the newspaper had established itself among the expatriate community as the most credible source of news in Indonesia. But while the newspaper was fulfilling its original mission to be Indonesia's face to the world, and was popular with the foreign community, the paper could not grow without trying to reach the educated Indonesian middle class. And to do that it had to change the reporting culture in the newsroom.

A 1991 survey had shown that 62 percent of *The Jakarta Post's* readers were expatriates. The survey had also found that Indonesian readers saw *The Jakarta Post* as another *Kompas* in English. "I thought if we had to depend on expats, we will never grow and be influential," Susanto said. "I had the spirit of *Tempo* in me. *The Jakarta Post* would never expand to a paper in the hundreds of thousands, but I thought the way to grow would be to change it to a more daring and aggressive newspaper.

Susanto's early life had prepared him for living on the edge. His father, a bank director in Blora, Central Java, was killed in the 1948 communist-led Madiun rebellion, an anti-Sukarno mutiny by a group of leftist army officers that went nowhere but was a precursor to the events of 1965. Susanto was just 9 years old then. Like *Kompas* Chief Editor Jacob Oetama, Susanto went to Gadjah Mada University's communications school during the turbulent 1960s, when the student movement was at its height. He moved to Jakarta in 1966 working for the Japanese news agency JiJi, covering the decline and fall of Sukarno as part of the presidential palace press corps. It was then that he met Megawati Sukarnoputri, often at the Bogor palace, the splendid 250 year-old Dutch-built mansion in the volcanic hills outside Jakarta that was Sukarno's weekend home.

"In 1966, Mega was 18 and I was young," Susanto recalls. "Sukarno was very personal with the press. I'd wave to her when I saw her and after a few months we got to know each other. We became friends." She called him by his family nickname, *Mas Cus*. "She knew my sister-in-law and brother. It was only after she joined politics in the 1980s that we met again. We used to have lunch or dinner together, talking about the political situation, how the Suharto regime didn't like her. People were afraid to meet her then, but I'm a journalist and an old friend and I wasn't afraid."

It was Amir Daud who recruited him in 1977 to *Tempo*, where he worked for the next 14 years, becoming first national editor and then managing editor, earning a reputation as one of *Tempo's* leading writers on the prestigious National Desk, often taking charge of the cover story.

Susanto told me all this over a beer at a bar at Plaza Senayan, one of the most up-market malls in Jakarta, a place to see and be seen. Built with Japanese money in 1996 in the Senayan district, it is not far from *The Jakarta Post*, where he never goes these days. Susanto is a heavyset man, soft-spoken, with a gentle manner. Like so many Indonesian journalists I have met over the years, he is an intellectual and an art lover, prone to philosophical ruminations. His tone, as he recalls his salad days at the *Post*, is a bit wistful and defensive. He did not part on the best of terms with management before following in Sabam's footsteps and taking up an ambassadorship – in his case to Moscow. He visibly shudders and his face falls as he talks about his time in Russia, from where he has just returned. "It was sooo cold," he moaned. And he got fat there.

Susanto found a like-minded soul in Raymond Toruan, who had at that time just been named publisher of the *Post*. If Susanto wanted to push the envelope of press freedom, Raymond wanted to push the cause of democracy by hooking up with the non-governmental organization (NGO) movement. They worked unusually closely together as publisher and editor, both driven by the same ideal: to put *The Jakarta Post* at the forefront of coverage of an emerging pro-democracy movement. The early 1990s were bright with possibility (and impossibility). He and Raymond took their proposal for a bolder and more daring approach to Jusuf Wanandi and the board of directors, who, somewhat to their surprise, gave them a mandate to change the newspaper.

"We succeeded in convincing the board...that the newspaper should try to reach more Indonesian readers," Susanto recalls. "In short, we wanted to reinvent the *Post* into a critical and influential newspaper, though small in circulation, but reaching the decision-makers, the cream of society. We began to be more daring and bold, and as a result, I got summoned to the ministry of information many times."[1]

Raymond, meanwhile, had worked out a deal with *Kompas* to build a new two-story office building on the site of the old laundry room-turned-newsroom (the cause of Susanto's confusion his first day), financed by the *Kompas* pension fund. He then kitted out the new offices with state-of-the art word processing computers "better than *Kompas*." The board was inclined, at least then, to look upon Raymond as their golden boy.

"Ah, we built a really beautiful team, Susanto and I," Raymond says today.

Susanto and Raymond's more adventuresome course was, in some ways, sailing with the prevailing winds of the times. The fall of the

---

1 Getting warned could be an unpleasant experience. I was twice summoned to the Director General of Information's office when I was with Reuters for browbeating sessions. The late Janner Sinaga, who claimed to be a former journalist, sat me in a chair in the middle of his office and bellowed and berated, insulted and threatened me for not adhering to the right formulations on sensitive topics (e.g. Indonesia "integrated" East Timor, not invaded it). It was a gruesome experience and all the more so because Indonesians typically avoid scenes like that. The following Christmas, he sent the Reuters bureau a musical tape he had recorded of Indonesian love songs.

Berlin Wall in 1989 had signaled the end of the Cold War. By August of 1991 the Soviet Union had collapsed. "Desert Storm" in Iraq had demonstrated the United States' new status as, what the French had begun calling, a "hyper-power". The West would no longer be so willing to turn a blind eye to Indonesia's poor human rights record because of its staunch anti-communism in the Cold War struggle for hearts and minds in the Third World.

U.S. ambassador Paul Wolfowitz got tongues a-wagging on the Jakarta cocktail circuit with a speech just before his departure in 1989 to take up a Pentagon job in the new administration of President George Bush. Wolfowitz bluntly called on Suharto to embark on political reforms alongside the impressive economic liberalization measures his government had undertaken. *The Jakarta Post* heartily approved.

"His remarks on the need for more political openness in this country as a logical consequence of its increasing economic dynamism triggered by a series of deregulation measures are not as earth-shaking as one might think," the *Post* said in an editorial entitled "Wolfowitz parting advice." Precisely because of the New Order's success under President Suharto, "the set of socio-political institutions that have been effective so far in moving the nation forward is becoming obsolete." The editorial concluded that "we ought to appreciate Ambassador Wolfowitz' wise counsel."

Less appreciated in Jakarta was U.S. Vice President Dan Quayle's meeting with Indonesian dissidents in June 1989 that was meant to signal, in a ham-handed sort of way, Washington's support for pro-democracy forces.

A massive influx of foreign investment, which grew 10-fold between 1986 and 1991 as the Berkeley mafia liberalized the economy, was adding impetus to a more outward-looking Indonesia. The economy had become more connected to a world that was offering new ideas, trends and communications channels. "Desert Storm" was broadcast live on satellite television even in places such as Indonesia. The government was almost powerless to stop people from putting satellite dishes atop their roofs or jacking into the World Wide Web

New Boredom

A man clad in blue pajamas flew off the top of a second-story building in a Jakarta neighborhood, landing with a loud clatter in a pile of boxes and prompting a young Chris Noth to turn to me and say: "Whoa, that's gotta hurt."

It was late 1987, and Noth, the future "Mr. Big" in the hit television series, and movie, *Sex in the City*, was then 32. An alumni of the Yale School of Drama, Noth had landed his first starring role in a film, an action thriller called *Jakarta*, written and directed by camp horror film-maker Charles Kaufman.

Jakarta was an unprecedented American-Indonesian film production, the first Western-made feature film to be shot on location in the world's (then) fifth-most populous country, and certainly one with some of the most exotic locations.[†] Up until then, Indonesia under Suharto had been distrustful of foreign film-makers, fearing they might portray the country – and its government – in a poor light. The New Order was also wary about inducting Western values into its traditional society. Local films generally had a nationalist or historical theme until the 1980s, when frothy and sometimes steamy love stories and action thrillers came into vogue.

Movie stunts such as the building leap scene in *Jakarta* were long on bravado, if a little short on technique, in Indonesia back then. Indeed, this venture was meant to upgrade indigenous movie-making skills. Indonesia would now welcome foreign film-makers willing to "exchange technology," Suharto (no relation to the president), the ministry of information's director of commercial films, told me then. The government had decided it was high time to expand the cultural, if not the political, boundaries a bit and to give its flagging film industry a boost.

But since this was New Order Indonesia there were plenty of catches. Scripts had to be vetted by the ministry, and directors and crew members had to have Indonesian counterparts, among other things. As a result, *Jakarta*, which was supposed to be wrapped up in two months, dragged on for more than eight in production in Indonesia.

Noth had been getting into character by reading *Under the Volcano*,

Malcolm Lowry's classic novel about alcoholic madness. He told me he felt like he had been living under a volcano himself. "Jakarta is hot and throbbing, and feels like a coiled spring," he told me "But in some ways there is more creativity here than in New York." Noth was like a coiled spring himself, and I was only too happy to trail along with this babe magnet to various Jakarta watering holes, especially the Jaya Pub, near Merdeka Square, where he sang the blues and played harmonica.

I had become acquainted with Noth because my house on Jalan Kudus was deemed suitably nondescript to be chosen as the setting for a CIA safe house in the movie, thanks to Jeremy Allan, the gonzo Canadian who took me on his Harley across Java and who had reinvented himself as a "location scout" for this film and the other foreign ventures he was sure would come.

As it happened, almost no other Western film was made in Indonesia during the rest of Suharto's regime.[†]

In *Jakarta* Noth played a CIA agent whose life was spinning out of control in New York before he was drugged and abducted to Jakarta, where he tries to unravel the mystery that broke him three years earlier. The movie was long on pyrotechnics – a movie-set village is blown up, a car bomb destroys a Jaguar automobile, a taxi hurtles over a truck into a brick wall, thugs on motorcycles have grisly accidents – and short on script, in keeping with the New Order zeitgeist. While Noth had some steamy scenes with his Chinese-American co-star, former Penthouse Magazine Pet of the Month, Suzie Pai, it was a movie he probably would just as soon forget. Christopher Null, for example, wrote on the web site flimcritic.com: "Simply put, this is one of the worst movies you'll ever see."

If the government intent was to give Indonesia's film industry a boost, that effort was also a flop. Nan Achnas, who began her career as a cub reporter for *The Jakarta Post* in 1984 and is now a leading documentary film-maker, says the decade between 1985 and 1995 represented the dark ages of the Indonesian film industry. From about 110 films a year in the 1970s and 1980s, film production dwindled to a mere handful each year in that lost decade, she says. Things got so bad the Indonesia

Film Festival had to be cancelled in 1993 for lack of any films to show.

First there was all the hassle of making one – getting scripts approved by the director of film and television, making sure government union people were in the crew, getting the necessary shooting permits, Nan says.

And lets face it, creativity and expression did not thrive under the stultifying, *Pancasila* dictat of the New Order. Indonesia's artists, writers, filmmakers and intellectuals were closely watched, as it was assumed they generally had leftist (or at least democratic) leanings. Indeed, the relentless anti-intellectualism of the New Order yielded almost nothing in the way of memorable literature, plays and films – something the government had begun to recognize and address to a degree with the "openness policy" of the early 1990s.

At the same time, television was exploding with a raft of new stations and an open skies policy that let foreign broadcasts come in with the latest popular comedies and dramas. Pirated videos alone practically killed the domestic industry, Nan says. "The poor Indonesian film industry was really outdated and producing vastly inferior work compared to what was happening in TV," Nan tells me at a coffee house near the Indonesian television and film institute, where actors, producers and directors hang out .

About the only customer for films was the government, which needed a steady stream of them to show off its achievements, she says. The industry began to change, especially with the fall of Suharto, but even before that the novelty of foreign television programs was wearing off. "People wanted to see their own images and their own voices on the big screen. They got fed up with foreign TV and wanted to hear their own stories in their own language," Nan says.

As for Noth? The last time I saw him, in 1990 in New York, he had just finished doing a pilot for a new kind of television detective series that he was excited about. For the next five years he co-starred as detective Mike Logan on *Law & Order.*

† The 1985 Academy-award winning film *The Year of Living Dangerously* was actually shot in the Philippines after Jakarta gave it the thumbs-down.

on personal computers (The Indonesia top-level domain .id was granted in 1991.)

Suharto, under pressure from the powerful military as well as from his erstwhile Cold War supporters, began to experiment with a more liberal policy towards contrarian views as the new decade began. In August of 1990, in his annual Independence Day speech, he proclaimed the need to have more open airing of opinions in Indonesia.

The New Order's overweening obsession with security and *Pancasila*-based "consensus" politics had not only snuffed out dissent, it had also stifled the kind of creative and analytical skills Indonesia would need to compete in a rapidly inter-connecting world. "The government's response was to promote a kinder, gentle approach to dissent, a policy shift which came to be known as *keterbukaan,* or openness," Adam Schwarz wrote in *A Nation in Waiting.*[2]

But was it really about responding to the forces of globalization and the new post-Cold War realities? Or was Suharto, as he so often did during his 32-year rule, trying to flush out his opponents? Bobbing and weaving, left to right, he could seem like a heavyweight boxer toying with a lightweight opponent, before delivering a crushing blow to the solar plexus. Ten years after his fall from power, and even after his death, his motivations, his meanings, remain as enigmatic as that smile he always wore.

Life could be highly uncertain under the New Order. You could suddenly have your land taken away because the army needed it. You could be a labor activist kidnapped by government goons on the street and interrogated for days, your family never knowing what had befallen you. You could be a petty thief stealing food for your family and be executed "mysteriously" in a crime sweep. You could be a transmigrant, taken from overcrowded Java to live on one of the outer islands, and have your home burned down or even your head chopped off by resentful locals. You could be a reporter, investigating a case of illegal logging, found dead in your car of multiple stab wounds. You could be a Chinese shopkeeper worried about being a

---

2   *A Nation in Waiting, Indonesia's Search for Stability,* Adam Schwarz, Allen & Unwin, p. 231

target. Or you could be just an upstanding middle-class citizen in the wrong place at the wrong time getting shaken down by the police.

But Suharto was no tin pot banana republic dictator and the New Order certainly was not the Third Reich, or the "Killing Fields" or even the Burmese junta. Suharto brandished his iron fist in a velvet glove. Indonesians were willing to forgive much or look the other way as long as the country kept growing at the seven percent annual clip it had maintained through most of *Bapak's* years in power. Self-sufficiency in rice, the staple crop, was no mean feat, either. The 17,000 islands boasting hundreds of ethnic groups, languages, religions, and indeed, ancient rivalries and resentments, was largely at peace with itself and its neighbors. It was as if the country was on tranquilizers and the drug was *Pancasila*.

Almost everybody had to take P4, as *Pancasila* classes were called. It was the propaganda machine that underpinned Suharto's autocracy. *Pancasila* was drummed into students to such an extent that an entire generation has grown up reacting to it, mostly in a deeply cynical way. Anything could be twisted around to fit the rubric of *Pancasila*. As H.R. Dharsono, the retired general and co-founder of the Petition of 50 dissidents group, once famously said: "There is a basic contradiction between the tolerant nature of *Pancasila* and its actual intolerance in practice."

Harmoko, who continued to keep a small stake in the *Post*, once explained the government's view of the press and *Pancasila* in an interview with an Indonesian magazine. "Publications which don't reflect the values of *Pancasila* and the 1945 Constitution and instead propound different views, including liberalism, radicalism and communism, are prohibited. In practice, that means their SIUPP (press license) will be cancelled, a step which is allowed by law."[3]

Thus the limits of the "openness policy" almost immediately became evident. You could be open about things the same way a cowed child could be open with a particularly strict Daddy – very carefully. Certainly, any talk of succession was way out of bounds.

In October of 1990 police in Jakarta closed down the theatrical

---

3 *A Nation in Waiting*, Adam Schwarz, p. 241

comedy *Suksesi*, a Nano Riantiarno play about a king who is unable to choose a successor The *Post* in an editorial wondered why assign police officers to act as New Order theatre critics. "The timing of the police decision is indeed unfortunate since what is considered as an ongoing debate in our country, whether we should proceed with more openness in order to enhance Indonesia's political development, or whether we should restrain ourselves, is followed closely by foreign observers."

A week later, Harmoko closed down the entertainment tabloid *Monitor* without the usual prior warnings, for publishing a popularity poll that ranked several celebrities and political figures – including Suharto, Iraqi President Saddam Hussein and even the Catholic editor of the magazine – over the Prophet Muhammad. That touched off days of street protests by Muslims during which the *Monitor's* office was stoned. The editor Arswendo Atmowiloto was convicted of blasphemy and given the maximum sentence of five years in jail.

Around the same time, students demonstrated at Gadjah Mada University in Yogyakarta against the conviction of a fellow student for distributing the works of Pramoedya Ananta Toer, a perennial Nobel literature nominee who was jailed for years after 1965 for being a suspected communist.

Partly in response to these events, a "Democracy Forum" comprising journalists, lawyers, Muslim intellectuals and academics was founded in April 1991 to campaign against restraints on freedom of speech and to promote a looser political system. Led by *Nahdlatul Ulama* (NU) Chairman Abdurrahman Wahid, the forum was to give impetus to the growth of NGOs, a movement that Susanto and Raymond were seeking to tap into.

The forum was also partly Wahid's response to the establishment of the government-supported Indonesian Association of Muslim Intellectuals (ICMI) the previous December under the leadership of Research and Technology Minister B.J. Habibie, who was even then thought to be a front-runner as Suharto's chosen political heir.

Wahid, whose NU mostly represented rural-based Muslims – many of whom had incorporated *kebatinan* beliefs into their religion – feared that ICMI would come under the control of fundamentalists, and could also be used as a political tool for Suharto. He also clearly saw it as threat to NU, which had a membership of 30 million and ran traditional *pesantren*, or religious schools, in Java's heartland.

By the early 1990s Suharto seemed to have abandoned his fascination with *kebatinan* beliefs and had embraced orthodox Islam, going on the *haj* in 1991 and becoming ICMI's patron. Suharto saw ICMI as giving Muslim intellectuals a role in "national development," but others saw it at the time as a transparent attempt to bring Islamic leaders within the orbit of officialdom and further reduce any potential political threat ahead of the 1992 elections.

Wahid was becoming alarmed at signs of an intolerant and anti-secular brand of Islam taking hold in Indonesia and in March 1992, a month before general elections, led a *rapat akbar* (great assembly) of some 200,000 NU followers in Jakarta. It was far less than his hoped-for 1-2 million, because the all-important license to hold the rally at Senayan sports stadium was only granted the day before.

In a letter to Suharto afterward, Wahid lamented that the goal of the rally, an Indonesian Islam characterized by openness and pluralism, was not getting a wider endorsement in the New Order society, even as he reiterated support for *Pancasila,* which he had by now cleverly hijacked as a vehicle for change. "If we follow the contemporary discussion and debates in mosques and Islamic councils, it is clear that the issues of sectarianism, such as fear of something called the "Christianization movement" and the like (are prominent in society today)."[4]

This period of *keterbukaan* and incipient political ferment seemed a propitious opportunity for Endy Bayuni to return to the fold of Indonesian journalism, since it promised the opportunity to write and edit stories with less constraints than in the past. So, true to Sabam's prediction, he came back to the *Post* in 1991, as night editor, after seven years with Reuters and the French news agency AFP.

Suharto by the early 1990s had come to the conclusion that

---

4 *Politics in Indonesia: Democracy, Islam and the Ideology of Tolerance,* by Douglas E. Ramage, Routledge, p. 41

Indonesia should open up the economy and tap into the new forces of globalization. This would please Indonesia's aid donors, who constantly harped about the need to liberalize the economy. It would please the Americans, who had begun pushing a "Washington consensus", a set of market reforms promoted by institutions such as the World Bank, IMF and the U.S. Treasury Department under the Clinton administration. But mostly it would please Suharto's family and cronies who would be given first crack at the sweet privatization deals and licenses to do business with the foreigners." But having set the economic ball rolling, the president had raised expectations for political openness as well, Endy said. "He had liberalized the economy and deemphasized centralized planning. What about political freedom? So though in fact there was no political freedom, we created the space for public debate about *keterbukaan* – the media, the NGOS, the intellectuals. The government never said they were going to accept more criticism. It kind of evolved and the pressures were both external and internal."

The pressures were coming from various corners. Foreign investors wanted more transparency, legal certainty and rule of law. Foreign aid donors kept banging on about human rights. Students were embracing a new kind of activism on campus. The NGO movement was beginning to spread throughout Indonesia and was becoming a force in what some political scientists were calling the creation of a "radical centre" in Indonesia.

"*The Jakarta Post* and *Tempo* saw themselves as part of the movement for more democracy in Indonesia along with the NGOS and along with our friends in the universities," Endy said.

"We were working together with them. Susanto and Raymond were cultivating relations with them, hosting lunches and dinners and forums for those NGOs," Endy continued. "And in those years we needed to have friends. We didn't want to be perceived as fighting alone in this battle. We didn't want to the government to see us as being alone in this battle. We felt much better with friends."

When *The Jakarta Post* was started in 1983 people naturally associated the newspaper with its majority-owners: the Wanandi brothers, with CSIS and Ali Murtopo, and by extension, Suharto.

"CSIS became more credible after Murtopo's death, and certainly by the 1990s," Endy said. "Murdani had told Suharto to control the children and was then made defense minister in the 1988 cabinet. Then came Jusuf's memo."

It was a psychological break for the newspaper and its staff.

"We started writing about human rights violations in Indonesia in the opinion pages," Endy says. "We started calling for opening up the political corridors to public debate. As long as it was limited to academic debate in the opinion pages, the government was okay with it. And this is why in the 1990s some of the scholars became famous – Juwono Sudarsono, Dewi Fortuna Anwar, and others – because they were leading the debate on political reform and we were printing it on the opinion pages. The government said we can live with that because it's an academic debate and it doesn't change anything on the ground. Golkar is still dominant, the elections are fixed and the only change is that the debate has become more lively."

By the early 1990s *The Jakarta Post* added four pages and was now a 12-page newspaper with more space to devote to domestic stories. "The front page was no longer dominated by foreign news," Endy says. "There was a shift in priorities, partly because of Susanto's personal preferences, and partly because Indonesia was evolving. *The Jakarta Post* in the 1990s became a political newspaper. But while we were focusing on political stories, we still had restrictions imposed on us."

Now it was no longer individual generals or spokesman ringing up to warn editors away from certain stories, such as the odd bombing of a barracks. The military and government officials were summoning chief editors for "briefings" that basically set the ground rules on what or what not to cover. They were never explicit about what was out of bounds. The referee was showing the red card to the players without telling them the rules. They left it to the editors to guess, and usually they erred on the side of caution. "This was where chief editors had to be good at guessing what the line was," Endy says. "The line was never defined. We had to interpret where it was."

Under this system, the government could plausibly suggest that official censorship did not exist in Indonesia. But the sword of Damocles held above the head of editors was the SIUPP license, which the ministry of information could always revoke, as it did with *Sinar Harapan,* for any transgressions.

The Jakarta Post in a 1991 editorial noted that journalists were so careful "they do not even have enough courage to print any stories about not-so-sensitive issues, let alone anything involving anti-*Pancasila* ideology which would mean a pointless and stupid suicide".

If the media did have something sensitive to report they would find ways of burying the news. Typically such stories would lead with a long official version of an event from the most high-ranking authority that could be obtained. During the 1980s, for instance, quoting Benny Murdani at length on stories such as the Tanjung Priok riots was the safest way to go. If the story had a nugget or two of information that contradicted the official version, it would be stuck in the middle of the story, with a vague or passive sentence structure – just the opposite of how journalism is practiced in the West. As Susanto said: "We had to publish the official version first. That was the first rule. Otherwise I am banned."[5]

If Suharto could not tolerate discussion of succession in the media, he was even more intolerant about any unflattering reportage in the press about his children's growing business empires. In November 1990, the *International Herald Tribune* and *The Asian Wall Street Journal* were pulled from distribution in Indonesia for that transgression.

One of the most blatant examples of first family avariciousness came the following month when the president's youngest child, Hutomo Mandala Putra "Tommy" Suharto, acquired a monopoly on clove-trading. The spice is a key ingredient in *kretek* cigarettes, an industry worth an estimated $3 billion a year at the time.

A government decree ordered cigarette manufacturers to buy all cloves from a new Clove Support and Trading Board at set prices starting January 1. The Board was primarily controlled by a company owned by Tommy, thus giving him an effective monopoly on the clove trade. Tommy's brainstorm was to almost double the

---

5   Interview with Janet Steele in *Wars Within*, Equinox Publishing, p. 99

price paid to clove farmers for the spice – and quadruple the price charged to *kretek* cigarette manufacturers. Economists predicted that consumption would be bound to fall, while supplies soared, which is exactly what happened.

To finance his clove stock management company, known by its Indonesia initials as BPPC, Tommy wrangled $350 million loans from a reluctant Indonesian central bank, after the president intervened on his son's behalf. But cigarette companies had quickly bought up huge stocks of the spice and were refusing to buy cloves from Tommy. In February 1992, Tommy admitted to parliament that the venture had failed. His solution was to have farmers burn their crops to reduce the excess supply. This was apparently too much for even Suharto's rubber-stamp legislature and that plan was abandoned. Meanwhile, Bentoel, one of the largest *kretek* cigarette manufacturers, was left with debts of $370 million, partly from buying up clove stocks in its battle with Tommy's monopoly. The company's suspension of payment on some of its debts even led some offshore lenders to reconsider their exposure to Indonesia.[6]

It's hard to imagine a case of a business license wreaking so much economic havoc on the blatant behalf of a favored son. Farmers got burned. An industry that employed some 4 million factory workers was threatened. Tax revenues from the lucrative cigarette industry could have been jeopardized, never mind the money the government had to pump into Tommy's enterprise at a time when the central bank was engaged in a tight monetary policy to curb inflation. It also made little political sense to sour core constituencies such as farmers and factory workers. But this kind of patrimonial love and rule was to be *Bapak's* Achilles heel in the years to come.

The Jakarta Post published a carefully written editorial in September 1993 after BPPC finally repaid its loans to the central bank, making most of these points. "Most economists had predicted as early as 1990 that BPPC was doomed to fail because it was assigned to do something which ran counter to market forces and to carry out a mission which is not only irrelevant for a private institution, but which even most

---

6   *Indonesian Politics under Suharto* by Michael Vatikiotis, p. 152

international commodity pacts have failed to accomplish. We think, as the government's economic reform measures have shown since the mid-1980s, the best solution to the clove problem is letting the market signals, rather than a monopoly, guide the farmers."

This was treading close to the edge for a New Order newspaper, but typically the editorial argued purely the economics of the case – certainly not the delicate issue of abuse of power, conflict of interest and distortion of markets to pamper a favorite son. Suharto clearly felt his children were entitled to be in business. No one could argue that, but plenty of people could take issue with the flagrant favoritism. Maybe Suharto felt people would not begrudge the "Father of Development" some indulgences for his children after all the peace and prosperity he had brought to the nation over the years.

Whatever the case, Suharto soon found himself in the "how about me" dilemma familiar to many fathers. In July 1990, RCTI television, owned by Suharto's son Bambang Trihatmodjo, was given a nationwide license to broadcast programs and commercials through the airwaves without requiring a decoder. This not only ended state-run TVRI's television monopoly, it marked the first time commercials could be broadcast to a mass audience, something the government had wanted to avoid up until then, fearing it would create a consumerist culture in a nation where most of the population had little disposable income.

Six months later, Suharto's oldest daughter Siti Hardiyanti Rukmana (or "Tutut") jumped into the TV sweepstakes, founding the TPI educational television network. The sweet part of this deal was that TPI was allowed to use the now beleaguered TVRI's facilities without charge. Bambang trumped them all by getting his father in March 1993 to end the state PT Telkom monopoly on telecommunications. The government awarded licenses for international direct-dial and mobile phone services to Bambang's Satelindo company – and the best thing for Bambang was that he got the licenses for free.

All of this, of course, was done in a context of privatization and deregulation and spun as such. A government audit in June 1989 had shown two-thirds of state-run businesses were financially unsound.

Privatization made eminent economic sense: It kept the World Bank and the aid donors happy, and if family and friends had access to capital, well, who's to stop them, the President must have reasoned. "The children and cronies were the chief beneficiaries of this openness. They were getting all the concessions from the government. They were getting the lucrative contracts," Endy says.

A glimpse at the extent to which state companies could function as piggy banks for Suharto's cronies came in 1992, after a 15-year legal battle over the will of a Pertamina oil executive and the Indonesian government. The Singapore High Court ruled that $80 million that had accrued with interest over the years in a Bank Sumitomo account – and into which German firms had paid as kickbacks to Pertamina executive Achmad Thahir – belonged to Pertamina and not Thahir's heirs. Their case rested not on any contention that the money was illegal – as the man's salary was $9,000 a year it obviously was – but that such "commissions" were a common and accepted practice in Indonesia.

Commenting on the decision *The Jakarta Post* made a similar point, saying "there are many 'Thahirs' around us even now. Here we can see how so many people – mostly government officials – live in grand style. These officials own a mansion, or mansions, probably worth billions of rupiah, located in first-class residential areas, ride in pricey cars such as Mercedes Benz or BMWs and take vacations abroad with their entire family in tow. Yet their civil servant's salaries are only around a million rupiah ($500) a month."

But as long as some of the wealth was trickling down to the countryside through development projects, the New Order mandarins clearly felt they could be forgiven a few excesses, especially if now and again *Bapak* sternly lectured about the evils of corruption. To drive home the point, the government in 1993 issued 50,000 rupiah banknotes with Suharto's portrait on them, describing him as "*Bapak Pembangunan Indonesia*" or the "Father of Indonesian development." The notes were withdrawn from circulation after his resignation a few years later.

The Father of Development sought to deflect any anger about the sweet deals that had become the hallmark of his rule onto some of the wealthy Chinese clans and *cukongs.*[7] In March of 1990 Suharto gathered 30 of the top businessmen in Indonesia to his Tapos ranch in West Java, and, with the television cameras rolling, he told them publicly that they should sell up to 25 percent of their businesses to "cooperatives."

Sofyan Wanandi was one of those called to the ranch.

"He gave us a nice meal and he slaughtered his best cows, and in the meantime he is asking questions about this and that, and then how about giving 25 percent of your wealth to the cooperatives. I'm the one who has to tell the president what we can do and can't do. And the President is telling me, hey before the New Order you had nothing but the yellow jacket[8] and now you're a conglomerate head. And I said *Pak*, you started out with your green (army) jacket and now you're President."

In the end, Sofyan negotiated the divestment down to a mere 1 percent, but not before the strange event threw the business community for a loop. "Suharto was trying to manage public opinion and political pressure and to do something for the SMEs (small and medium enterprises), otherwise there would be jealousies," Sofyan says. The problem was that the cabinet had no prior warning of this bombshell. They were busy over the next few days trying to downplay the president's plan as something aspirational and not to be taken too literally. Not a month later, Suharto called in his *cukong* chits. Bank Duta, 70 percent owned by charitable foundations connected with Suharto, announced losses of US$420 million from foreign exchange trading. Liem Sioe Liong and timber baron Prajogo Pangestu put up $490 million to cover the losses.

The expansion of the newspaper to 12 pages, and the government's fit-and-start "openness " policy was allowing more room in the newspaper for local stories, and that in turn was putting strong pressures on the little "check desk". By 1993-94, it had grown into

---

7 A Chinese word meaning master or lord, it referred to the Chinese entrepreneurs that the military relied on to raise capital. Suharto's ties with Liem Sioe Liong was a prime example.
8 Student protesters in 1965-66 were identified by their yellow University of Indonesia jackets.

a full-fledged copyediting desk staffed by up to a half-dozen native English-speaking foreigners. "After about 1988, we started to get people out on the streets," Maggie Agusta says. "We had bright people and they were coming back with incomprehensible stories."

Maggie, married to an Indonesian poet and living in Indonesia since 1979, was asked to set up the copyediting desk and head it up, a role she never anticipated when she showed up for work with zero experience as a journalist in 1984, with her two year–old boy in tow. Maggie is a large, reserved and plain-speaking woman from the corn state of Iowa. Like almost every foreigner who has made their way into and out of *The Jakarta Post,* she had to undergo her intercultural acclimation phase in the newsroom. "Put anybody different – race, culture, religion – in a corner and isolate them and put them in a position of dubious authority, no one is going to like them very much," Maggie says. "And that's what happened to the check desk. You're the traffic cops, the bad cop. Copy editors would be the ones that got blamed for mistakes in the story."

Creative tensions typically prevail between editors and reporters on any newspaper. When the editors are Westerners and the reporters Indonesian, it throws up other issues, as well. Maggie recalls a day in 1986 when former managing editor Thayeb Sabil called her into his office. "He told me I wasn't 'Indonesian enough', that I was rude, too critical, and too straightforward when I told people what was wrong with their copy. I said, okay, I get it. But you need to know one thing. I'm 33 and I spent 27 years in America and you cannot expect me to be Indonesian."

It was a tricky position to be the foreign copy editor in an Indonesian newsroom. Expats were the native speakers, and supposedly the writing experts. They could make reporters, and editors, look bad by catching egregious mistakes and funny English – and also by introducing errors themselves. Egos had to be massaged, and senior Indonesian editors – generally much older than the young, backpacking foreign copy desk editors who arrived in the newsroom typically with little journalism experience – did not like to be shown up. "Some of the reporters say these guys change my stories, they introduce errors in my stories, who needs them," Endy says. "Beyond that there's the cultural clash – the foreigners on the copydesk versus the Indonesian staff. And the Indonesian editors are always saying when we have a fight with them we always lose. " It's a truism in any news organization: the desk always wins.

Jason Tedjasukmana, an Indonesian-American who grew up in a wealthy Detroit suburb, was hired, like many of his predecessors, virtually on the spot in 1995. He had come for vacations, mostly to Bali, when he was growing up but knew little of the country and nothing of the language. When he graduated from the University of Michigan with a degree in history and wanted to travel through Indonesia, he stopped off at *The Jakarta Post* to see if he could find work for awhile to help finance his journey.

"It's one thing to go to Bali, but it's quite another to work in an office with Indonesians and participate in that culture," says Jason, whose father is Sundanese from West Java. "I was impressed with how committed people were. They were fighting the New Order and challenging the one-party hegemony and militaristic culture."

He picked up his Indonesian at the *Post*. "What better place to learn a language than in a newspaper with open-minded and curious people." He, too, had to learn how to adjust to the Indonesian way. "Just because few of them can speak or write English better than you, or that you went to a prestigious university, doesn't mean you understand the story better than they do. It was a humbling experience for me," Tedjasukmana says. "But you learned some of the more mundane and arcane things about Indonesia. They gave me a chance to do features, travel and the arts, which are the kinds of stories I mostly do for *Time* these days."

The Jakarta Post created an idiosyncratic newspaper culture that emerged from bringing together Indonesians of various ethnic and religious stripes from across the vast archipelago and adding a few Westerners into the mix. "I've always liked the pluralistic nature and moderate atmosphere there," Tedjasukmana says. "*The Post* was especially conscientious about respecting peoples' views. I still feel like I'm welcome there. It's still a big family."

By the mid-1990s, management realized they could no longer just throw hapless foreigners into an alien environment and let them learn by trial and (mostly) error. So the foreign copyeditors were given a three-day workshop on how to work in a multicultural environment, how to speak and interact with Indonesians properly, and taught the basics of copy editing.

Much of the learning still came on the job – editing in the autocratic New Order regime was as much an art as a science. "You had to learn to edit between the lines to avoid censorship," Tedjasukmana said. "It was all about reading between the lines, steering the reader in the right direction, letting them figure it out for themselves. It was a real art and there was some serious rewriting going on."

Maggie developed techniques for reworking copy and a theory about why stories were written in such circuitous style. She would interview reporters to find out what happened at the event they were covering and learned to spot certain patterns in the writing. "There was chronic vagueness. It's what happens when you take a language that has a special logic, where everything is connected. It's nonlinear. You start at a centre and move out in spirals. It's very different from the pyramid style," she said, referring to the Western news writing style of arranging facts in a story in descending order of importance.

"Things kept falling through the cracks because of the implied and intuitive thought process of the Indonesian language. In my early years, I was learning why certain patterns kept emerging and certain mistakes kept coming."

Western journalists are trained to write short sentences in the active voice. Indonesian reporters often write in the passive voice, in which the subject of the sentence is nowhere to be found. Partly this is a stylistic issue: Indonesian, like many Asian languages, tends to put the subject discreetly at the end of a sentence or drops it altogether. It's especially impolite for personal pronouns to thrust their way to the start of a sentence. But the passive voice was also a nifty device to hide the reporters' sources to protect them.

Chief Editor Susanto said the usual technique was to use phrases such as: "It was reported", "it is understood" or "according to sources." The maddening "they said," or "*konon*" in Indonesian, was a favorite in the Indonesian media, but usually didn't make the cut at the *Post*.

Another way of beating the censor was to begin a controversial story with a long introduction giving an official's version of the story before introducing contentious matter. The idea was to mislead a censor – they were not among the best and brightest to begin with – into thinking the story was a paragon of *Pancasila* journalism, before his attention wandered onto something else on the page. "It softened the impact and also made (the story) more objective," Susanto said.

Bruce Emond, now the weekend magazine editor, was one of the few foreigners hired in the early 1990s that actually had some experience as an editor, having edited the campus newspaper at Grinnell College in Iowa before interning at the respected *Des Moines Register.*

"When I came here, the big thing I noticed was the redundancy you see in Indonesian, the lack of directness, the roundabout way of explaining things. But it wasn't ever horrendous. I just edited the stuff because that was your job. When I think back on it…I just remember being very happy. It's a unique environment. The reporters are all Indonesian and so are all the page editors, but they are all working in a second language. I don't think there are many jobs in Indonesia where a foreigner can have such an interaction with Indonesians and learn so much of the country from them."

Some of the stuff the copy editors learned could never make it into the newspaper, including the simmering conflicts in remote parts of the archipelago. Power in the New Order was highly centralized, hierarchical and patrimonial, with Suharto occupying a regal epicenter. But along the periphery of Indonesia, the state of the nation was entropic. East Timor in 1991 remained untamed 15 years after Indonesia's invasion, a low-level rebellion rumbled on in what was then called Irian Jaya, and tribal resentments were growing in Indonesian Borneo. By 1990, long simmering grievances in the far north province of Aceh, rich in oil, gas and timber, had erupted into rebellion.

The public rarely heard about these conflicts because the domestic press was not allowed to write about them. The foreign press was rarely given permission to go to places such as East Timor, and when they were, minders both seen and unseen were on them like green on bamboo to ensure they didn't stray far. But the burgeoning NGO movement was taking up these and other causes in the early 1990s and becoming press savvy as well, at a time when media technology was making it ever more difficult to keep the world in the dark about the depredations and deprivations taking place in even the most far-flung places on the planet.

On the morning of Nov. 12, 1991, a memorial service was held in Motael church in East Timor's capital of Dili for Sebastiao Gomes, a student killed during a military raid on the church. Along the route of the funeral procession that was taking his body to Santa Cruz cemetery were ranks of grim-faced Indonesian soldiers with assault rifles. The mourners and demonstrators took that opportunity to unfurl pro-independence banners and the flag of the rebel group Fretilin. Scuffles broke out. An army major, who was not in uniform was stabbed. The funeral procession continued to the cemetery.

The events of that day were disputed, but unlike most such incidents in Indonesia, this one was witnessed by foreign reporters with television cameras.

According to their reports, a column of Indonesian soldiers marched up from the route the funeral procession had taken, while a truckload of soldiers arrived from another direction. Without warning they fired into the crowd. Some Timorese tried to escape over the back wall of the cemetery but soldiers, who had surrounded the area, began beating and bayoneting them.

Hundreds more sought refuge at the residence of Dili bishop, Carlos Belo, who would share the 1996 Nobel Peace Prize with East Timor's future president, Jose Ramos Horta. Human rights groups say up to 200 people were killed and secretly buried in mass graves.

Indonesia at first admitted to only a handful of deaths. The armed forces commander, Try Sutrisno, was unrepentant. He told a military seminar that the incident was the work of "ill-bred people who have to be shot," and that his troops had showed great restraint but were goaded into anger. "In the end they had to be shot…And we will shoot them."

A decade earlier, the military might have gotten away with such appalling statements, but as Suharto was about to find out, the world was undergoing a "new order" of its own. Televised footage of the "Dili massacre," as it came to be known, was beamed around the world, giving a huge lift to the flagging East Timor independence movement. NGOs were energized to the cause.

Stunned by the international outcry, Jakarta formed a commission to look into the massacre that included officials and judges but no international representatives of NGOs. Its findings, however, surprised many because they directly contradicted the military's account. The commission said 50 were killed, 91 injured, and at least 90 others unaccounted for. Suharto sacked his two top commanders in East Timor and ordered his military to conduct courts martial. Suharto later expressed condolences to Timorese families of the victims. Some soldiers were in fact tried, but received light sentences. Meanwhile those accused of organizing the demonstration were given long jail sentences. The commission also came under scorching criticism abroad for failing to address the widespread accounts of mass graves.

Suharto's response to the tragedy was probably influenced to a great extent by the outcry in Europe, where Indonesia's aid donor group was based and which had become ever more pointed about its human rights concerns in Indonesia. So the old general must have felt chagrined that his conciliatory gestures for a tragedy in which his military had caused him a loss of face did not in least tamp down criticism of his human rights record.

In April 1992, Suharto unilaterally abolished the Inter-governmental Group on Indonesia (IGGI), the foreign aid consortium, based in the former colonial power, the Netherlands, which was giving more than $5 billion a year in grants and soft loans. He told the Dutch in particular to "go to hell" with their aid, a remark that was surely meant to echo Sukarno's popular stance against "neo-colonialism" in the 1960s.

Then in a classic Suharto move he feinted back to the left and surprised everybody by setting up a National Human Rights Commission in

1993. Again much to everybody's surprise, he appointed credible people to the panel. The move clearly had a political dimension to it and showed Suharto was still cocking an ear to popular opinion. Wahid's Democracy Forum had resonated well among the middle class and the *rapat akbar* at Senayan stadium had shown the power of the rural masses behind the idea as well.

Whatever ground was swelling under the democracy movement posed no threat to Golkar, however. It captured 70 percent of the vote in the June 1992 elections. Suharto took over in September as chairman of the Non-Aligned movement for a three-year term. In March of 1993, he was elected to a sixth term as President, again belying expectations that he had been planning to retire as he had so often intimated.

His new Cabinet reflected the rise of the nationalist's camp, led by B.J. Habibie, who favored developing indigenous strategic industries – ships and planes in particular. And while the President named the now retired army commander Try Sutrisno as his vice president, his government featured fewer military men. Harmoko had became Golkar chairman, as well as information minister, and was now one of the most powerful civilian men around Suharto.

The Jakarta Post, sensing a widening information space and in the spirit of *keterbukaan,* hosted a round table on human rights on its 10th anniversary in April 1993 after the new Cabinet was formed. The newspaper sponsored a survey of leading NGOs and academics about the state of human rights in Indonesia, and to nobody's surprise the results were hardly flattering to the regime. Nevertheless, the story about the survey and round table was given a prominent place on the front page. If the newspaper thought Harmoko was going to give it a little slack just because he was at the 10th birthday party, they were wrong. *The Jakarta Post* received a rare written warning for its sin of giving human rights in Indonesia an airing.

It was often said around the Jakarta cocktail circuit that Suharto's dilemma about stepping down from power was like that of a man riding a rampaging tiger: dismount and he would be trampled; stay on and he would eventually be eaten. His government's challenge was how to manage Indonesia's spectacular growth in the 1990s at a time when the world was becoming more interconnected and when Indonesians themselves were chafing at their restraints.

❧

CHAPTER FIVE
DARKENING OF THE LIGHT

Suharto glances at his watch, but not impatiently. It is more of a cool and deliberate gesture meant to convey to the media horde crammed into a grandstand on the grounds of Bogor Palace that President Bill Clinton, the most powerful man on earth, is coming to *Bapak* President's house. And he is late, as usual.

Clinton's bullet-proof limousine pulls up in front of the palace, the last of the 18 heads of state to arrive for the Asia-Pacific summit Indonesia is hosting. He takes his time getting out of the car, shaking hands and beaming for the cameras. "Oh, it's so embarrassing," mutters one Jakarta-based TV cameraman. Suharto doesn't appear to mind. He can wait. He's always played a waiting game, letting his foils and opponents make the first move...before he pounces.

Clinton is bounding up the steps of the Palace, built by the Dutch colonial power in 1745 in the volcanic hills of Bogor as a nice, cool place for the governor to live. Clinton and Suharto are wearing matching gold batik shirts as they shake hands on a huge ornate carpet on the palace verandah before heading inside for this Asia Pacific Economic Cooperation (APEC) summit.

It is a crowning moment for Suharto after nearly three decades in power. He is head of the 111-nation Non-Aligned Movement, and now APEC chairman this year; Jakarta has won a rotating seat on the U.N. Security Council, and the World Bank is hailing Indonesia's economy as part of an "East Asia miracle."

Bapak President has prepared this event carefully. Jakarta has swept the usually teeming streets of sidewalk vendors and beggars, transvestites and prostitutes until after the summit. Clinton, who had been jogging and shaking hands with passers-by in the vast park near the Indonesian National Monument that morning (probably accounting for his tardiness,) would have seen an improbably squeaky clean Jakarta.

I have come back to Jakarta for the first time in four years to help cover the APEC summit for Reuters and my, how the city has changed. Jakarta still looks like the world's biggest village in some respects. The *kampung* neighborhoods sprawl higgledy-piggledy along reeking canals or nestle under tropical shade trees. But cranes loom over construction sites everywhere. Dozens of new office towers glint in the sun. New toll roads snake towards industrial sites, Tanjung Priok port and the international airport.

Home to 10 million people, Jakarta is at the epicenter of Indonesia's economic transformation, and is all too often its main beneficiary – at the expense of resource-rich provinces that sent far more money to the capital than they got back in development projects. "Indonesia's economic performance has been one of the best in the developing world," the World Bank gushed in its 1994 annual report on Indonesia. Over the past 25 years, average GDP growth exceeded 6 percent, and poverty had been reduced to 14 percent of the population from 60 percent. But the Bank and others also warn the income gap is widening at an alarming rate, and Indonesia's debt, which had tripled to more than $90 billion from a decade earlier, is most worrisome, indeed.

Still, Suharto, at the age of 73, could feel pleased on this overcast morning of Nov. 16, 1994. Even the skies have not rained on his parade, though Bogor with its 157 inches of annual rainfall is known as "rain city" and one of the wettest places on the planet. The government had called in a *"pawang hujan,"* or rain shaman, to ensure the 18 leaders could stroll without umbrellas through the palace's world famous Botanical Gardens, amid gamboling deer, peacocks meandering about the lily ponds, and mist coming off the hills.

Yes, as Suharto took the leaders on a tour of the white palace – which the Dutch governor who built it had named *Buitenzorg,* or "free of cares," and where Suharto's careworn predecessor had spent much of his time – carefully skirting the room of nude paintings that the flamboyant Sukarno had collected over the years, he could feel proud, almost contented.

If it wasn't for those annoying East Timorese, it would have been perfect. For President Suharto had to share the spotlight at this second APEC summit with East Timorese protestors, who were squatting in the U.S. embassy compound after scaling its railings four days earlier. Dili had witnessed unprecedented rioting over the three days previous to the APEC summit after clashes with security forces in the wake of a demonstration to mark the third anniversary of the "Dili Massacre."

With television crews from around the world preparing to record a boring economic summit, the storyline suddenly became how rag-tag groups of East Timorese had stolen the mighty Javanese king's thunder and how a country of nearly 200 million people had yet to conquer a half-island of 800,000 after 20 years of warfare. The unrest brought political and human rights concerns, often thrust to the side by the region's governments as their young economies boomed, back to center stage at APEC.

It was clear that East Timor was considerably more than what Foreign Minister Ali Alatas famously called a "pebble in our shoe." Rebel leader Xanana Gusmao (today the young nation's prime minister,) jailed for life after his capture in 1992, sent a letter to Clinton from his prison cell asking him to raise the East Timor issue at his meeting with Suharto. Clinton duly did so and said Indonesia's human rights record could be "a limiting factor" in ties between the two countries. Then he gave Suharto a matching pair of Chihuly blown-glass artworks.

The message was definitely mixed. Clinton and his entourage declined to meet with rights groups in Jakarta, and the centerpiece of the bilateral visit was the $40 billion in business deals that corporate America signed with Indonesia – including $35 billion for Exxon to develop the Natuna gas fields off Indonesian Borneo.

Indonesian activists had come under strong pressure not to use the APEC occasion to promulgate their causes. The independent

Indonesian Labor Welfare Union (SBSI), whose leader Mochtar Pakpahan was jailed for three years in the weeks before the summit, promised to behave itself at the APEC party – and it did. Indonesian NGOs tried to organize a press conference for foreign journalists but were refused permission.

The prevailing mood in Indonesia's disparate dissident movement was one of cautious pessimism. The tone had been set in June when Harmoko closed down three popular news magazines, bringing the fit-and-start period of "openness" to an abrupt close. It was becoming clear that unflattering coverage of B.J. Habibie – the bug-eyed, hyperkinetic "mad scientist" in Suharto's cabinet – was right up there near the top of the list of taboo topics for press coverage.

On June 11, 1994, *Tempo* and two other news weekly magazines published a story on frictions within the government over Research and Technology Minister Habibie's plan to buy 39 used warships from the former East German navy. The purchase of the aging warships, in fact, was only a small part of the $1.1 billion deal that also involved refurbishing 15 shipyards, building a new deepwater part and acquiring oil tankers. The story exposed a rift between Finance Minister Ma'rie Muhammad and Habibie over the issue, as well as gripes from the Indonesian navy about being bypassed in the decision-making. Habibie had basically gone around the economic ministries and the military by taking the plan directly to Suharto for approval.

The first hint of government displeasure came when Suharto, speaking at the dedication of a naval facility in Lampung, Sumatra, on June 9, said the government would take "firm action" against certain publications that he said were jeopardizing "national stability" by making an issue over the purchase.

A fortnight later, the information ministry informed *Tempo* and the weekly magazines *Editor* and *Detik* that they no longer had a license to publish. The June 21 letters to the three magazines gave no explicit reason for canceling their SIUPP licenses, which essentially put them out of business permanently. The letters merely said the magazines had endangered "national stability" and failed to safeguard the Pancasila press.[1]

The Jakarta Post took umbrage in a June 23 editorial that represented one of the newspaper's strongest criticisms of Suharto's regime to date. "It never crossed our mind that right in the middle of the newly found climate of openness the government would go so far as to ban these publications." The editorial complained about the vague reasons for the banning. "One thing that makes it rather difficult for the press, of course, is that no clear-cut guidelines have ever been outlined on what constitutes acts that disrupt or endanger the nation's stability. Surely, most people would agree that so far there have been no indications that the nation has been destabilized or in any way in danger…It was indeed a very sad experience to have to helplessly watch our colleagues being punished and fall victim to certain debatable aspects of our society, as we agree with the view that a legal course should always be taken to settle disputes or violations of any kind."

The editorial concluded that the media were still "in a period of living dangerously" and it would be "naïve to expect that the authorities would shrink from any step they felt necessary to maintain their treasured national stability". The termination of the magazines would slow down the speed with which political openness had been progressing. "But in the end, we believe that democracy will be recognized for what it is: an unstoppable phenomenon, beneficial to all," the Post declared.

Goenawan Mohamad and Fikri Jufri, University of Indonesia classmates during the 1960s campus ferment, founded *Tempo* in 1971. They were an "odd couple" partnership that created probably the most influential publication in Indonesia of its time. Goenawan, a reserved and reflective man who had already acquired a reputation as a poet and essayist at the university, was the writing persona of the magazine. Fikri, a political economist, was the extroverted networker, the weekly news magazine's organizational face.

Tempo's goal was to be the *Time* magazine of Indonesia and to that end it adopted a cover design almost exactly like its American counterpart, including the trademark red border.[2]

---

1   *Wars Within*, Janet Steele, p.234
2   The similarity would prompt a *Time* lawsuit in 1973, which was eventually dropped.

In its early years, the magazine was hardly anti-establishment. "We were products of the New Order," Fikri says in a 2008 interview. *Tempo* carved out a loyal readership base that ultimately grew to more than 100,000 based on its strong coverage of the arts, literature, culture, and especially socio-political stories that were often featured on the cover. It was widely viewed as expressing the aspirations of the educated middle class who had been largely responsible for helping Suharto come to power, but were now becoming disillusioned with the New Order's political repression and gaming of the economic system. Over the years, *Tempo* had been banned – for two months during the 1982 election for reporting on campaign violence – and warned numerous times.

Tempo was finding support throughout the country in its death throes. In the days after the announcement, art students in Yogyakarta wrapped the *Tempo* bureau in white, the traditional color of mourning. Hundreds of journalists and activists marched to the information ministry demand that the bans be revoked. When their request to meet officials was turned down, they showed up the next day with an even bigger demonstration. Riot police waded in with swinging clubs, inflicting several injuries and arresting 32, including leading poet and dramatist, W.S. Rendra.

In the *Tempo* newsroom, Fikri Jufri had called a press conference on June 23 in what would be the last working day at the magazine for more than four years. He clambered up on his desk and addressed the staff. "It's a violation of the Basic Press Law," he declared, and poured scorn over a statement from the information ministry that *Tempo* had been given six written warnings, three stern warnings and 33 oral warnings. "From where is he counting? Since *Tempo* began to publish?"[3]

The last time *Tempo* was banned in 1982, it was Fikri who worked his connections to undo the damage. He kept pursuing information minister Ali Murtopo, who was avoiding him, before finally cornering his adjutant in a hotel in Bali. Fikri had known Murtopo from his student activism days in 1966, and told the adjutant: "Just tell him I want to meet the man I knew when he was captain. I want to meet the Ali Murtopo I knew in 1966, 1967." He eventually got through to Murtopo, who acknowledged his debt, saying: "Fikri, you're my boy."[4]

But this time Fikri was not only friendless in the Suharto inner circle, he was the target and so he was doomed. The press conference was Fikri's last hurrah. When he dropped down from his desk and walked out the door, he ended his career as a working journalist. From then on, he devoted his energies toward helping to run *The Jakarta Post* as a board member.

The government, as in the case of *Sinar Harapan*, attempted to revive *Tempo* with an offer it could well refuse: *Tempo* could publish again, if it dumped Fikri, who had assumed the duties of chief editor in 1992 after Goenawan took an indefinite sabbatical. The offer was conveyed by Prabowo Subianto, Suharto's ambitious son-in-law, who was about to be appointed head of the controversial Special Forces, *Kopassus*.[5]

A chief editor had to have the recommendation of the Indonesian Journalists' Association, or PWI – which of course was under the sway of the information ministry – to attain and keep his position, so pressure certainly could have been exerted. The government viewed Fikri as someone who had been too close to Murdani, and too opposed to Habibie, to lead a revived *Tempo*. But Goenawan refused to throw his old friend and partner under the bus. "By then I realized we had to fight this government," Goenawan said. *Tempo* would not publish again as a magazine until after the fall of Suharto.

Fikri, who bears a passing resemblance to Henry Kissinger, is deeply pained by any suggestion that he was taking anybody's side in the murky and Machiavellian political machinations of Suharto's New Order. Of his relationship with Murdani, Fikri says: "He can chat with you, he's fluent in English, and he's sharp. Who doesn't like him? Of course, we disagreed on many things, too. But don't forget we are journalists and working as a journalist you have to know the difference between activist and journalist."

The Jakarta Post, meanwhile, was taking every opportunity to

4 *Wars Within*, p. 110
5 *Wars Within*, p. 258

show solidarity with one of its key shareholders by giving coverage to the pro-*Tempo* demonstrations – which was against New Order rules. Janner Sinaga had been replaced by Subrata, a gentler Javanese soul, as Chief Scold at the information ministry. While the warnings under Subrata were more nuanced, the threat of being shut down was always implied, Susanto recalls.

"There was a big demo after the ban. This was something new. Students and lots of people joined in. We reported that and published a picture of the poet Rendra and the union leader Mochtar (Pakpahan) at the demo. I was summoned and told that we were giving the impression abroad that things were not peaceful in Indonesia. They especially did not like the picture of Rendra. So the next time there was a demo, I instructed (editors), go ahead and print a picture, but don't show any celebrities. And nothing happened. So we learned a new lesson about the limits of freedom."

Some *Tempo* journalists joined other publications after the magazine was closed down. Bambang Harymurti and a group of *Tempo* journalists formed a company that put out the Sunday edition for the daily *Media Indonesia*. Some started or joined underground newsletters and Internet publications, a phenomenon that the military and the government proved helpless to stop.

Something had profoundly changed in Indonesia. When *Sinar Harapan* was banned, people reacted in sorrow. When *Tempo* was given its death sentence, anger erupted. And it found potent expression when the government-sponsored PWI issued a statement saying it could understand the decision. On Aug. 7, 1994, a group of journalists, outraged over that statement by the toady press union, founded the alternative Alliance of Independent Journalists (AJI). Meeting at a *Tempo* guest house in Sirnagalih, a West Java hill station just outside Jakarta, they issued the *Sirnagalih Declaration* that stated in part:

> *We acknowledge freedom of speech, access to information and freedom of association as a basic right of all citizens.*
> *We recognize the history of the Indonesian press is*

*marked by press struggles to uphold truth and justice as
well as to oppose all types of oppression.*

*Indonesia is a constitutional state. Because of this, the
Indonesian press bases its struggles on legal principles
rather than power. Based on the above mentioned
principles:*

*~We reject all kinds of interference, intimidation,
censorship and media bans which deny the freedom of
speech and open access to information.*

*~We reject all efforts to dissipate the spirit of the
Indonesian press venturing to fight for their concerns.*

*~We reject one-sided information advanced for the
benefit of individuals or groups in the name of national
interest.*

*~We reject the concept of a single compulsory
organization for journalists.*

*~We proclaim the establishment of the Alliance of
Independent Journalists as an organization which
upholds the struggles and concerns of the Indonesian
press.*

Among the 58 journalists who signed the Declaration were *Tempo*
editors Goenawan, Fikri and Harymurti, along with Aristides
Katoppo. At least 15 staff members of *The Jakarta Post* attended the
meeting as well, including Andreas Harsono, then a cub reporter
with the *Post*, who would soon become a spokesman for AJI. An
Indonesian-Chinese from Jember, East Java, Andreas had joined the
Post along with a group of cadets nearly a year earlier. All but he had
graduated from the standard probationary period and made full-time
employees. Weeks after becoming a founding member of AJI, Andreas
was given the sack at the *Post*. Susanto told him his journalistic skills
were not in doubt but the editors were troubled by the "partisan"
approach he was taking in his news writing, which was not in keeping
with the principles and news values of the newspaper.

On his website, Andreas said Susanto had caved into pressure to
fire him. "He said that my skills as a journalist were not in doubt; they

were beyond what *The Jakarta Post* required. He said he was satisfied with the features I had written, though not with my handling of 'straight news' which tends to be 'unbalanced.' Susanto stressed that this decision was not taken under any pressure from outside. Mas 'Santo also said the dismissal had nothing to do with AJI, though he acknowledged that people outside would make the connection. I have been told that one person on the management of *The Jakarta Post* has been talking about the need for quick action against any members of staff who have joined AJI. If this is true, I am the first victim. I am a signatory of the *Sirnagalih Declaration* and an AJI activist which makes me one of those who need to be 'excised.'"[6]

AJI, in an October 1994 statement, then seemed to accuse *The Jakarta Post* of doing the government's dirty work. "Terror tactics against AJI members have started to occur via pressure from chief editors at various publications. And *The Jakarta Post* has triggered this action," the statement read.

Susanto and Raymond dismiss this, and point out that *The Jakarta Post* had a number of AJI members on staff throughout the remainder of the Suharto's regime, and they did their best to protect them. Susanto said the probationary period for Andreas had been extended twice, even before the banning of *Tempo,* over his "partisan reporting".

"He was not impartial. His reports were always one-sided and we always advised him on that but he did not improve," Susanto says. "We had a lot of AJI members at *The Jakarta Post*, including Ati Nurbaiti." Ati, then a staff writer, and now a managing editor at the *Post,* was chairwoman of the AJI. But Susanto acknowledged he was under considerable pressure to conduct a witch hunt in his newsroom. The government said it would begin enforcing a rule that all Indonesian journalists must belong to PWI – and that no member of PWI could belong to AJI as well. Shortly after that, PWI Chairman Tarman Azzam telephoned Susanto demanding that he fire all AJI members at the *Post* and even supplied him with the names of suspected members, including Ati Nurbaiti.

---

6 See his blog at http://andreasharsono.blogspot.com/1994/10/jakarta-post-dismisses-aji-member.html

"So I summoned Ati and told her if someone asks you about AJI membership, you just tell them you are no longer in the newsroom, but actually I want to you to stay there and continue on. You just say like that. We could not surrender to PWI! And then a week or two later, Tarman called me again. Have you discharged these AJI members? I told him I have moved them from the newsroom, it's not a problem. They never asked me about it again. But we actually had many AJI members and sympathizers in the newsroom."

Raymond says he called the AJI members into his office and handed them two letters. "One letter is telling them they have been reassigned to work in the library because of their work in AJI. And then they started to get upset, and I immediately gave them another letter. This one says they have now been reassigned back to the newsroom. That one they took away, and I kept the first letter in my desk drawer."

It may well be that Andreas Harsono, who has gone on to an award-winning career as an advocacy journalist in Indonesia, would have been let go at the *Post* in any case for his "partisan" news writing style, but he probably can't be blamed for thinking of himself as a scapegoat–or as, perhaps, a sacrificial lamb that helped ease the pressure on other AJI members at the *Post*.

Andreas joined Fikri and Goenawan in starting ISAI – the Institute for Studies in the Free Flow of Information – to document the harassment of the Indonesian press. Its biggest funder was USAID, which was working closely with many different Indonesian NGOs in the 1990s. "It was a new way of circumventing the information blockage by the government," Goenawan says. "We published instant books on current affairs. They were usually banned after about a year, but by then they had been circulated clandestinely, including to campus newspapers all over the country."[7]

AJI meanwhile had begun publishing an unlicensed underground magazine called *Independen,* which gained a small but influential readership for its coverage of such sensitive topics as presidential succession, and the wealth of the president's family and Cabinet ministers.

---

7 Goenawan Mohamad interview in *World Press Review* with reporter Charles Stokes.

At that point, the government decided to crack down. On March 16, 1995, Jakarta police rounded up several journalists at a party hosted by AJI to celebrate the end of the Muslim fasting month. Among those detained was AJI chairman Ahmad Taufik and the outspoken former parliamentarian Sri Bintang Pamungkas. At their trial in June, they were each sentenced to 32 months in jail (it was raised to three years on appeal), under a colonial era "hate-sowing" law for publishing an unlicensed magazine.

A day after the arrests, PWI expelled 13 signatories to the *Sirnagalih Declaration*. Since membership in PWI was compulsory, the move effectively put them out of work. Editors began getting a stream of warnings from information ministry mandarins, ordering them to lay off stories critical of PWI and Harmoko, and to stop writing stories that painted the new Indonesian Democratic Party (PDI) leader, Megawati Sukarnoputri, in a favorable light.

While AJI was challenging PWI's "monopoly" on representing journalists, *Tempo* journalists led by Goenawan and Fikri contested the legality of Harmoko's withdrawal of the magazine's publishing license. It was the first such challenge in Indonesian history and was indicative of the new-found boldness and outrage that had begun to reverberate in the industry. In a decision that rocked the media world, the Jakarta Administrative Court ruled in favor of the *Tempo* suit, agreeing that the banning did indeed violate the 1966 Basic Press Law. The victory was short-lived. On appeal, the Supreme Court overturned the decision. *The Jakarta Post* reported that about a thousand people crowded into the courtroom for that ruling. Goenawan, wearing a white shirt and black armband, spoke to a throng of journalists and supporters afterward: "For me, the struggle for freedom of the press by legal means ends here. Now the struggle must take another form."[8]

Tempo was the second of *The Jakarta Post's* hydra-headed ownership group to be permanently banned after *Sinar Harapan*. The Wanandi brothers had by then fallen into disfavor with Suharto. Harmoko still retained his five percent, but he had shares in many different media companies, and nobody doubted his willingness to

---

8 *Wars Within*, Janet Steele, p. 258

pull the plug on the *Post*. The ever-circumspect *Kompas* was still printing the paper, but could not be counted upon to stick its neck out for *The Jakarta Post,* which was pushing into dangerous territory as the New Order began to grow brittle and show cracks.

And if Suharto was becoming politically tone deaf in his old age and somehow unaware of the building anger over the rot in his regime, he certainly got an earful on a trip to Dresden, Germany in early spring of 1995.

Suharto had been planning his trip to Germany for months, which gave activists abroad plenty of time to plan an ambush. When Suharto arrived in Dresden on April 5 to visit a castle and art museum complex, he was "welcomed" by two German activists groups. One group, pretending to be students on a school tour, unfurled banners, shouted rude slogans, banged pots and blew alarm whistles. One person even got close enough to slap a rolled-up newspaper on Suharto's umbrella. Suharto broke off his tour and retreated back to his hotel until it was time to have dinner with his host, the Saxony prime minister. The demonstrators were lying in wait again. They surrounded the bus taking the president and his entourage to dinner, and rocked it back and forth for a few minutes. They then kept a din outside the restaurant throughout his evening.[9]

An infuriated Suharto blamed Indonesian groups for aiding and abetting the German activists. "These people are insane, irrational. They are selling out their own nation to another country," he told the local media when he got home, and advised authorities to take firm measures against them. The last time he was this blunt *Tempo* and the other two magazines were shut down.

The government later identified Goenawan, Sri Bintang and student activist Yeni Rosa Damayanti as the ringleaders providing "material support" for the Dresden protests. "Do demonstrators abroad really need to be supplied with material in the age of information when they can use e-mail and news services?" Goenawan retorted. The Legal Aid Institute said the accusations against the three meant they were effectively being tried in the press and the government should

9   Human Rights Watch report, "Soeharto retaliates against critics", May 18, 1995.

not be making scapegoats of activists for the short-comings of their security agencies. The institute also noted that if Indonesia was going to take an increasingly high profile internationally, it would have to expect greater scrutiny of its human rights record.

The Jakarta Post underlined these points in an editorial that was hardly sympathetic to Suharto's sensibilities. "Who was responsible for allowing the President's entourage to enter into such a vulnerable situation," the newspaper said in an April 17, 1995 editorial, which also deplored naming the three activists in connection with the Dresden protests.

"After all, we always pride ourselves in being citizens of a country which respects the law. Thus everybody must be considered innocent until proven otherwise by the law." The editorial pointed out the vagaries in the government charge that the activists were "giving out materials" to foreign parties, asking "what materials are considered 'negative' or 'harmful'. "We have to remember that in this age of information, the world has shrunk to an extent that information can be easily obtained through any electronic means...The foreign press, embassies, and other international organizations are free to file their reports. Hence, any information can be easily obtained without necessarily having to pass through the hands of our own nationals... The conclusion is, we have to be ready to face criticism on practically anything, particularly in relation to any perceived misdeeds," the editorial said in a thinly veiled reference to Suharto himself.

Misdeeds? That word surely meant Susanto would have to trudge on down to the information ministry to catch an earful again.

The banning of *Tempo* and the crackdown on the press that ensued brought together the media and the NGO community in a common cause of regime change. By the mid-1990s, the number of registered NGOs had grown to some 8,000, working in a plethora of disciplines across the archipelago.

The New Order had encouraged to some extent the growth of those NGOs that furthered its overriding goal of economic development: voluntary organizations working on projects in education, cooperative housing, rice self-sufficiency – anything, in short, that was non-political. Suharto had come to power with the firm idea that confining politics to a small military-led clique was a necessary precondition for rapid economic development.

The ban on politics on university campuses caused intellectuals and would-be student activists to turn their energies to NGOs, which emerged in the late 1980s and 1990s as strong critics of the government's development strategies, particularly when it came to forestry and the environment. Emil Salim became Indonesia's first environment minister in 1978 and went on to become a pain in the New Order butt for the next 15 years, as he pushed, prodded, harangued and implored forestry, mining and other resource extractors to pursue "sustainable development" of Indonesia's rich resources. This put him in direct conflict with people close to Suharto, notably Bob "the plywood king" Hasan.

Because his ministry was chronically under-funded and in the political outer circle around Suharto, Emil turned to NGOs and their foreign donors for support. Indonesia's Environment Management Act of 1982, in fact, explicitly called on NGOs to play a "participatory role" in the development process and "recognized the right of NGOs to act as community institutions for environmental management and development".[10] Hundreds of environmental NGOs mushroomed during this fertile period.

Foreign aid groups meanwhile had discovered that NGOs were far more effective, energetic and honest about implementing aid projects on the ground than the lethargic and corrupt bureaucracy and preferred to channel their money through grassroots groups, which also helped the movement to grow.

Many of these groups began focusing on issues – equitable income distribution, broader decision-making in society better resource management – that was annoying to Suharto's people. NGOs, however, were severely circumscribed in what they could do by a 1985 law on mass organizations (known in the New Order's penchant for Orwellian acronyms as ORMAS). The law required NGOs to be licensed by the government and made it more difficult

---

10 "NGOs, the Environment and Political Pluralism in New Order Indonesia," by Joshua Gordon, Explorations in Southeast Asian Studies.

for them to receive foreign aid. Yet they were getting assistance, and they were being critical, and Suharto began seeing them more as anti-government organizations than non-governmental ones.

Debra Yatim had become involved in environmental activism after leaving the *Post* around 1986 and was working with the Indonesian Environmental Forum (WALHI). Trained in radio and television in Australia and the recipient of a journalism fellowship at Stanford University under the U.S. National Endowment of the Humanities, she was putting those skills to use in providing advocacy skills to grassroots NGOs. Ironically it was one of Suharto's big successes – his family planning program – that helped spawn the grassroots movements that would sow the seeds of his own downfall, along with other groups such as WALHI, the Legal Aid Institute, the independent labor movement and the Islamic NGOs. "These organizations became the focal point for vocalizing everything that was bad about the New Order," says Debra, an author and documentary filmmaker, who now runs a public relations consultancy, *Komseni,* that specializes in public campaigns for culture, gender equality and environment. "WALHI in particular managed to convince (environment minister) Emil Salim that without a civil society voice the country won't work. Emil went to many international fora with NGOs to see how that works, so he championed the idea that a thriving civil society needed a thriving NGO force," Debra says.

In 1994, after the crackdown against the media and a new independent labor union, Suharto issued a presidential decree that put NGOs on notice. An NGO would be shut down if it was found to be "undermining the authority (of the state), discrediting the government...hindering the implementation of national development" or upsetting "political stability or security."[11]

The NGOs were coming to realize as well that they needed a media strategy to market their message. *The Jakarta Post,* for its part, saw the NGOs as source material for the kinds of stories it wanted to cover in the 1990s. Aristides Katoppo, who had been effectively blacklisted in the newspaper industry after *Sinar Harapan* was banned, became a leading figure in bringing the NGOs closer to the media in the 1990s.

---

11 "High Anxiety", *Far Eastern Economic Review,* September. 29, 1994

"I know how effective this cooperation can be," Aristides told me in February 2008, after helping to launch a new magazine at the Legal Aid Institute, one of the most outspoken human rights NGOS of the New Order period. "At the time, I was wandering around, seeing NGOS, trying to help them. And they asked how can we be effective? I said use the press. Write letters to the editor. Find out the editor's name and address it to him personally. Go visit the newspaper regularly. But don't go in a big group, just one or two of you. Insist on seeing the chief editor, and make sure you know his name. Better still, go to the newspaper just when he's leaving his office for the day and doorstep him. Organize photo opportunity events, like Greenpeace does. Make sure you invite the editor to your event. In other words, I gave them tips on how to be good reporters. Most likely, you won't see the chief editor, but you will start to penetrate the newspaper. After all, they're looking for news. When you link with the press, your message is magnified a thousand-fold."

If the NGOs were eager sellers, *Jakarta Post* Managing Director Raymond Toruan was a motivated buyer. He wanted NGO people to hang out with him and other reporters in the office. "We were a bit political. We knew we couldn't go on with Suharto. But we also knew the country was not prepared for democracy. We had had a dictatorship since 1955. Our philosophy was to help develop a new Indonesia, a civil society. So what we were doing at the time was to help grow elements of civil society to help prepare for a change of regime to a more democratic one."

He had known Legal Aid Institute head Adnan Buyung Nasution and Emil Salim from his days as a reporter at *Kompas*. "*Pak* Emil was one of the ministers who initiated the NGOS in Indonesia, so I kept in touch with those guys. But we kept the impartiality in the paper. We never contributed money to the organizations. We sponsored meetings at hotels, and such. After a while we built a trust and so they started showing up at the office. What we did was provide a place where they could get together and have talks to further their organization and help set up networks among themselves."

Years later, however, when Jusuf Wanandi took over the day-to-day operations of the newspaper he was aghast at what he saw in the books and says Raymond and Susanto threw money at their NGO friends.

Raymond Toruan had been enrolled in a Jesuit seminary – like his mentor and patron, Jacob Oetama, the chief editor at *Kompas,* and *Jakarta Post* Managing Editor Vincent Lingga – though he dropped out after airing certain philosophical differences with the school rector.

It was 1967 and it was the economic dark ages in Indonesia when Raymond left Yogyakarta and arrived almost penniless in Jakarta looking for work. He was selling coconuts at a street stall in Jakarta, and applying for newspaper jobs all over the town, when *Kompas* called him in for an interview. He almost didn't go, he said, because he had nothing to wear.

"I didn't need much more than a singlet, shorts and sandals to sell coconuts," Raymond recalls. So he borrowed a neighbor's shoes, shirt and trousers, nailed the interview and won the job. He moved from desk to desk at *Kompas* over the years, eventually specializing in business reporting, before becoming one of Jacob Oetama's most trusted hands. In 1982, Jacob asked him to act as general manager for the *Post.*

Entering the 1990s *The Jakarta Post* began to worry that it had reached a plateau with a readership oriented mainly to expatriate readers. Ad revenues, after taking off during the late 1980s, were also not growing, mainly because the new television stations that had sprang up in the wake of deregulation were grabbing a much greater share of the advertising market.

"To keep growing in terms of circulation, we had to explore a new audience and penetrate the Indonesian market," Raymond says. It necessitated a reorientation of the *Post*'s editorial content. Foreign readers had different tastes, interests and needs from Indonesian ones. The newspaper needed to strike a cultural balance, catering to its Indonesian readers while accommodating its loyal expatriate subscribers.

The *Post*'s new marketing strategy coincided with a more repressive information regime under the New Order that followed the banning of *Tempo* and the other two magazines. The *Post* found itself alone on some stories – and still standing afterward – due to the quirks of censorship. "We could report stories that other Indonesian newspapers did not dare publish, with the government's press watchdogs daunted by the prospect of poring over an English-language article."[12]

The strategy worked and, by 1994, two-thirds of the *Post's* readers were Indonesian. The newspaper's surveys also revealed that its readership was in the highest brackets of educational attainment and income and had become one of the 10 most sought-after newspapers for advertisements.

In the midst of the government crackdown on the Indonesian media, *The Jakarta Post* published its first Sunday edition on Sept. 18, 1994 that, paradoxically given the climate of the times, aimed to be a showcase of the kind of bolder in-depth and analytical reporting the newspaper was attempting to write in its quest for Indonesian subscribers. With some trepidation, the newspaper decided to look more closely at The First Family and Friends. (see box story)

Hutomo Mandala Putra, better known as Tommy Suharto, never met a monopoly he didn't like. While his five older siblings were all worth hundreds of millions of dollars from the generally sweet business deals that had been handed them, the fast-living youngest (and by all accounts favorite) child of the Indonesian president was trying to get rich in seemingly the most outrageous ways. He was still battling to keep his clove monopoly when the playboy, rally-car driver bought Italian sports car manufacturer Lamborghini from Chrysler. With this, he staked his claim to produce Indonesia's "national car."

The national car policy announced in February 1996 was probably the shabbiest example of nepotism in Suharto's Indonesia. Tommy's Humpuss company was given the right to import South Korean Kia cars free of all import duties and taxes, add a few accessories and slap the brand name "*Timor*" on the car and sell it in the local market at a huge discount to the mostly Japanese competition. He was allowed to do this while *Timor* built its own car manufacturing plant. Indonesia

12 "Building a newspaper on the public's trust", by Raymond Toruan, *Jakarta Post*, April 25, 2003

Family rules

Vincent Lingga is not a crusading journalist, not a shoot-from-the-hip kind of reporter. He is an editor by personality and trade, the business editor of the *Post* from its inception in 1983 to his retirement some two decades later. Moreover, he is prone to intellectualizing, perhaps a result of his training at a Jesuit seminary. Though the stocky Batak can appear grim in his cogitations behind his black horn-rimmed spectacles, he is a gentle, if wise-cracking soul.

Indonesia was becoming a more outward looking country in the 1990s, taking leadership of the Non-Aligned Movement and APEC, while inviting foreign investment on a massive scale. This was taking place during the information technology revolution and Indonesia was finding it harder to hide behind the mysteries that always seemed to cloak controversial events and transactions in the country. *The Jakarta Post*, probing the limits of New Order censorship, began reporting in more detail the business activities of the President's family and friends. But Lingga got the fright of his life when he decided to look into Mohamad "Bob" Hasan's plywood monopoly.

When Indonesia in 1985 banned the export of logs, forest concessionaires rushed to build plywood mills. The country's plywood capacity expanded from a mere 19,000 cubic meters to more than 10 million cubic meters by 1994. This eventually led to a price war among Indonesian mills as overseas buyers, particularly in North Asia, played one plywood company off against the other. Hasan stepped in at that point, and with the support of the government set up an export quota and pricing system for the Indonesian Wood Panel Association (Apkindo). No company could export even a piece of chip board without Apkindo's approval. Hasan had declared war against lumber mills in Japan, South Korea, Taiwan and other countries.

Indonesia's plywood exports rose steadily to 9.7 million cubic meters by 1992, about three-fourths of the global market for plywood, using methods his critics described as "predatory pricing".

Then he got really greedy. Apkindo set up its own marketing arms in the buying countries, duplicating the cartel on the buying side that had been created on the sell-side. Indonesian plywood companies had to go through these exclusive importers, who charged fees ranging from $5 to $6 a cubic meter, and accordingly to Indonesian plywood companies, also marking up the price to the buyer. It was not exactly clear where all this money was going, but the Apkindo chairman was controlling it. Lingga wrote a series of stories based on research in Indonesia and in the importing countries of northeast Asia that explained all this and the deleterious effect it was having – Indonesia's plywood exports had begun to decline after importers in North Asia decided to look elsewhere for plywood, or for substitute materials.

In an editorial after the series came out, *The Jakarta Post* noted that plywood companies had predicted after the sole importing agency was set up in the major importing countries that Indonesia's preeminent plywood exporting position – and by 1994 plywood was accounting for an astounding 14 percent of Indonesia's exports – would be challenged by other suppliers. "It is regrettable, though, that none of them was willing to speak openly for fear of upsetting the politically well-connected Chairman of the Indonesian Wood Panel Association, Mohammad (Bob) Hasan...We are afraid if the present monopoly system is maintained, we will continue to lose our market share..." the editorial concluded.

Hasan, an ethnic Chinese who converted to Islam, was then a very powerful man in Indonesia. As Suharto's golfing buddy, he was known as "first friend" and his connections in the sporting world won him a coveted seat on the International Olympic Committee in 1994. The term "timber tycoon," frequently used to describe Hasan, did not do enough justice to his control over some of the world's richest forest lands. And his influence extended way beyond the timber business. In early 1997, he took over as chairman of car-maker Astra International and a few months later brokered a deal to develop a gold mine at Busang in the jungles of Borneo, parceling out shares for himself, the government, the U.S. mining concern Freeport McMoRan Copper & Gold Inc. and a now infamous Canadian company called Bre-X Minerals Ltd. The deal exploded spectacularly when Bre-X and the mine were exposed as one of the biggest frauds in gold mining history.

Hasan wasted little time in hitting back at Lingga. He suggested in parliament that the author of *The Jakarta Post* articles had been bribed by the South Korean plywood importers. Lingga started getting scary telephone calls. "There were calls with veiled threats against me from reporters close to Bob Hasan," Lingga says. "They were telling me to stop writing stories critical of Apkindo. I was quite afraid because they made a point of saying that Bob Hasan had a driver who was former Special Forces. I took it seriously."

Lingga called an editor at *Kompas* who knew Hasan well. "I asked him to explain to Bob that I will not do anything more about this issue. This editor said when Bob Hasan meets reporters he either gets angry or gives them money. I didn't want either of that from Bob Hasan."

As it turned out, Vincent Lingga would be the least of Hasan's problems when it came to his plywood cartel. Apkindo would be closed down as one of the conditions imposed by the International Monetary Fund in exchange for its massive bailout of Indonesia during the 1997/98 Asian financial crisis.

In 2000, Hasan was sent to an infamous prison island known as Indonesia's "Alcatraz" for misusing $75 million in forestry funds in the early 1990s, a rare instance when one of Suharto's cronies was prosecuted for corruption. The former trade minister and the only New Order cabinet minister of Chinese descent was released on parole in February 2004 at the age of 73, after serving two-thirds of a six-year jail term.

When it came to reporting the business activities of the First Family and its friends, the *Post* tried to stick to just the facts, and not make any obvious attempt to connect the dots, Lingga says. "If there were any critical reports, like from the World Bank, we would hide behind them. We could criticize them in editorials, not from the standpoint of crony capitalism, but you criticized it on its economic rationale."

But it was always a fraught decision in any New Order newsroom: How far could you go? And what consequences were you prepared to face?

justified the policy as a way of kick-starting an automotive industry that had long been dominated by foreigners (i.e., Japanese). Priced at just $15,000, or about half the price of comparable sedans, Tommy was poised for a killing in the market. But instead of thirst-quenching lemonade, Tommy got a lemon. As was the case with his clove caper, the public soured on the *Timor*.

The Jakarta Post practically begged its readers not to buy the car.

"How can the government, which often boasts of international recognition of its prudent macroeconomic management, treat a sedan made in Asan Bay, southwest of Seoul, as a national car simply because it will bear the national brand name *"Timor"* and some Indonesian labor content?...The new privilege simply reflects the government's determination to push ahead with what it calls the national car program at almost any cost to duty and tax revenues, and the credibility of its policymaking mechanism....

"The success of the scheme depends on the reaction of the Indonesian consumer. The consumer who has been prodded by the government to buy domestic products in order to curb import growth amid the worrisome rise in the current account deficit, has enough sense to make a sound judgment. The privileges granted to *Timor Putra* through so many government regulations in the form of Presidential instruction, Presidential decree and ministerial rulings may damage the company's image and consequently tarnish its national car."

Suharto had won plaudits as host of the APEC summit for promoting free trade. Manufacturers in other industries began to worry that maybe the rules of the game would be changed for them as well to benefit another Suharto child or crony.

What nobody realized at that time was that a monumental financial crisis was just around the corner and soon nobody would be buying cars and the IMF sheriff was coming to town to try and shoot down Tommy's monopolies.

The story of 23-year-old Marsinah exposed the ugly underbelly of Indonesia's "miracle" economy and the searchlights that human rights groups and the media were training on the Dickensian conditions of Indonesia's own industrial revolution. Marsinah was found dead in a remote hut by a roadside on May 8, 1993, three days after leading a strike at the P.T. Catur Putra Surya watch factory in Surabaya, East Java. Wounds on her neck and wrists indicated she had been severely beaten, had suffered internal bleeding and had been raped with a blunt instrument before dying.

Such an incident was not so unusual in New Order Indonesia. Those who dumped her body in public view may have wanted to instill fear and dread in anybody thinking of doing what Marsinah did – much like the "mysterious shootings" of the 1980s were meant to send a message to criminals. But because Indonesia had become more open to the outside world and because incidents like this one were now getting attention through the NGO networks, Marsinah's case took an extraordinary course. Only after the United Nations conference on human rights in Vienna and the International Committee for the Protection of Human Rights took up the case of Marsinah's "mysterious death" did the authorities begin to act. "The case got a lot of international play," says Debra, who worked with activists on the Marsinah issue. "By that time, we NGOs were already savvy using the Internet. It was also a labor case and the international labor platform had a lot of ammunition."

Nine managers and security guards from the factory were convicted of the murder, although circumstantial evidence at the time indicated the military had kidnapped and killed her. Their trial was farcical. Several key witnesses "mysteriously" disappeared. Then one by one, all the defendants retracted their confessions, saying they were made under duress. Some of the remaining witnesses also tried to recant their testimony. The trial judge dismissed all those attempts as lies and subterfuge.

The government prosecutor tried to make a case that the company had feared Marsinah would reveal that the firm had used false trademarks in their watch production. In a country where trademark piracy was rife, this did not seem very plausible. The fact that she had begun organizing workers at the plant and protesting labor conditions was much more likely to draw retribution. The justice minister refused to order a new investigation. Then to everyone's surprise the newly formed National Commission on Human Rights decided to show a little gumption and promised to get to the bottom of things.

The Jakarta Post in a March 7, 1994 editorial endorsed the commission's stance. "Since the Marsinah murder case has by now caught extensive worldwide attention, not only is our reputation as a nation at stake, our national dignity is at risk as well. Our sense of justice and our judicial system are now in question and this is a matter we have to respond to seriously and courageously...Moreover, human rights is the central issue in the world today. Failure on our part to find the Truth would certainly draw us deeper into the vortex of world displeasure."

The *Post's* editorial sets out an argument its editors often made when criticizing the government, which was that Indonesia risked alienating its friends, neighbors, potential investors and strategic partners by the way it was conducting itself.

This could resonate only in a country that was becoming dependent on foreign capital, and that certainly was the case in Indonesia in the 1990s. Beyond that, however, the case highlighted the issue of labor exploitation in Indonesia, something foreign investors were getting pressured about. Indonesia approved a record $39 billion in foreign direct investment in 1995, much of it for projects in light manufacturing, chemicals and consumer products (compared with about $310 million in 1985). Because the government was tightly controlled and labor unions, save for the one run by the government, were banned, foreign (and domestic) manufacturing outfits were able to take huge advantage of the cheap labor force without fear of any backlash from the government or opposition parties. Critics in the NGO community focused on the widening income gap and pointed out that the political and economic structure of the country was stacked against the worker, leaving a few favored domestic firms and foreign investors to mainly reap the benefits of the country's prosperity.

After Marsinah's death, the new independent Indonesian labor movement grew more intense. In April 1994, tens of thousands of angry workers rioted in Medan, Sumatra, protesting low wages and a lack of freedom. The demonstration turned violent and the mob of workers, as all too often happened in Indonesia, turned their animosity on ethnic Chinese; one ethnic Chinese businessman was killed. Hundreds of protesters were arrested, including Mochtar Pakpahan, the chairman of the independent labor union SBSI, who was accused of inciting the violence.

The United States and Europe took up cudgels on behalf of labor rights in Indonesia in the 1990s, and though Washington hinted on occasion that it could sever the United States' $600 million trade with Indonesia, it also was working hard to help U.S. companies set up businesses in the country that aimed to exploit the cheap labor pool. In fact, Indonesia's greatest resource by the 1990s, was not its dwindling oil reserves and disappearing forests, but its huge and ever-growing workforce that was earning less than $2.00 a day in the mid-1990s.

The Marsinah case remains unsolved. In May, 1995, the nine people found guilty of the crime were released from jail, their convictions overturned. Soon after the fall of Suharto in 1998, the Indonesian National Police reopened the investigation into her murder, based on the admission of a military captain that she was killed at the district military command (Kodim). The case has yet to come to trial.

In April 1996, Suharto's wife of nearly a half-century, *Ibu* Tien, died of a heart attack and some Indonesian watchers saw it as a sign that the president's time in power was now at an end. It was she, born to minor royalty in the ancient kingdom of Solo, that truly held the *wahyu,* or mystical power in the family, they said. She certainly was viewed as the one trying to keep some measure of decorum among her children fighting over the riches of the kingdom. Two months after her death, Suharto was hurriedly flown to Germany with an undisclosed illness. It turned out to be kidney stones, but rumors that he was dying posed the relentless question about his succession.

When Suharto came back he took aim at the daughter of his old nemesis, Sukarno. Megawati Sukarnoputri was winning hearts and minds among younger folks at the grassroots level for her populist stances and the democratic procedures she had introduced in the PDI. Looking ahead to the 1997 general election, the party was expecting to get significant support from 20 million new voters, about a fifth of the electorate.[13]

Megawati Sukarnoputri was a meek figure, a rather boring speaker, who assiduously tried to steer away from controversy – the very antithesis, in fact, of her father, and a bit like Suharto himself. But she had become a lightning rod for broad anger and resentment against the New Order. Apparently fearing that Megawati might do the unthinkable and pose a challenge to Suharto for the presidency, the government ordered her party to have a congress in Medan in June – without her and her supporters on the party's executive board. This faction of the party, following orders from on high, named Suryadi as their new chief.

The ham-handed move completely backfired, and only added to Megawati's allure in the end. Her supporters took over PDI headquarters in an old Dutch colonial mansion in an upscale Jakarta residential area, holding free-speech forums, beating the drums for democracy, and basically preventing Suryadi from claiming the party's prime piece of real estate. Hundreds of Megawati fans swarmed outside, many wearing motorcycle helmets, expecting to get beaten soundly for their insolence. The military fielded the thugs and street louts that always came in handy for these occasions and forcibly took over the offices on July 27 1996, igniting violence that quickly spread to other neighborhoods. The two days of riots left five dead, 149 injured and 23 missing, not to mention considerable damage to property. The day would become known as "Black Saturday" and mark the beginning of a renewed crackdown by the New Order government against supporters of democracy, who had now rallied around the banner of *"reformasi"* or reformation.

The Jakarta Post blasted the government's handling of the case in an editorial. "The massive protests against the government's handling of the PDI affair show that society has changed and that our citizens are more politically aware. The free speech forums held in the PDI office compound reflect a growing crisis of confidence in the authorities and in the ability of the current political system to solve today's problems. Given that our society has become used to

13 Adam Schwarz, *A Nation in Waiting*, p. 322

violence, it was plain to see that the PDI affair had the potential to erupt. And that is exactly what happened. We should take note of the fact the riots were joined by a group of young people who feel entirely left out of the economic development process. These youths took part because it was rare opportunity for them to vent their pent-up anger at the government, whom they blame for the current economic situation. When both the politically and economically frustrated opt for violence, there must be a breakdown in communication in the political system."

The Jakarta Post had swarmed reporters to the story who were breaking news, and at times, leading coverage of the story. "People were looking for copies of *The Jakarta Post* because they thought we were telling the real story of that incident," Endy Bayuni recalled. "We learned this because Harmoko called in Susanto and showed him a photocopy of *The Jakarta Post* and asked him: 'How did this wind up in a village in East Java?' We didn't distribute there, but it showed that even people in the villages were aware of us. After that, the information ministry and the government started watching *The Jakarta Post* closely. They thought *The Jakarta Post* was read only by foreigners, a small audience of English speakers with no influence. We had used that advantage to become more critical and then wound up selling more and more copies to Indonesian readers."

The government laid the blame for the July 27 incident on the tiny People's Democratic Party (PRD), which had formed an alliance with labor groups and had organized wildcat strikes across Java. Suharto and the military quickly branded them as communists out to overthrow the government, and banned the party. Some 18 months later, with the regime teetering on the brink of collapse, elements of the military would try to make a case against Sofyan Wanandi by linking him to the PRD after he made critical statements about Habibie and the Suharto regime.

The Jakarta Post had been getting away with hard-hitting commentary and reporting on politics, human rights and dissent because, as noted earlier, the authorities were not overly worried about getting the educated middle-class riled up, and the bureaucrats in charge of looking for transgressions in the press were generally not well-versed in English.

Habibie was reading the paper, however, and again he was not happy. The technology and industry minister threatened to take *The Jakarta Post* to court over its coverage of the fatal crash of one of its CN235 planes in May 1997. Habibie, the president of state-owned aircraft manufacturer P.T. Industri Pesawat Terbang Nusantara (IPTN), accused *The Jakarta Post* of publishing a "slanted" report about the crash in West Java that killed six people, including one American. He was quoted by the *Suara Karya* daily as saying that he would use "legal means" because the report "could have a negative impact on our competitive edge." Habibie said it was "completely wrong" to suggest that a propeller broke and a fire started before the plane crashed. A parachute rope that snapped inside the plane caused the aircraft to lose balance and crash, he maintained. The aircraft crashed at the Gorda Serang air base in Serang, West Java, while conducting a test to parachute-drop four tons of cargo.

The Jakarta Post issued a correction and apologized for not checking on information it obtained from an unnamed source. Habibie went ahead with the suit anyway seeking hundreds of millions of dollars, Endy Bayuni says, far more than enough to bankrupt the newspaper or hand it over to the minister in a court judgment. Ironically, Habibie's lawyer was Buyung Nasution, the Legal Aid Institute chief with whom Raymond was hob-nobbing. The suit, though, was quietly dropped months later. Habibie had other things on his mind, apparently. Suharto had just proposed him as his new vice president, the first civilian in that post in two decades. Had *Bapak* President finally named his successor?

CHAPTER SIX

FIRE OVER WATER: REVOLUTION

Things fall apart; the centre cannot hold;
Mere anarchy is loosed upon the world...
And what rough beast, its hour come round at last,
Slouches towards Bethlehem to be born?
— W.B. Yeats, *The Second Coming*

Bruce Emond stood atop the roof of *The Jakarta Post* building and watched the Palmerah pasar burn. People had raced out of the market "like a swarm of locusts to pick the buildings clean of everything and anything they could get their hands on." Then they set the buildings afire. He watched two looters fight over a single shoe. Children were hauling away TV sets. Men were carrying away refrigerators on their backs. People had draped themselves with bundles of clothes, scurrying down the narrow lanes leading from the market looking like ambulatory laundry baskets. "To me, watching from my safe perch in the office, the festive atmosphere accompanying the mayhem was like something from a grotesque Bosch painting or Fellini movie."

It was May 14, 1998. Riots roiled Jakarta. Suharto was desperately clinging to power. The rupiah, depreciated to a fraction of its value, could buy little – if there was anything even to buy. Essential commodities were in shortage and terrified shopkeepers had shuttered their stores. The morning had dawned bright and fine, but the air was crackling with tension. Four protesting university students had been killed two days earlier by sniper shots, a climactic event after months of burgeoning demonstrations across the country against Suharto's sclerotic New Order.

The Jakarta Post shuttered itself after columns of black smoke began spiraling into uncommonly blue skies across the capital. The large TV screen was whisked away from the lobby and fire hoses rolled out in the newsroom. The staff that had arrived that morning would remain there for the next three days, sleeping on the floor of the newsroom, as the New Order began imploding in an orgy of fire, looting and random violence fueled by decades of anger, envy and resentments.

"Cordoned off in my ivory tower, I felt sick to my stomach. I can say honestly that I did not fear for my personal safety, but instead the impending loss of my livelihood and the creature comforts I have come to enjoy," Emond wrote in a column for the *Post* afterward.[1]

At work on the copy desk during the riots, he gazed dispassionately at a photo of a charred body, probably that of a looter removed from one of the gutted shopping plazas, thinking of a caption to write. "I found it extremely difficult to sympathize. I walked around for a couple of days with a self-righteous sneer on my face, wondering if everyone who passed was enjoying their ill-gotten gains." The three army trucks parked by the *Kompas* compound did much to assuage his fears and then he began to see the irony of it all.

"While my insular middle-class sensibility rejoiced at the sight of soldiers in combat uniform to keep the riffraff at bay, I had not blinked an eyelid as 'looting' on a much grander scale went on during the past few years. It was all so pat back then. The country's riches may have been raped and pillaged, its banking system used for private largesse, but it did not affect me if it was not in my own backyard. As long as all the terrible excesses, the greed and insincere protestations to upholding democracy had no direct effect on my immediate life. It was quite all right, thank you. But, of course, what goes around, comes around, and our lives can never be detached from the injustices surrounding us, even if we build big walls and guard ourselves with private armies."

The riots in Jakarta and other cities in May 1998 were climaxing another "year of living dangerously" in Indonesia. If the first such year in 1965 saw a little-known general emerge as the Hero in a battle

---

1   Bruce Emond, "By the Way," *The Jakarta Post*, May 27, 1998

against Evil Communism, this second would find him absorbed in his own regal image and hubris, putting family over nation and reviled by people yearning for democracy and justice.

Alarmed at a *dukun's* (shaman) prediction that "the nail of Java has come loose", Suharto in February 1997 ordered a massive *Ruat Dunia* (Cleansing of the World) ceremony near Borobudur, the stunning 9th century Buddhist monument in central Java. It came nearly a year after the death of his wife of 48 years, Siti Hartinah, who was distantly related to the Pakubuwono (nail of the world) royal family. This came after an eruption of Mt. Merapi in Central Java, one of Indonesia's most dangerous volcanoes, often taken as a bad omen. The year had gotten off to an ominous start. Dayaks, a former head-hunting tribe on Indonesian Borneo, had run amok after clashes between Muslim migrants from Madura island, east of Java, setting fire to their settlements after a series of incidents between the two groups. Hundreds of people were killed amid reports Dayaks had taken heads and cut out the hearts of the resented new settlers, a practice that had died out after Christian missionaries came in the mid-19th century. Those fires would be a grim portent of the coming conflagrations.

The May general elections saw some of the worst electoral violence in Suharto's long reign, renewing questions about his grip on power, and fire was again the motif. In the worst incident, rioters rampaged through Banjarmasin, a timber town on the southern Borneo coast, attacking hotels and shopping malls – icons of New Order wealth. Looters, afraid of police massing outside the shopping mall they were pillaging, barricaded themselves inside and burned to death when rioters set the mall ablaze. At least 130 died in the inferno.

The five-yearly "festival of democracy" was the one chance for Indonesians to let off steam. But this time it seemed to be erupting in a geyser of anger and resentment over the widening income gap, endemic corruption, the brutish sidelining of mild-mannered Megawati, the rapacity of the First Family and their cronies, and the lack of any succession plan for the 76-year-old Suharto. Whatever, Golkar won by its usual by its usual wide margin, capturing 74 percent of the vote.

The election showed once again Indonesia needed the kind of political regulation the economy had been undergoing; indeed, economic liberalism had reached a dead end without reforms to an autocratic system that dispensed business favors with utter disregard to the overall health of the economy. "This nation has a split personality: economic liberalism and political authoritarianism," said Amien Rais, leader of Muhammadiyah, the second-largest Muslim group. "As long as this discrepancy is not solved, the cronies will get fatter and the people's alienation will grow."[2]

The bonfires of Borneo began in July 1997 during a cyclical El Nino drought, and within a couple of months nearly 1 million hectares of rainforest were blazing out of control, mostly due to timber and plantation groups clearing land through illegal burnings (it's the cheapest and fastest way.) Suharto "deeply apologized" to Indonesia's angry neighbors for the smoky haze from the fires that had spread as far north as Thailand. Even he described it as an unprecedented natural disaster. Suharto rarely had to say sorry and again people saw signs of weakness.

Fire is the manifestation of power in Javanese mysticism. The ancient Hindu kings of Java were said to have derived their power from Agni, god of fire and son of Brahma the creator. Agni was also known as the king of men. The uncontrolled fires on Borneo were seen by some Javanese schooled in the ancient ways as a sign of Suharto's loss of power and the passing of his *wahyu*.[3]

Natural disasters tend to follow when leaders lose their power, according to traditional beliefs. In 1963, Sukarno was invited to attend the most holy Hindu ritual on Bali, called *Eka Dasa Rudra,* a purification rite that takes place only once or twice a lifetime at the mother temple Pura Besakih, which sits on the upper slopes of Mt. Agung. In the middle of the month-long ceremony, the volcano erupted spectacularly for the first time in 140 years, killing more than 1,000 people and destroying a number of villages. Some at the time saw it as a signal of Sukarno's imminent loss of power.

---

2 Running 'amuk': Indonesia's riots put focus on the Iron rule and future of Suharto", *The Wall Street Journal*, by Peter Waldman and Richard Borsuk, May 27, 1997

3 Cynthia Mackie, then working as vice president of Conservation International in Jakarta, makes this point in her 1997-98 journal

The bombshell disclosure of the Bre-X gold mining scam would be a portent, too – of the financial crisis that would soon engulf Asia's high-flying emerging economies. The discovery in Indonesian Borneo of what was being touted as one of the richest gold finds in history was exposed in May of 1997 as one of the all-time greatest mining scams, and became a metaphor for cronyism, corruption and collusion in Indonesia.

By mid-1997, Indonesia's economy was still a darling of the emerging markets crowd – even with all the corruption and opaqueness supposedly priced in. Economic growth had averaged 6-7 percent for decades and per capita income had crossed $1,000 a year. Host to tens of billions of dollars worth of foreign manufacturing joint ventures, Indonesia had, in the 1990s, started to attract Western and Japanese banks to its shores after it deregulated the financial industry. On their heels came legions of investment bankers, drawn by what then seemed to be an undervalued rupiah currency. The market capitalization of the Jakarta Stock Exchange soared from $2 billion in 1990 to $117 billion at its peak in July 1997 – the start of the Asian financial crisis.[4]

It is ever the case that as surely as a hangover succeeds the wild party, the time of plenty was sowing the seeds of catastrophe. In July 1997, the Thai central bank, its foreign reserves depleted, surrendered after a long battle against foreign portfolio investors who had decided that Thailand's corruption-ridden credit markets had become too risky and had beaten down the baht to bargain basement prices. After the baht was freely floated – and in free fall as well – investors saw the same scenarios at work in the Philippines, Malaysia, Indonesia, and finally in South Korea. The "Asian contagion" crisis was full-blown in a matter of weeks, featuring collapsing financial and property markets and a chain reaction of bankruptcies of overleveraged companies.

As Indonesia's economy expanded in the 1990s on the back of foreign investment, the business opportunities and capital tended to flow to the people who seemed best placed to get things done in Suharto's Indonesia, namely the people he had designated for that

---

4   *Reformasi*, by Kevin O'Rourke, Allen & Unwin, p. 24

purpose – selected military officers, ethnic Chinese business clans, and his relatives. They built mega-projects, some of which were actually needed, but whose main purpose was to create opportunities to siphon money and pad accounts during the building and development phase. They left uprooted people, bulldozed communities and anger and envy in their wake.

An accepted feature of doing business in Indonesia was providing kickbacks, bribes, unofficial levies, or gifts of shareholdings to well-placed individuals to grease the New Order wheels. The students who had come out of New Order hibernation and were becoming restless on the campuses had a name for this: *korupsi, kolusi, nepotisme* (corruption, collusion, nepotism) or KKN for short.

The most spectacular manipulations involved Suharto ordering his central bank to provide lines of credit to friends and relatives – Tommy Suharto's *Timor* car project, for instance.

Still Indonesia was generally not seen as susceptible to the kind of meltdown that Thailand was experiencing. Its balance of payments was strong, and unlike the Thai baht and Korean won, the rupiah was actually seen as undervalued. But when Bank Indonesia widened the trading band of the rupiah on July 11, within days the currency had dropped 7 percent to the weak end of the band – and stayed there rather stubbornly.

At the time, Indonesian companies owed creditors abroad about $80 billion, or about four times the country's foreign exchange reserves. Companies started scrambling for dollars, fearing the rupiah would follow other regional currencies and go south – which it did, in the kind of vicious circle that characterized the Asian crisis. Investors stampeded out of the Jakarta Stock Exchange and dumped other Indonesian assets.

Finance Minister Ma'rie Muhammad announced a package of measures, including public spending cuts that initially calmed the market. Among the projects that were supposed to be shelved were Tutut Suharto's unlikely plan to build a bridge across the Malacca Strait, and her idea of a subway in swampy Jakarta, along with some other crony projects. But soon the cycle of rupiah depreciation, share market sell-off and capital outflows amid a climate of fear and pessimism resumed. By October, stocks had lost two-thirds of their value in three months and the rupiah had weakened to 3,800 to the dollar from around 2,300.

That's when Indonesia called in the International Monetary Fund. The rescue package announced on Oct. 31, Halloween day, was almost scary in its scope: The Fund would provide up to $43 billion in exchange for some tricky structural reforms. These included dismantling some of the more outrageous arrangements of the New Order: Bob Hasan's plywood cartel was supposed to be churned to sawdust. Tommy Suharto's national car program? Take it to the junkyard. His clove monopoly? Up in (*kretek*) smoke. Liem Sioe Liong's flour-milling monopoly? Grind it to pieces. The National Logistics Agency (Bulog) that handed out various commodity monopolies? Uproot it. The Fund also demanded the closure of 16 insolvent banks, including at least two controlled by Suharto's children and relatives. The IMF, had metaphorically speaking, dropped a bomb on Jalan Cendana, the President's home that symbolized his business connections. At least it looked that way on paper.

But the IMF was being taken for a ride by Suharto's family and cronies, who demanded to be the exceptions to every rule and became the biggest stumbling blocks to resolving the crisis. Public subsidies continued for Tommy's *Timor* car. Bambang reopened his closed bank under a new name with the help of Suharto's oldest and closest crony, Liem Sioe Liong. A power plant project involving Tutut was revived. Bambang accused the IMF of being in cahoots with those trying to bring down his father. "I see this as an attempt to sully our family name in order to indirectly topple my father, so that *Bapak* won't be chosen as president again," he told reporters on November 4.[5]

The bank liquidations, which were meant to restore confidence by showing that no cow was too sacred to be slain, had the opposite effect when depositors took the view that things must really be dire if the president's son and cronies had to give up their vaults. With no system of deposit insurance, people began making panicky withdrawals and the fear that had been gripping the financial markets spread to the banking system.

---

5   O'Rourke, *Reformasi*, pp. 44-47

The rapidly unfolding events were bewildering not only to journalists and market analysts but to policymakers as well. Then *Jakarta Post* Managing Editor Vincent Lingga says his newspaper used the prescriptions of the IMF and other multilateral institutions as cover, and "suddenly had the courage to launch harsher, straightforward criticisms against the Suharto authoritarian government. Since Suharto's bargaining position vis-à-vis the IMF and other major supporters of the bailout program became weaker and weaker, the press hid behind the demands and analyses of these multilateral institutes in attacking Suharto, his greedy family members and crony businessmen."

The Jakarta Post and other major newspapers were greatly assisted by the transparency in which the multilateral agencies, especially the IMF as the leader of the bailout program, managed its programs in Indonesia, Lingga says. "Obviously, the IMF and other multilateral agencies needed the mass media to exert public opinion pressures on Suharto, and the media in turn used these multilateral institutions as their protection in shooting out criticisms against the government which they did not dare say during the heyday of the Suharto power." Even cabinet ministers later acknowledged they, too, had used the IMF in pressuring the government to take bolder reforms which they would not have dared to suggest before 1998, Lingga says.

The Jakarta Post, confident that the weakening Suharto government would not risk further jeopardizing its position by closing critical newspapers, hired Kwik Kian Gie, an economist in the opposition camp who would later become chief economics minister in the Abdurrahman Wahid presidency, to write a weekly column on the economic and political crisis.

As virtually the only English-language newspaper left in Indonesia after the onset of the economic crisis, *The Jakarta Post* became the main source of news and analysis on Indonesia's economic and political crises for foreign residents in Indonesia and those overseas, Lingga notes.

Capital was fleeing Indonesia faster than a three-legged cat from a pack of hounds. About $8 billion left Indonesia in the fourth quarter of 1997 compared with net inflows of $3 billion before the crisis.

The rupiah had plunged to 5,800 to the dollar in December, a level that would leave much of corporate Indonesia technically bankrupt at end-year book-closing time.[6]

The country was in recession, inflation was rampant, food shortages and hoarding had begun. Conditions seemingly could not get any worse as Suharto began preparing to be installed for a seventh term as President in March. But they did.

Armed Forces Commander Feisal Tanjung called a press conference on Jan. 14, 1998 to demand that the owners of 13 large conglomerates bring their dollars back from abroad and convert them to rupiah to bolster the free-falling currency. That was code for "Ethnic Chinese are taking their fortunes out of the country when they should be trying to rescue the rupiah" (See box story). Two weeks later the leader of the military faction in parliament, Lt. Gen. Syarwan Hamid, put it more bluntly. He called the conglomerate heads "rats" with no patriotism, who were salting away "the fruits of national development." Suharto's son-in-law Lt. Gen. Prabowo Subianto, in widely reported remarks at a Ramadan fast-breaking event with Muslim leaders on Jan. 23, blamed the rupiah crisis on a political conspiracy aimed at bringing down the government. Others at that event explicitly linked the conspirators to "the conglomerate group." The government, unwilling or unable to explain to the people what the monetary crisis was all about, had opted for the old gambit of scapegoating Indonesian Chinese, a tactic with echoes of 1965, when the army suspected that ethnic Chinese were a fifth column for the China-backed Indonesian Communist Party.

By mid-January, the IMF had hammered out another agreement with Suharto and his technocrats, again trying to nail down the dismantlement of the cartels and monopolies underpinning the "KKN economy," including Bob Hasan's timber empire, Tommy's national car project, his clove monopoly, and the others. The central bank was supposed to be given more independence, government accounts were to be made more transparent so that accounting legerdemain, such as the infamous transfer of $600 million from the

---

6   O'Rourke, *Reformasi*, p. 50

Blaming The Wanandi Brothers

When a homemade bomb went off prematurely on Jan. 18, 1998 in a room belonging to students linked to the banned leftist People's Democratic Party (PRD) suspicion would not ordinarily have pointed to the Wanandi brothers. Jusuf and Sofyan Wanandi had helped lead the student movement that brought Suharto to power. Jusuf had for years provided long-term planning advice for Suharto. Sofyan, as spokesman for Chinese-owned conglomerates, raised money for various New Order projects.

But ethnic Chinese-Indonesians had once again become scapegoats for Indonesia's financial crisis and the food shortages it engendered, and the Wanandis, who had fallen from New Order grace, made convenient targets. Throughout Indonesia's history, ethnic Chinese have been the target of attacks, including by European settlers during the colonial era. In the aftermath of the 1965 abortive coup, which had been blamed on the country's communist party, Chinese-Indonesians were targeted for their suspected links to Beijing. People were slaughtered and Chinese shops and homes were burned and looted.

If ethnic Chinese were stigmatised as disloyal in the 1960s for being pro-Peking, their patriotism was questioned in early 1998 for not showing sufficient enthusiasm for an "I love the Rupiah" campaign led by Suharto's daughter, Tutut. Military officials publicly condemned Chinese-Indonesians, who made up less than four percent of the population but were thought to have owned 70 percent of the domestic economy, as "rats" and "traitors" for keeping money overseas.

Sofyan Wanandi, the informal spokesman for a group of Chinese conglomerates that had supported Suharto's New Order and a director of *The Jakarta Post*, was particularly stigmatized. As head of the Gemala Group, with interests in the automotive, pharmaceutical, chemical, property and financial sectors, Sofyan was a widely respected businessmen and board member of the think-tank, the Centre for Strategic and International Studies. He was one of the leaders of the student movement that mobilized mass demonstrations in 1965/66 that helped topple Sukarno. In the 1970s and 1980s, he had helped the military manage some of their business units.

But the political clout of CSIS had begun to wane after its executive director, Jusuf Wanandi, suggested Suharto give some thought to his succession and more empowerment to his economic ministers. It got worse after Research and Technology Minister B.J. Habibie, with Suharto's support, founded an association of Muslim intellectuals (ICMI) that was meant to counter the Catholic-dominated CSIS, but which raised concerns about the increasingly Islamic tilt of the Suharto regime.

In late 1997 and January 1998, Sofyan Wanandi had made no secret of his misgivings about the impending choice of Habibie as vice president or his criticism of the "I love the Rupiah" campaign. Sofyan says his relations with the Suharto regime began to deteriorate when he went on a Finance Ministry road show to the United States in 1997 and took questions about who would likely be Suharto's successor. "I said the next vice president should be from the armed forces, but Suharto wanted Habibie." The president was not amused, and asked his old friend Lim Sioe Liong – one of the biggest conglomerate owners – to sack Sofyan from his position as spokesman for the president's Prasetya Mulya Foundation.

Sofyan was typically outspoken about Tutut's "I love Rupiah" campaign in early 1998, saying the financial crisis would have been better solved if the government was less corrupt and more transparent. In connection with that campaign, 13 business tycoons were reported to have received "threatening phone calls" from the military. The Armed Forces chief also met with Indonesian journalists and editors advising them to write articles critical of ethnic-Chinese Indonesians

When Armed Forces Commander Feisal Tanjung said Chinese business leaders were not doing enough to help the country and should bring home the $80 billion he claimed they had stashed overseas, Sofyan called the remarks "divisive". Indeed, it was ironic that the "I love Rupiah" campaign was led by one of Suharto's children, since the combined wealth of the first family far exceeded that of the wealthiest Chinese conglomerate owner.[†]

It was against that backdrop of Sofyan's spat with the military that Jakarta military commander Maj. Gen. Sjafrie Sjamsoeddin claimed an e-mail message had been found on a laptop in the room where the bomb went off, linking the students to Sofyan Wanandi. A week later, on Jan. 25, Yunus Yosfiah, the head of the social and political section of the armed forces, told reporters the military suspected a "political conspiracy" behind the rupiah crisis aimed at overthrowing the government.[††] The next day, in answer to a summons, Sofyan went down to the internal security agency, Bakorstanas, and afterward told reporters he was pleased with how his interrogation had gone. Sofyan underwent further questioning mid-February after returning from a trip to Australia, and on February 13, his brother Jusuf was grilled at the notorious interrogation center, Kodam Jaya, in Jakarta.

In late January, scores of students, arriving on chartered buses, staged a series of demonstrations outside CSIS, calling for its dissolution. Shouting "hang the Wanandi brothers", they blamed Sofyan and Jusuf for the financial crisis. It seemed like 1974 all over again. Youths also demonstrated outside the office of the daily *Media Indonesia*, which had run an editorial suggesting that the allegations against Sofyan Wanandi were a fabrication by the military. The *Media Indonesia* editor-in-chief was called in for questioning.

Amnesty International and Human Rights Watch Asia severely criticized the attack on the Wanandi brothers, suggesting that it appeared to be a ploy to divert public attention away from the cronyism and corruption that had increasingly come into focus during the crisis by using the timeworn tactic of scapegoating the Chinese.

Jusuf took it in stride. He had seen it all many times before, and decided to give his young interrogators from military intelligence and Gen. Prabowo Subianto's feared Special Forces (Kopassus) a lesson in history. "They asked me about PRD and our involvement with students. I said when did you graduate from the academy? And they said, the 1970s and 1980s. I said you know when I was an activist in defining this country my counterpart was Suharto, and we are the ones who made him President and now you accuse us of anything under the sun? So don't tell me you have all this evidence, because I have helped make Suharto! Then I gave them a lesson on 1965. I did all the talking not they, for five hours. I lectured them about how I helped Suharto and how close we were. After two interrogations with them and one with the police they didn't move on anything. All they said was 'stay in town.' Nothing ever happened and after several weeks I could travel again."

He shakes his head, as older brothers will do when they talk about headstrong younger siblings. "The problem with Sofyan is he cannot stop himself from talking," Jusuf says. "He is very outspoken."

Sofyan had mentioned to Prabowo that Suharto should choose a strong and competent military man as his vice president, to get the trust of the armed forces and Suharto's ambitious son-in-law thought Sofyan was suggesting he was just the man for the job, Jusuf says. "Prabowo later said he was instigated by Sofyan to stand up against his father-in-law."

---

† *Sydney Morning Herald*, 16 February 1998
†† Yunus would become information minister in the Habibie government and oversee the dismantling of New Order press curbs.

reforestation fund to Habibie's aircraft plant, wouldn't happen again. Pictures of the signing ceremony, splashed on the front page of *The Jakarta Post*, showed IMF Managing Director Michel Camdessus standing above a seated Suharto, arms folded and wearing a frown. For Indonesians used to seeing Suharto's guests bowing and scraping in gestures of deference and obeisance to his regal presence this was a real shocker.

Suharto, in any case, blithely ignored the agreement when he was sworn into power for a seventh term and unveiled his crony cabinet in the weeks to come. *The Jakarta Post* foresaw that and argued in a Jan. 16 editorial that economic reforms in the absence of political reforms were doomed. "Many may worry that a government under the same leader might easily return to its old habits. The risk of a recurrence of corruption, collusion and market distortion is indeed quite big with the children and close relatives of so many top officials, provincial leaders, high military offices and retired generals quite active in business." The editorial warned against further backsliding on IMF reforms. "The grave crisis we are in now should have rudely awakened the government to the likely horrendous cost of another mistake or capricious attitude. The writing is already on the wall: Reform now or collapse."

The writing on the wall was quite literal in Jakarta during this time: rude messages about Suharto were being spray-painted around the capital's neighborhoods. The rise in prices of basic goods such as rice and cooking oil led to food riots on Java in January that spread to other islands throughout the archipelago the following month. Chinese-owned shops, homes and businesses were the main targets. It wasn't just the poor who were feeling desperate. Well-off Indonesian women were taking to the streets as well. In Jakarta, a group of educated, middle-class women was hauled off to a police precinct and underwent hours of interrogation in February after staging a demonstration against shortages of baby milk powder. "We could have used the shortages as a good excuse to promote breast-feeding," quipped Debra Yatim, the former Jakarta Post page editor and founder of a feminist NGO that was supporting the protest.

"But it was probably better to use it against the New Order. After that incident, civil disobedience became an acceptable tactic for the middle class."

Bapak Presiden meanwhile was making it quite clear to the IMF his family would remain the conspicuous exception to its rules. On January 22, the day the rupiah breached 10,000 to the U.S. dollar, the mines and energy minister commissioned Indonesia's biggest ever power project, a $6 billion coal-fired power project in Sumatra. Its shareholders included Nusamba, the holding company that Bob Hasan controlled on behalf of the Suharto family.[7] At the 10,000 exchange rate, Indonesia's per capita income in dollar terms had fallen to the level it was when Suharto came to power in 1966.[8] Weeks later, the president sacked his newly independent central bank chief because the fellow refused to support the president's unconventional plan to stabilize the rupiah. The currency had halved in value in 1997 and had halved again in January alone, prompting Suharto to seriously consider implementing a currency board system (CBS), in which the rupiah would be rigidly pegged to the U.S. dollar and the Indonesian economy would essentially become dollar-based. Any increase in the rupiah supply would have to be matched with foreign reserves.

Under such a system, the government would no longer be free to set interest rates or inject liquidity into the economy at will. Financial markets and companies would have to make massive adjustments. Indonesia's creditors saw it as completely unworkable and a prescription for more financial market contagion. *The Jakarta Post* explained in an editorial: "Given the rigid market discipline CBS requires, the biggest question – or rather the greatest doubt – is whether such a system could be credible and sustainable for a long time under a political leadership notoriously known for its huge vulnerability to cronyism, nepotism and corruption." It was bound to fail because "two key fundamentals for a CBS success do not yet exist in the country: a sound banking system and strong public confidence in the political leadership's capability and willingness to consistently take painful reform measures to cope with the economic crisis."

---

7   O'Rourke, *Reformasi*, p. 54
8   George Aditjondro, Multinational Monitor, January 1998.

Youth was hardly feeling served by an antiquated New Order that felt Suharto, the only president they had ever known, was mortgaging their future to cater to cronies. Student protests had begun to rumble on campuses. With the food riots showing no sign of abating and even middle-class mothers marching in the street, Suharto decided to circle the wagons ahead of his reappointment as president by the rubber-stamp assembly in March. To make sure his security was in good hands, he appointed a general he had been grooming for years, Wiranto, as both armed forces commander and defense minister – an unusual arrangement. Lt. Gen. Prabowo's Special Forces took care of the dirty work, abducting a number of dissidents and taking them to secret interrogation centers to be tortured.

This kind of thing was not unusual in the New Order, but for reasons that are not quite clear until today, some of these dissidents were released weeks later to tell their chilling stories. Months later, 11 Kopassus operatives were found guilty of kidnapping and torturing nine of the activists who had disappeared and sentenced to 22 months in jail. Their commanding officer, Prabowo, would later admit to ordering the abductions.

Students on campus held rallies featuring a slogan that commented on Suharto's refusal to contemplate succession, "*tujuh kali sampai mati*" (seven times until he dies). But otherwise the President's seventh anointment went smoothly in the MPR (House of Representatives). Suharto then unveiled his infamous "screw you" crony Cabinet that thrust a metaphorical stiff middle finger at the IMF and his growing legion of critics. Oldest daughter Tutut, who helped her father hammer out the dubious lineup, slotted herself in as social affairs minister, the first time a family member was made a minister. Her partner in the Sumatran power project, Bakrie & Brothers executive Tanri Abeng, was made minister of state-owned enterprises. The highly regarded Ma'rie Muhammad was kicked out as finance minister and replaced by the obliging director-general of taxation, Fuad Bawazier, who had cheerfully provided tax exemptions to Tommy's car project, and who had also served with Bambang Suharto on a foundation that skimmed 2 percent of taxable income from all Indonesian taxpayers.[9]

But the appointment that caused the most outrage was that of Suharto's old golfing buddy and bag man, Bob Hasan, as minister of trade and industry. The very personification of the KKN economy, the First Crony was to be put in charge of the crisis. He was quick to show his colors, describing structural reform as a plot to weaken Indonesia. "Foreigners are nice to us only if they want something from Indonesia – but if they no longer benefit from our commodities, or if they feel threatened by our exports, they start attacking us," *The Jakarta Post* quoted him as saying.

In early April, a student protest on the campus of Gadjah Mada University in Yogyakarta turned into a huge melee with troops firing tear gas and swinging batons. At least 88 were injured. That touched off a series of campus protests throughout the month, culminating in simultaneous rallies on 25 university campuses across the country on April 25. With the opposition political parties cowed and sidelined, and erstwhile New Order critic, the NU's Abdurrahman Wahid, strangely silent and seemingly ambivalent about the chaotic events rapidly unfolding in the world's largest Muslim country, it was the students that were spearheading a "People Power" movement, following in the footsteps of their parents in the 1965 generation.

Jakarta Post reporter Emmy Fitri raced out to prestigious Trisakti University on May 12 after hearing that students had been shot dead during a protest. A standoff between thousands of students and police in full riot gear had seemed to be averted and students were moving back to campus when they were fired upon from a flyover overlooking the university. Four students died in the early evening twilight. Whether it was police or a Special Forces unit, and why they fired with live ammunition at that point, seem destined to remain yet another of those New Order mysteries. [10] Another *Jakarta Post* reporter, Budiman Moerdijat, made it through the swelling and angry crowd of students to a hospital morgue near

---

9 O'Rourke, *Reformasi*, p. 75

10 Two police officers were later tried for misconduct in connection with the Trisakti shootings

the university to view the bodies. *Jakarta Post* cartoonist Bernard Napitupulu, who had been one of the main liaisons between the newspaper and the student movement, was already there helping to guard the bodies. They prevented an army doctor from conducting an autopsy, fearing the results would be "doctored", then editor-in-chief Susanto Pudjomartono recalled. "So Bernard invited one of the best Indonesian doctors to do an autopsy. While the autopsy was in progress several army doctors came to the hospital and wanted to do the autopsy, but Bernard and his friend prohibited that because they suspected foul play...They were afraid the army would remove the evidence". The evidence, in fact, showed that students had been shot with live rounds, and not with rubber bullets as per riot-control protocol.

Wire services and other Indonesian media were reporting six students had been killed and stayed with that figure for a full day, but the *Post* reporters who were in the morgue with the students could see the four beds, each with a student covered with sheets speckled with blood, and kept insisting to duty editor Endy Bayuni to stick with four dead, which turned out to be the correct number.

The killings spawned an orgy of rioting that convulsed the capital for nearly two days and which mainly targeted hapless Chinese traders and shop-owners. Chinatown was gutted. According to Jakarta police around 1,200 people died in the capital, many of them trapped in burning buildings, and 2,000 were arrested. The riots destroyed more than 5,000 shops, banks and offices, more than 1,000 homes, 40 shopping malls, 11 police stations, 15 markets and two churches. Riots erupted in the country's second largest city of Surabaya – where mobs burned a showroom of Tommy Suharto's *Timor* car – Yogyakarta and Solo in Java, and Bandar Lampung and Palembang on Sumatra.

Post publisher Raymond Toruan, whose ambition had been to have the newspaper be at the center of the NGO movement, was hosting a meeting of student leaders in his office on May 13 during the memorial service for the four Trisakti students and the riots that followed later that afternoon. "I was in the office and somehow, all of these guys, the student leaders, turned up in my office. It's about 1-2 p.m. and there are about nine persons in my office." They were following the reports that *Jakarta Post* reporters were phoning in about the memorial service at Trisakti, the riots that had begun erupting near the university and which quickly spread to Chinatown, and giving the latest sightings of where the military was being deployed. "Around 3 p.m., my son called from Trisakti University," Raymond says. "He said there were 1,500 students there and they had no more food and water. I called the Indonesian Catholic Women's Association and they collected 2,000 *nasi bungkus* (cooked rice packages). Hunger has no religion. I got commitments from other friends to send them aqua bottles, and not one cent of that came from the *Post*. I asked for volunteers at *The Jakarta Post* to help distribute food and water to the students. We had to sneak it past the military."

The smell of smoke from fires hung heavy in the air as soldiers patrolled the streets with orders to shoot at unruly mobs, who were raping, looting and burning Chinese in their shops and homes. *The Jakarta Post* published a front page photo of a contingent of Indonesian marines marching through Chinatown with raised fists, but the caption said it was a gesture of solidarity with the neighborhood, and residents were relieved to see uniformed security in their neighborhoods. Months later, a government commission would find that individuals or elements in the military, including Special Forces, and members of paramilitary outfits such as Pancasila Youth, had been hired to help provoke the riots. The apparent purpose, according to *The Post,* was to give somebody an opportunity to declare martial law and step in as the Hero, much the way Suharto had in 1965.

Ethnic Chinese and expatriates were leaving Indonesia by the thousands after the riots, fearing the country was spinning out of control. Convoys of buses ferried them from assembly points in the city to the rapidly overcrowded airport. My brother Jim, back in Indonesia on another USAID project, his wife Cynthia and their son Kevin made their way to the American Club, after the U.S. embassy ordered a mandatory evacuation. Hundreds of confused people milled about there, hauling the one oversized suitcase they were allowed to take with them, leaving pets, servants, friends and valuables behind. Cynthia recalled bursting into tears at the sight, and of leaving her beloved Indonesia behind in a state of anarchy, wondering when she would ever return. "Margaritas are the only way to deal with an evacuation," Cynthia recalls. "We got funnier and funnier as the night went on, practically falling into the pool." Frank Sinatra died that day, and his music played like a weird soundtrack to the crisis...*I did it my way...*Suharto certainly did.

Suharto had cut short a trip to Cairo and arrived back in Jakarta on May 15 after the riots had ebbed. A convoy of 100 armored vehicles escorted him home, past shattered glass, gutted buildings and burnt cars. Something he said in Egypt had caused a sensation back home as well. *Jakarta Post* reporter Kornelius Purba was with Suharto when the president spoke to the Indonesian community in Cairo. "If I am no longer trusted, I will become a *pandito* (sage) and endeavor to get closer to God. I will spend my time to guide my children, so they become good people." That made front page headlines, because it seemed to imply he was ready to step down, though the idea of the anti-intellectual Suharto announcing plans to be a sage was surely a tip-off he could not be serious. In ancient times, Javanese kings might give up power to become a sage (though they usually didn't announce it in the midst of mayhem) and it appeared that Suharto was again invoking kingship and Javanese mysticism in dealing with the crisis. But Indonesian officials would later say he was not stepping down; it was just his way of expressing anger about the situation back home.

Kornelius knew he was in deep trouble. "I could not stand up from my seat for 30 minutes after one of Suharto's most trusted aides, his photographer, told me (Suharto) was very angry with the report and I was not allowed to fly home with him," he said years later. Kornelius was let onto the plane in the end, where another aide made grim jokes that he would be disembarking somewhere over the Bay of Bengal.[11]

As traumatized Jakarta residents tried to clean up from the riots, Suharto's old comrades-in-arms and erstwhile allies had decided that

---

11 Kornelius Purba, writing in FT Online/Pacific Media Watch, after the death of Suharto in January 2008

it was time for the old general to make his final retreat, even as a potentially horrific clash was looming between students and soldiers at the parliament building.

On May 19 Speaker Harmoko stood before the House of Representatives and, flanked by leaders of the main parties and factions, called on Suharto to resign. It was a stunning announcement coming from one of the president's most loyal retainers, and meant that the House was threatening impeachment. "The fact that House Speaker Harmoko…had been a staunch opponent of the type of reform called for by the student movement, and that the House had long been branded as a rubber stamp legislature, are noteworthy when viewing this sudden decision," *The Jakarta Post* said. That evening, former chief editor Sabam Siagian was given a statement from his neighbor, Gen. (ret) Kemal Idris, on behalf of an armed forces association, also calling on Suharto to resign, giving the *Post* a little scoop.

Students were pouring into the grounds of the national parliament from every direction, singing and chanting. The ring of security around the compound was letting them come through after showing their school identification cards. It was May 20, National Awakening Day, marking the 90th anniversary of the birth of Indonesia's nationalist movement against Dutch colonial rule.

Emmy Fitri was wandering among the thousands of students who had been camping out around the compound for the past week, since the shootings at Trisakti University and the riots that engulfed Jakarta afterward. The scene was carnival-like. Some students, half naked and bodies painted, were doing comic skits. Others were singing and dancing, playing guitar, or reading poetry. Vendors wandered through the crowd selling drinks and snacks. The word, spreading like wildfire around the parliament compound, was that the president, the only one they had ever known in Indonesia, would make an important announcement the following day. Surely, this time he was really going to quit. This day's protest was their boldest yet.

"There was an avalanche of students coming from every direction, and the number kept growing bigger and bigger until they finally outnumbered the police and soldiers," Emmy recalls. She had been brought up in a New Order family, and she herself was not much older than the students she was covering. "My father and mother were civil servants and pro-government and to me it was all so unreal." She had hung out with the students the day before, gone to the office to write her story that evening, and then had spent the rest of the night with the students. Now they were swarming inside the parliament assembly hall, sitting atop the green domes of the roof, and everywhere in between – an estimated 30,000 of them. "It was so wild," Emmy said. "They were sitting on the desks inside, smoking, singing and playing guitar, dancing. It was very lively." Outside the parliament building, non-students shouted support for the students, and chanted "*Reformasi, Reformasi.*"

It was weird. Police and soldiers, who a week earlier had been in a tense standoff with students at Trisakti University in Jakarta where the four students had been shot dead, were now protecting them inside the parliament compound as they pressed the case for Suharto's ouster. Inside the parliament hall, Amien Rais, head of the Islamic Muhammadiyah organization, was at the speaker's podium demanding Suharto step down immediately – inside the very hall where the president's puppet parliament two months earlier had given him a seventh term in office.

The centre of Jakarta remained sealed off by barbed-wire barricades. Tanks from Lt. Gen. Prabowo's Kostrad strategic reserve command (he had recently been promoted from Special Forces commander) were guarding major roads to government buildings and the presidential palace. The massive military clampdown had precluded an anti-government march that Amien Rais was organizing and which had been expected to draw one million people to Merdeka Square on May 20. Prabowo's commanders threatened to shoot Amien if he went ahead with the march. They were also preparing to organize pro-Suharto goon squads to forcibly eject the students from the parliament compound.[12]

Suharto had told the nation the day before that he was not

---

12 "How a titan fell," *Tempo,* Oct. 15, 2006

interested in staying in power against the people's will. He promised to name a new reform cabinet and a "reform council" in charge of organizing new elections "as quickly as possible". But skeptics wondered if the president was just playing for time to do what he had done very well for 32 years: manipulate the political situation. The students said they would not leave Parliament until Suharto quit. They spent the night in tents or sleeping on plastic sheets.

The Jakarta Post summed up the mood in an editorial that day headlined *More turmoil ahead?* "As the crisis of confidence in the government reaches extreme proportions, many critics are no longer willing to put their trust in the president's integrity, suspecting he might merely be trying to buy time with his latest reform plan," the editorial said. "It looks as if we may be heading toward a time of mounting pressure, growing disorder and economic distress."

As night fell across the tense city of some 10 million, people wondered would the man who would be Javanese king really quit, or was it all just a trick?

Back in *The Jakarta Post* newsroom, Susanto and other editors were furiously working the phones calling their contacts in the military and the presidential palace long after the front page had been sent to the composing room.

Deputy National Editor Meidyatama "Dymas" Suryodinigrat was taking a stream of calls from palace reporter Kornelius Purba late into the night. "I think it was close to midnight that I made the last call to Kornelius who quoted an off-the-cuff response given to him as [State Secretary] Saadilah Murshid passed by: 'Let it be, its not going to be long now, it's over.'"

Susanto did what every editor dreams of doing at least once in his life. He told the night editor to stop the press. *The Jakarta Post* was about to tell the world Suharto was quitting. But in fact the night editor had been holding the front page for just this eventuality.

That morning's edition was, however, already in production and getting ready to be printed, as a team of editors, including Raymond and Susanto, crowded around the front page layout, where National Editor Santi Soekanto was furiously rewriting the lead story. "She was writing the top half of the story and adding things as it came as *Pak* Raymond and Susanto stood carefully looking over and sometimes helping pick words, while Lela Madjiah came by every so often on what her sources had told her," Dymas said. "For me it was a rare sight to see some of the most senior people at the *Post* huddled in such away. Something I've never seen again and probably never will."

At 2 a.m., the printing presses began rolling with a story saying informed sources had told *The Jakarta Post* that Suharto would hand over the presidency to Vice President Habibie at the State Palace at 9 a.m. "We had the biggest scoop in Indonesian press history," Endy says. "Nobody else had the story."

Except for *Kompas*. But typically it pulled its punch when it came time to presenting the story. Dymas recalls *The Jakarta Post* editors being quite nervous about being alone on a story such as this and so he was dispatched to find out what *Kompas* was going to print. "I distinctly remember walking over to the *Kompas* printing/production area after midnight after we put the story to bed to check the first plotter of *Kompas'* headline. By coincidence we both ran similar headlines, except in typical *Kompas* 'Javanese' style they were less up front about declaring Suharto would resign. *Kompas* was saying that a new Cabinet would be formed and suggested that Suharto afterwards may resign. JP was more frontal saying he would resign at 9 a.m. at the Palace. It was the presentation style, more than the facts itself that gave us the scoop."

Shortly after 9 a.m. on May 21, President Suharto stepped before a microphone at the presidential palace, joined by Gen. Wiranto, Lt. Gen. Prabowo, the supreme court chief justice and his daughter Tutut. In a terse five-minute speech, he conceded the impossibility of forming a government. In line with article 8 of the 1945 Constitution, he said, "I have decided to hereby declare that I have ceased to be the president of the Republic of Indonesia as of the time I read this on this day, May 21, 1998." In Catholic liturgy, it was the day marking the Ascension of Christ to heaven, and it was now the day marking the descension of the Javanese king.

Suharto, enigmatic to the end, then invited Habibie to take the oath of office before the Supreme Court chief justice, and walked out of the room, briefly shaking hands with him, but declining to say anything. In his book *Decisive Moments,* Habibie said he had a "lively discussion" with Suharto the night before about naming a reform cabinet, following which Suharto said he would resign. "What is my position as vice president?" Habibie asked. "What happens, happens," the president gruffly responded, and dismissed Habibie.[13]

Habibie actually was not sure until the morning that Suharto resigned that he was meant to fill out the remainder of *Bapak* president's term. Habibie recalls sitting with the media in the State Secretariat, waiting for Suharto to arrive. "I was sitting there with media people and wanted desperately to see the president to discuss the problems. But Suharto barely acknowledged his vice president during the ceremony. I wanted to discuss with Suharto, but he went by me and avoided eye contact. Then it was just the time for me to be sworn in."[14] The two men never spoke again. Even as Suharto lay lying in a Jakarta hospital in January 2008, Habibie was refused permission to see him.

In newsrooms across the country, reporters and editors were trying to decipher what Suharto was really trying to say. Most news organizations translated his remarks as saying he was resigning, or withdrawing as president. *The Jakarta Post* had decided to prepare a special afternoon edition of the newspaper and Susanto showed Raymond a dummy of the front page, entirely devoted to the story under the headline: "I Resign."

"I disagreed," Raymond recalls. "He was saying he has 'stopped as president'. I said we both know that Suharto is a Javanese general and Javanese generals do not step back. So what he is saying in Javanese terms is that it's no longer worth my effort. That is Suharto. He will not resign. He quit. And Susanto agreed. We went upstairs (to the newsroom) and listened to the recording again and heard him saying 'I stop'. Every other newspaper had him resigning. They were wrong."

---

13 Interview with B.J. Habibie, USINDO Brief, Jan. 29, 2008
14 Interview with Habibie, U.S.-Indonesian Hegemonic Bargaining: Strength of Weakness, by Timo Kivimaki, Ashgate Publishing, 2003

"I Quit" in 80-point characters, was the headline in the *Post's* special edition.

Raymond and Susanto then held a traditional ritual feast. "We went out and slaughtered two goats for the occasion," he said.

Suharto, true to his character until the end, departed in a shroud of mystery over how he wanted to exit the national stage. *The Jakarta Post* reported that Armed Forces Commander Gen. Wiranto, 51, visited Suharto the night before his resignation to deliver a message from the military leadership asking him to resign now that his cabinet had quit rather than face impeachment in parliament. House Speaker Harmoko had given Suharto a Friday deadline in the name of Parliament to step down or face impeachment.

Suharto had found it impossible to set up the interim cabinet he had hoped would give him the graceful exit he craved. His senior economics minister and the longest-serving cabinet member, Ginandjar Kartasasmita, along with 13 other ministers had all refused to join. State Secretary Saadilah Mursjid came to Suharto's office shortly before midnight on May 20 to break the news. "Who's in the cabinet?" Suharto asked. "It's just you and me," Mursjid replied. Suharto sighed, and after a long pause said, "Well, that's it then."[15]

The end-game for Suharto had played out like a *wayang* play, of course, featuring feuding generals, chaos in the streets and betrayal. In Javanese lore, the king is always betrayed by his right-hand man. Suharto, perhaps, blamed Habibie for failing to prevent the mass resignations of his Cabinet – what political observers say was the knife in his back.

Years later, it was disclosed that Suharto had written a letter transferring executive powers as head of a National Vigilance and Safety Operation Command to Gen. Wiranto. It was modeled on the March 11, 1966 *"Supersemar"* letter that Sukarno supposedly wrote to Suharto, handing over power. Suharto told Wiranto, when handing him the letter shortly before midnight on May 20: "It's up to you whether or not you use this letter," a *Tempo* magazine source, present in the room, quoted Suharto as saying in Javanese. "No one,

---

15 Schwarz, *A Nation in Waiting*, p. 308

including Habibie, was aware of Suharto's letter to Wiranto until much later," *Jakarta Post* Chief Editor Endy Bayuni says. "Suharto probably intended that Habibie would resign along with him since they had been elected on the same ticket two months earlier."

So why didn't Gen. Wiranto force the issue? For one thing, he had his hands full keeping the military together. Within hours of Suharto's resignation, he had removed Prabowo, the Suharto son-in-law and Kostrad commander, and assigned him to a military staff school in Bandung. Prabowo, well-known as a Habibie ally, felt double-crossed. In an angry show of force, Prabowo mobilized some of his troops and showed up at Habibie's home that night to complain. "He asked me what to do, and I told him to obey his commander," Habibie said. But as a precaution, he said, the new president and his family were moved for several hours that night to a safe house and his grandchildren were flown by helicopter to join him.[16]

Jusuf Wanandi believes that Suharto thought he still had things under control almost to the end, until the 14 ministers quit. "He was already old and his reactions were slow. There was not enough momentum from the rioting to have another *Supersemar.*" Jusuf says Prabowo, who like Suharto in 1965 was the Kostrad commander, was expecting the President to hand power over to him in midst of all the chaos. "But Suharto gave (the letter) to Wiranto instead, and Wiranto didn't dare act on it." This *wayang* story was quite different. "In 1965, Suharto was the hero, because six generals had been killed. The wind was behind him. But now the wind was behind the students this time."

Habibie cobbled together a Cabinet on May 22. Students still occupied the parliament compound, demanding that the German-trained engineer follow Suharto into oblivion. Emmy had been with the students the night before when rumors of a military coup – probably sparked by Prabowo's visit to the Habibie home – swept the compound. Soldiers with loudspeakers ordered students out of the compound. Some ran inside the parliament building, others tried

---

16 Indonesia's New Leader, Self-Styled Reformer, Hopes to Stay Awhile", Seth Mydans, *New York Times*, June 3, 1998

to escape the compound by scrambling over a wall, including Emmy and her editor.

She recalls being hung up on the wall, and people shouting at her to drop down, and being frightened that the long-feared assault to eject the students had begun. She had watched the resignation speech inside the morgue at the University of Indonesia's medical school, where students had planned a rally that day and had had mixed feelings. "I was thrilled, but at the same time, I wondered what would happen next. And it was answered when there were riots" in the months ahead. "I never thought people could be so cruel and criminal."

The Nail of the World had some loose. The center was not holding. Indonesia would lurch from one crisis to another under weak and erratic governments in the years ahead.

༄

CHAPTER SEVEN

DELIVERANCE AND REFORMATION

Emmy Fitri was with a roiling horde of student protesters at Catholic Atma Jaya University near the Semanggi cloverleaf in Jakarta when police and soldiers, firing tear gas and swinging batons, moved against them that "Black Friday" the 13th in November 1998. Students had been gathering all day at various campuses in Jakarta and the military was determined to keep them from hooking up. The students at Atma Jaya had been joined by residents of surrounding neighborhoods and the crowd had swelled to more than 10,000 by afternoon.

Down the road at the national parliament, the People's Consultative Assembly (MPR) was meeting for the first time since Suharto resigned in May. It was a stormy session, now that political parties were finally free to dissent after 32 years of New Order somnolence and torpor. The opposition Islamic-based United Development Party wanted the military excluded from the parliament, which the majority Golkar party was resisting. Parliament was also debating whether and how to investigate and prosecute Suharto and his family for ill-gotten gains, and setting a date for general elections. Students had demonstrated for days in support of these demands. They often wound up clashing with the tens of thousands of paramilitary youths the military had organized to help keep order in the city.

The Jakarta Post, whose editorial leadership had staked out their pro-democracy credentials during the anti-Suharto agitation, stood clearly with the students. "Providing military officers with unelected

Student-led protesters crouch on the street as soldiers with assault rifles advance on them to break up a protest near Atma Jaya University in November 1998. Students were demanding that Suharto be investigated for corruption and that the military withdraw from politics.

Hutomo Mandala Putra, better known as Tommy Suharto, smiles broadly as he arrives at the attorney general's office in January 1999 to answer questions in connection with a corrupt land swap deal for which he was later imprisoned.

An East Timorese militia man guards residents in September 1999 following a historic referendum in which East Timorese voted overwhelmingly to become independent of Indonesia. Pro-Indonesian militia rampaged in the weeks after the vote, which led to the deployment a multination peace-keeping force in the former Portuguese colony.

Abdurrahman Wahid greets a supporter on October 21, 1999 a month before he was elected president by the national parliament. Wahid, widely known in Indonesia by his nickname Gus Dur, had long campaigned for secular, democratic politics, as head of the country's largest Islamic grouping, the Nahdlatul Ulama.

Former president Megawati Sukarnoputri wearing traditional dress in October 2001, three months after becoming president.

Susanto Pudjomartono (R), chief editor from 1991 to 2001, greets people at the 10th anniversary party of *The Jakarta Post*. Standing next to him is then Publisher Raymond Toruan. The two led the *Post* into taking a more aggressive reporting approach to test the limits of New Order censorship during the 1990s.

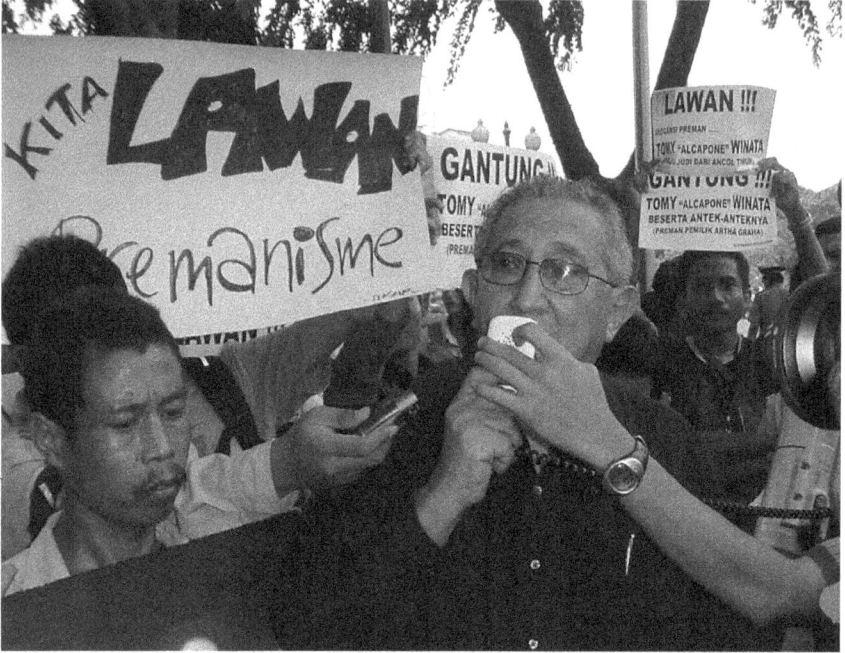

Tempo senior editor Fikri Jufri speaks at a rally on April, 22, 2003 protesting against the arrest of the magazine's chief editor Bambang Harymurti.

Former Armed Forces Commander Wiranto announcing his candidacy for the landmark 2004 presidential election.

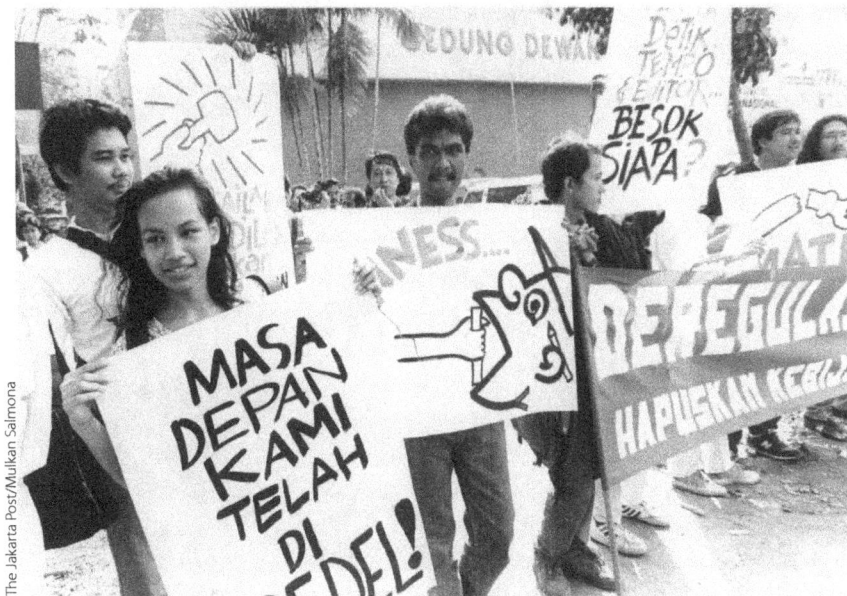

The Jakarta Post/Mulkan Salmona

Demonstrators hold protest banners following the banning of *Tempo* and two other weekly news magazines in June 2004. The demonstrations marked a turning point toward more open opposition to Suharto's New Order regime.

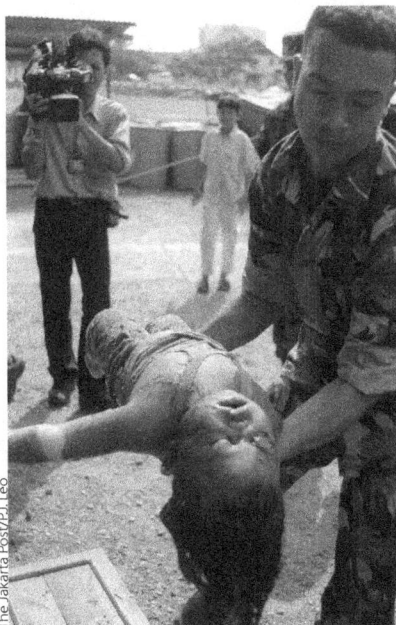

The Jakarta Post/P.J. Leo

A soldier carries a dead child to an emergency shelter in Banda Aceh on December 27, 2004, a day after a devastating earthquake and tsunami killed 170,000 people in northern Sumatra.

An elderly woman in Aceh collapses into the arms of sympathizers at an emergency shelter in Banda Aceh after learning that family members had died the day before in the December 26 tsunami that killed 170,000 people in the province in northern Sumatra.

A 9.15 magnitude earthquake and the unprecedented tsunami it unleashed wreaked havoc across a dozen nations along the Indian Ocean rim. Worst hit was Indonesia's Aceh province.

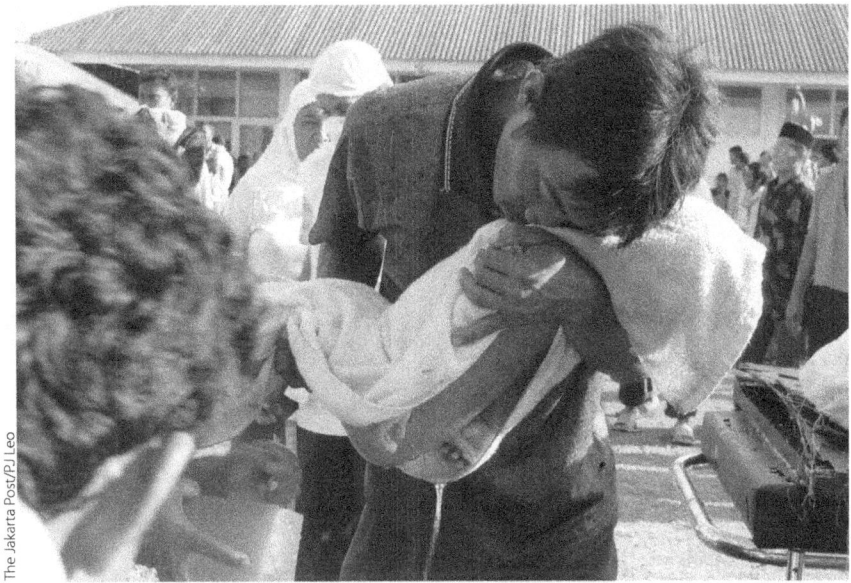

A father clutches his dead child a day after the earthquake and tsunami in Aceh. Women and children accounted for a preponderant number of vicims in the calamity.

The Indian Ocean tsunami raced at the speed of a train with waves as high as 10 meters pulverizing everything in its path.

Soldiers search for vicitms in the wreckage of a Gardua Airlines passenger plane that crashed and burned on the runway in Yogyakarta on March 7, 2007. It was the latest in a number of air and sea accidents that raised questions about safety standards in the country.

Former president B.J. Habibie gives a speech at the launching of his book *Legal Principles of the Indonesian State* in Jakarta on April 17, 2007.

The Jakarta Post/PJ Leo

Suharto golfing buddy and timber tycoon, Bob Hasan shown here in April 2007 about thre years after his release from prison on a corruption conviction.

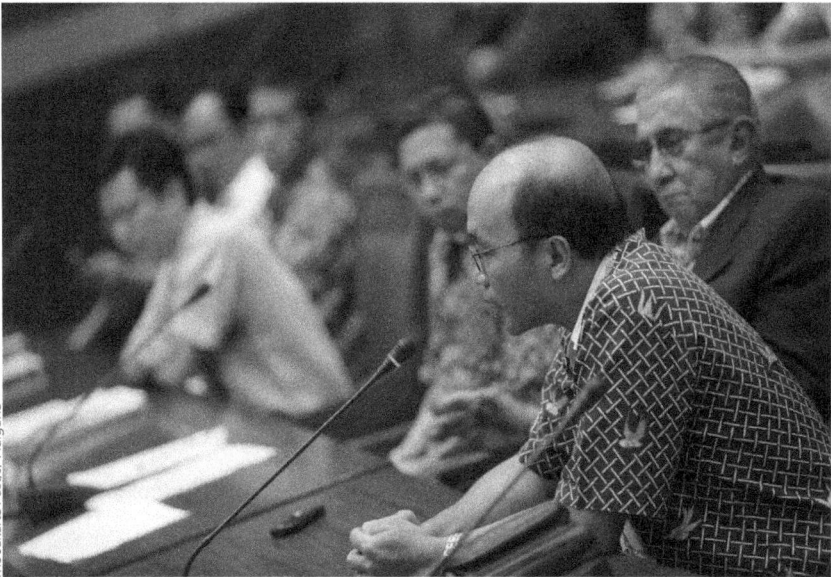

The Jakarta Post/J/ Adiguna

Tempo group chief editor Bambang Harymurti testifies before a parliamentary committee on press freedom issues on September 26, 2007. Bambang was sentenced to jail in 2003 after a court held him responsible as chief editor for a story that was deemed defamatory to businessman Tomy Winata.

Palestinian President Mahmoud Abbas, left, talks with Indonesia President Susilo Bambang Yudhoyono after their meeting at Merdeka Palace in Jakarta, Indonesia, October 22, 2007.

The "child of Krakatau" volcano in the Sunda Strait spewed steam and rocks on October 30, 2007. The caldera has been growing since the eruptions of August 26-27, 1883 the most violent volcanic events of modern times and the loudest sound ever recorded on earth.

The Jakarta Post /Arief Suhardiman

Abu Bakar Bashir, according to many in Indonesia and abroad, was the spiritual leader of the Jemaah Islamiyah militant group.

The Jakarta Post/Murdani Usman

Police inspect the ruins of Raja restaurant in Kuta Beach, Bali on October 3, 2005 after suicide car-bombs in south Bali that killed 129 people two days earlier. The attack was one of a series of suicide attacks blamed on Jemaah Islamiyah that began with the Kuta beach nightclub bombings in October 2002 that killed 202 people, most of them foreign tourists.

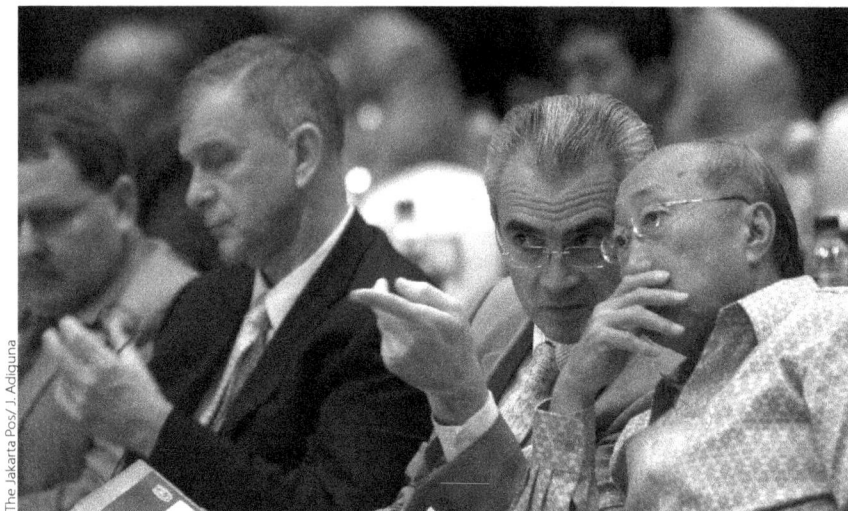

The Jakarta Pos / J. Adiguna

Sofyan Wanandi (R) listens to International Labour Organization Executive Director José Manuel Salazar-Xinirachs at a conference in Jakarta in March 2008.

The Jakarta Post/Mulkan Salmona

Acvitist Munir speaks at a seminar on Aceh in Hotel Cemara, Jakarta.

Sofyan (L) and Jusuf Wanandi. The brothers were leaders of the student movement that helped usher in Suharto's New Order, but fell from grace after urging political and economic reforms.

Kompas publisher Jacob Oetama (L) holds an animated conversation with *Jakarta Post* President Jusuf Wanandi (C) and Rahman Tolleng in a November 2007 gathering of the "66 movement" of activists who helped push Sukarno from power.

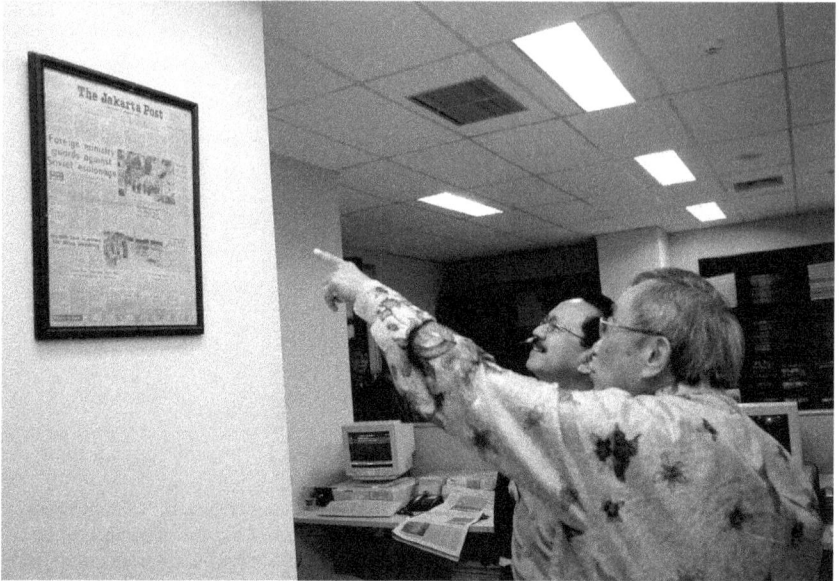

Jusuf Wanandi shows a framed first edition of *The Jakarta Post* to Jakarta Governor Fauzi Bowo on April 24, 2008. The governor official inaugurated the five-storey building.

Kompas Publisher Jakob Oetama (R) gazes at a painting in the newly opened office building of *The Jakarta Post* on April 24, 2008. To his left is Sabam Siagian, Jakarta Governor Fauzi Bowo, Jusuf Wanandi and Sofyan Wanandi.

Jakarta Post Executive Director Daniel Rembeth.

25 YEARS LATER: A new five-story office building on Jl. Palmerah Barat houses the entire operation of *The Jakarta Post*.

Sabam Siagian, the *Post*'s first chief editor (1983-1991) was the former deputy chief editor of *Sinar Harapan*. The paper's publishing company (PT Sinar Kasih) is a co-partner of the *Post*'s publishing venture. He is the first media editor appointed as full ambassador by President Suharto in 1991. Sabam is also the first Indonesian media editor awarded the Nieman Fellowship for Journalism at Harvard for the academic year 1978-1979 since the program was established in 1938. (picture taken in 1991 when Sabam left the *Post*)

Susanto Pudjomartono, became chief editor in 3 April 1993 until 1 August 2001. He was formerly the editor for national affairs at *Tempo* newsweekly, and was appointed by President Megawati Sukarnoputri as ambassador to Russia in November 2003.

Raymond Toruan succeeded Susanto as chief editor, increasing his responsibilities as he was also general manager of the *Post*'s publishing company PT Bina Media Tenggara. Before Susanto took over as chief editor, Raymond was the acting chief editor since Sabam left in July 1991.

Endy Bayuni is the current chief editor, taking over from Raymond on 3 August 2004. Endy started his career with the *Post* from the "bottom up" as he belongs to the first batch of reporters recruited in 1983. Like Sabam, he was a recipient of the prestigious Neiman Fellowship for Journalism at Harvard for the academic year 2003-2004.

seats in the House of Representatives is in naked violation of the 1945 Constitution and it has been a tragic irony to watch the Armed Forces, the defenders of our Constitution, gorging themselves on this forbidden fruit," the *Post* said in an early November editorial. "The problem with Indonesia today is that it still depends on the MPR, a body filled with reactionary advocates of the status quo who bear no resemblance to the majority of people for whom they purport to stand up for..."

The media, for its part, was gorging themselves on the previously forbidden fruit of press freedom. Information Minister Yunus Yosfiah, who had made his reputation during Indonesia's often brutal occupation of East Timor with the Special Forces, was the unlikely catalyst. Within days of his appointment, he had done away with the requirement that publications had to have a government license, and allowed independent press unions such as the Alliance of Independent Journalists, or AJI. The gloves had come off in the press as well as in parliament.

The military under Gen. Wiranto was still under a cloud of suspicion after the Trisakti University shootings and the horrific rioting that ensued – not to mention a host of other mysterious incidents during the New Order. But the brass hats were in no mood to see their political wings clipped in parliament or authority challenged on the streets. Gen. Wiranto, expecting trouble, had ordered Jakarta residents to "stay indoors" that Friday. The Golkar-dominated Parliament, in fact, had dodged the issue of how many seats the military should be guaranteed in parliament, though it did call for an investigation into Suharto-era corruption and set a date for elections in June 1999.

Tens of thousands of students had defied a heavy downpour and a massive security cordon the day before to march on parliament to protest. A policeman had died in one of the earlier clashes that also left at least three students with serious gunshot wounds among the more than 120 injured in fighting around the Semanggi cloverleaf. Built in the 1970s in the heart of a new Jakarta leading to the southern suburbs, the Semanggi intersection was the first such overpass bridge in Indonesia and immediately became an icon of New Order development. It was a strategic junction as well, commanding the arteries to parliament to the west and the seat of government to the north. Groups of students, joined by residents from the neighborhoods, were trying to converge on the cloverleaf from the south and the north to join the protests at Atma Jaya University that Friday.

Clashes had quickly escalated with students hurling rocks, Molotov cocktails or anything they could get their hands on. Security forces fired warning shots and tear-gas canisters. Emmy had been covering the student protests for weeks, and it had acquired a certain routine: Try to stay behind military lines when things turned nasty; put toothpaste on the face when tear-gas was fired. "There was a degree of numbness. This is going to happen every day and you have to deal with it," Emmy recalled years later.

It was getting mean and ugly on the streets by the afternoon of Friday the 13th. Emmy tried to cross a street to get behind the military lines to get away from the intensifying scuffles, but soldiers stopped her. "They were saying things like 'you slut, get away!'. They didn't care if you were a journalist." Armored personnel carriers were firing water cannons. Helicopters had dropped snipers onto the roofs of office and commercial towers around the cloverleaf. "We could see the snipers' infrared (targeting) beams moving around and around the crowd," Emmy said. "We were really scared, and I was ordered back to the office for safety reasons."

Police and soldiers began firing round after round of rubber bullets into the crowd of protesters and still the students kept pushing into the lines of security forces. The shooting began at 3:40 p.m. and did not end until 10:30 p.m. Down the road, President B.J. Habibie was giving his closing speech to parliament in the early evening – around the same time live ammunition was fired into the crowd of students. Saturday's edition of *The Jakarta Post* carried a banner headline "Black Friday" over a story that said 12 people had been killed and dozens injured "as parts of the Indonesian capital turned into a virtual battlefield".

In an editorial a few days later, the *Post* laid the blame squarely on Wiranto and Habibie. "The question facing the nation today is how many more lives will be lost in the blind ambition to preserve the status quo...Like his mentor, the despotic Suharto, President B.J. Habibie refused to sincerely acknowledge student aspirations. MPR members remained blissfully ignorant of the bloody struggles occurring only a few kilometers from their building...Once again, students voicing their aspirations were painted as subversives."

In the aftermath of what became known as the "Semanggi I" incident[1], speculation focused on who was using the live ammunition and why, as was the case in the Trisakti University shootings. Police and military spokesmen said their forces were authorized only to use blanks and rubber bullets. But forensic experts said metal fragments had been found in the wounds of nine of the victims and appeared to be shot at high velocity from a relatively long distance – suggesting the shootings could have come from sniper fire.[2]

The media focused on the likelihood that the shootings may have stemmed from a power struggle that had been going on since Suharto's fall or even before that. Was the Habibie camp seeking to discredit Gen. Wiranto and replace him with someone more loyal to the president? Or was it the work of the elite presidential security guards, who may have retained strong personal loyalties to the Suharto clan and who were seeking to sow chaos to pave the way for the Hero's return? Semanggi I could now be added to a long list of mysterious shootings that have yet to be accounted for.

A government team formed to investigate the May 1998 riots had announced its findings several days before Semanggi I. The Joint Fact-Finding Team (known by its initials TGPF) called for Lt. Gen. Prabowo Subianto and the Jakarta Military Commander, Maj. Gen. Sjafrie Sjamsoeddin, to be investigated for the unrest. "I was not behind the riots," Prabowo says. "That is a great lie."[3]

Wiranto had already dismissed Prabowo from the military in August for his involvement in the abduction and torture of political dissidents earlier that year. The long awaited TGPF report linked the

---

1 Semanggi II would take place the following September when the military fired on student protesters at the same interchange, killing four and wounding dozens. The students were protesting parliament's passage of a bill giving the military sweeping emergency powers.

2 O'Rourke, *Reformasi*, p. 184

3 Interview with Jose Manuel Tesoro, *Asiaweek*, "The Scapegoat?", March 3, 2000

riots to an alleged conspiracy, including individuals and elements within the military, seeking to create an emergency situation which would justify the invocation of "extra-constitutional powers".

The TGPF, comprising members of the government, armed forces and NGOs, said preparations for the creation of chaos, including the Trisakti University shootings and subsequent riots, were "made at the highest decision-making level", *The Jakarta Post* reported in a front-page story. "The whole process preceding the riots had a very clear political dimension...including efforts to secure extraordinary powers based on (an existing) decree (which) would have given the president extra-constitutional powers to overcome any temporary emergency situation", team chairman Marzuki Darusman said. The report found a common pattern during the May riots – well-built young men in crew cuts, usually strangers to the area, seen inciting residents to riots; appearing to be well trained, highly mobile and equipped with gasoline cans and Molotov cocktails. It said the riots were a culmination of events that began with the violent 1997 general elections and climaxed with the shooting of the four Trisakti University students.

Yet firm evidence to support those scenarios has yet to surface, even a decade afterward, and what really happened in the final days of Suharto remains obscured in conflicting accounts. Prabowo himself has said little since his dismissal and spends much of his time abroad.

Security forces were also suspected in a wave of "Ninja killings" that had spread across East Java in the run-up to the November 1998 MPR session– so called because witnesses often described the perpetrators as wearing masks and black robes that covered all but their eyes in the fashion of Japanese assassins. Some 182 Muslim preachers and "*dukuns*" (shamans) had been killed in the heartland of opposition figure Abdurrahman Wahid's Nahdlatul Ulama (NU) between August and November 1998. Reminiscent of the "Petrus" killings of 1983-84, police and the National Human Rights Commission concluded it was, indeed, the work of hired assassins. An NU investigation in October accused security officials in East Java of backing the campaign and said the killings stemmed from conflict among factions in the political elite, with the goal of influencing the MPR session. Gen. Wiranto agreed conflicts among the political elite might have been behind the killing spree. But if the killings were designed to ignite a conflagration – and like the May riots attempt to provide an excuse for a Hero in the military to emerge to set things right again – they clearly failed. The communist bogeyman had been eradicated; a radical Islamic threat had yet to appear. But some in the political elite did fear the forces of Suharto revanchism.

Habibie tried to nail his reform colors to the mast shortly after taking over the ship of state from Suharto, especially with public opinion firmly behind the student movement. He allowed freedom of speech and assembly, and new political parties, and he freed political prisoners. He had promised the MPR open parliamentary elections, limiting presidents to two five-year terms, and reducing the political power of the armed forces. But while politics and the press had been liberated for the most part, the economic crisis continued unabated. Beggars were everywhere on the streets of Jakarta. Indonesia's middle class had been all but wiped out and millions had been thrown into poverty. Habibie did not score many points when he suggested the solution was for people to fast two days a week.

He also seemed to be resisting pressure to investigate his old patron, Suharto. In his first days in office, Habibie's government did put Suharto family businesses under scrutiny: the tax breaks for Tommy's Timor car were revoked and family businesses supplying Pertamina Oil company came under review, for example. But when Attorney General Soedjono Atmonegoro presented a report on widespread corruption in the foundations organized by Suharto and his family, Habibie fired him five days later. Habibie, in fact, went through eight attorney generals during his 15 months in power as he doggedly refused to investigate Suharto, the man who was like a father to him but who would never speak to him again after his ouster.

The German-trained aeronautical engineer – the longest-serving minister during Suharto's reign – had long been viewed with suspicion by the military. When he was nominated as vice president in January 1998, the rupiah fell to a record low on fears his spendthrift ways would further damage the economy. Support from his own Golkar party was lukewarm at best, and lacking any sort of popular mandate, Habibie's political shelf-life seemed destined to be short.

That was certainly the view of *The Jakarta Post*, which expressed exasperation with Habibie in an editorial after national police summoned opposition figures for questioning in late November on suspicion of trying to topple the government. "The police questioning of several vocal government critics…on charges of plotting a rebellion, and the use of armed force to quell anti-government demonstrations…are symptoms of an increasingly intolerant and repressive government. Habibie is now facing exactly the same standoff that beset Suharto in the last months of his rule: a crisis of confidence."

The student movement continued after the MPR session, though it had undergone some changes over the past eight months, *Jakarta Post* Chief Editor Susanto Pudjomartono said. "In the past, they always had some leaders. So every time the authorities arrested the leaders, the movement temporarily stopped. But now there were a lot of leaders, some of them under cover. So when one of the leaders is detained, then the movement continued. They used so-called field coordinators, who stayed behind (the protest lines) using cell phones." But Raymond's office was no longer the ad hoc headquarters for the student movement as it had been during the fall of Suharto. "We couldn't take the risk of using *The Jakarta Post* as their headquarters, because it might endanger *The Jakarta Post*, so they met somewhere else," Susanto said.

The Jakarta Post had never named a person of the year, but at the end of 1998, the newspaper awarded "students" as Men and Women of the Year. "The media was reporting it, but we remained cautious. It was the students who took the leadership to make this people power movement and *reformasi* possible," Endy Bayuni says.

In the last years of the New Order, Jusuf Wanandi had been growing more and more uneasy about his editor and publisher's courtship of the NGOs and student movement. He had watched up close his mentor Ali Murtopo's machinations with civil (and uncivil) society groups and he was not at all sure he wanted to see that in his newspaper. He was particularly worried that the impartiality of the newspaper could be compromised. On a personal level, his ties with the Suharto regime had deteriorated to such an extent that he and his brother, the controlling shareholders of the *Jakarta Post*, were even falsely accused of being in cahoots with a radical student movement plotting to overthrow the government.

Things came to a head at Jusuf's 60th birthday party in November 1997, Jusuf recalled. "Raymond and Santo (Susanto) were too involved. They gave money that we didn't know about to Muslim leaders, student leaders. It wasn't just the money; it was the credibility of the paper. So on my 60th birthday in November 1997, I said the task of *The Jakarta Post* is to be really for the truth and not to be partisan. I don't agree with you spending the time with all these grassroots because then *The Jakarta Post* is establishing an activist tradition." In fact, it had been long established. "People said my office was the headquarters of the student movement," Raymond conceded.

The newsroom generally supported the activist stance of their top managers, though some were a little uneasy with the intimate relationships that Raymond had developed with student leaders. "They would come here and have meetings in Raymond's room often from midnight to morning talking about the next moves – what issues to blow up, when the next rallies would be," says Harry Bhaskara, the opinion page editor at that time. "We in the newsroom supported Susanto's and Raymond's vision about the government. But I was surprised to hear some NGO people saying 'hey your boss gave us money.' I suppose it was going too far as a newspaper to give them money. We could agree with their vision, but not give them money. That's going too far."

Raymond maintains he gave student and NGO group's money – often from his own pocket – only to help sponsor some of their meetings. He insists that at a time when the New Order was monopolizing the usual channels of information, it was important to cultivate non-traditional and alternative views on the news. "The role of the NGOs was to create alternative forms of discussion outside the government, parliament and formal organizations that existed at that time," Raymond says. "NGOs became a meeting place where people from all walks of life could exchange views, news and comments. That gave the elements of democracy at the grassroots level. Our largest contribution was to provide a forum that gives proof that democracy was going on at the grassroots level."

Susanto said they pushed for more press freedom and an end to the Suharto regime in their personal capacity "but in our journalism, we maintained our impartiality. This was a very strict rule. We could not, and we would not, bend those rules…What is the role of the media? What is the role of journalists in a country like Indonesia? We tried to be objective and impartial when reporting about demos against Suharto or even the minister of information. But behind the scenes we did a lot of things."

What, perhaps, became more troubling at *The Jakarta Post* after the fall of Suharto were some questionable management practices and strategies. *Krismon* had hit the newspaper hard, particularly since many of its expatriate readers had left the country and had yet to return. Circulation had fallen from a peak of 51,000 in early 1997 to 28,000 in 1998. At a time when the economy had imploded, when newsprint prices had soared, when ad revenues had dried up along with the readership, *The Jakarta Post* went on a spending spree.

The *Post* bought *D&R* magazine from *Tempo* in October 1998 and it turned out to be a pig in the poke. Most of *D&R's* best journalists had left the magazine to join *Tempo* when it re-launched that month after a four-year ban. *D&R,* which had built a formidable reputation as *Tempo's* surrogate, had enormous debts and no longer had a franchise on daring stories now that the press had been liberated in post-Suharto Indonesia (see box story). No one was supervising the magazine, either, to try and give it a new mission.

Susanto himself was disappearing from the newsroom for days and sometimes weeks at a time, which raised some concern among staff. Susanto, then in his early 50s, says he often was resting at home on doctor's orders because he had developed hypertension and adult-onset diabetes. He also says his absence was part of a deliberate strategy to develop a new generation of leadership in the newsroom through "delegation".

Confusions of liberty

The King of Spades cover had to be one of the most memorable in the entire history of the New Order. Indonesia's rubber stamp parliament had anointed Suharto for a seventh straight term in March 1998 in the midst of a severe economic crisis that had spawned riots across the country. That week's edition of *D&R* Magazine, a surrogate for the banned *Tempo*, showed Suharto's visage superimposed on the king of spades card, in a not so subtle allusion to the aura he had tried to cultivate of a Javanese king.

The issue sold out in days. In fact, newsagents were selling the magazine at a premium to its cover price of 6,300 rupiah (60 cents). Information Minister Hartono said the *D&R* editors would be charged in court with unethical activities. One member of the Peoples Consultative Assembly (MPR) that reappointed Suharto said: "*D&R's* cover this week simply broke the camel's back after months of defiance." Surely it was just a matter of days before the axe would fall on *D&R*, just as it had on Tempo. But with the country in a mounting political and economic crisis, *D&R's* case of *lèse majesté* was put on the backburner and Suharto resigned before it could be resolved.

The magazine was born out of confrontation with the Suharto regime. *D&R's* predecessor, *Tempo*, was banned in 1994 for printing a story about divisions in the government over then-Research and Technology Minister Habibie's purchase of the former East German navy. *Tempo* owned the title and license of a magazine it had briefly launched in 1968 called *Detektif & Romantika*, which was supposed to specialize in cheap scandal and romance stories. *Tempo* re-launched it as *D&R*, which was generally understood in the newsroom to stand for "*Demokrasi and Reformasi*". That was also the slogan of the people power movement that ousted Suharto in May 1998. Most of the journalists at *D&R* had once worked at *Tempo*, including former chief editor Goenawan Mohamad. Since many of them had been banned from working as journalists, they used pseudonyms and changed them weekly to avoid detection.

D&R quickly became one of the top-selling magazines in Indonesia based on the kind of solid, in-depth and daring reporting that had been *Tempo's* franchise previously. Then came the revolution. Suharto fell and Habibie's administration threw off the shackles of press repression, much to everybody's surprise. Indonesia suddenly had one of the freest presses in Asia. "We didn't know what to do," *D&R* Editor Bambang Bujono said. "We could write anything. We didn't know what to write. It was a contradiction."[†]

Stories about corruption, abuse of power, the Suharto family's venalities, and human rights abuses that had long been the domain of *D&R* were now commonplace on the newsstands. In the year following Suharto's resignation, the government granted 718 new media licenses – versus 289 issued in the previous 53 years since independence.

D&R, born and bred in confrontation with the Suharto regime, was looking for a new mission, but the staff was imbued with the fires of the student revolutionary movement. When students took over parliament in the dying days of the Suharto regime in May 1998, most of *D&R's* two dozen reporters went there as well. "I had to tell them 'please, please, distinguish between your involvement and reporting the case. We have a magazine to put out," Bambang said.[††] *D&R* probably had one foot in the grave when the Information Ministry gave *Tempo* back its publishing license and the magazine re-launched in October 1998, with Goenawan back as chief editor. Most of his old staff came back as well from their four-year diaspora, including many of the journalists at *D&R*.

Jakarta Post publisher Raymond Toruan and Chief Editor Susanto Pudjomartono, who had admired the magazine's ethos during its New Order heyday, convinced their board to buy *D&R* from Tempo, which was only too happy to sell. It seemed *D&R*, with a shell of its former staff, was also saddled with considerable debts to its printer. *The Jakarta Post* did not know quite what to do with the magazine it acquired. By all accounts, nobody at *The Jakarta Post* bothered to supervise *D&R* at a time when its staff had been gutted by the re-launch of *Tempo* and when the magazine was trying to find its place in the new and freer information order. The magazine floundered under the new ownership. The fresh-faced journalists who had taken the place of *Tempo* veterans had no feel for the magazine, or deadlines for that matter. The magazine was always coming out late – not just a day late, but a week or more. In less than a year, *D&R* had become an abject failure and folded.

"Raymond and Susanto wanted to buy *D&R* to diversify," former chief editor and board member Sabam Siagian says. "None of them paid attention to it, however. They kept printing 60,000 copies and 50,000-60,000 would be returned, piling up in the storeroom. The problem was that after Suharto, being daring was no longer attractive or unique. It was a strategic blunder."

For Raymond, that blunder would mark the beginning of his end at the helm of the *Post*, and his tone is a bit defensive in trying to explain what happened. "It was decided by the board. I did not do it alone. I'm not saying I was not responsible, but at least they were part of it," he says. "I would not have done it without an introduction from Fikri, who said this is great journalism, but (*Tempo*) cannot afford it anymore," he said referring to *Jakarta Post* director and *Tempo* Senior Editor Fikri Jufri. "Looking back, it would have been better to start that magazine from scratch." Fikri said it was indeed a fine magazine, but with *Tempo* about to publish again, it was no longer needed. "We had to find jobs for those people (at *D&R*)."

Board Chairman Jusuf Wanandi said the main problem was neglect. Nobody was going over to the *D&R* offices to manage the newsroom and make sure a product was going out the door. "On this issue, Susanto and Raymond did nothing. We had a whole house full of back issues."

Journalists at both *Tempo* and the *Post* also saw another problem at *D&R*: a perception that the magazine was being used by Raymond and Susanto to push a political agenda. "I think they were using this for political reasons and to support Megawati and PDI-P," says one senior editor at *Tempo* who did not want to be named. Susanto rejects that completely and says whatever his political affiliations were – and he was never reticent about his admiration for Megawati – he kept a professional impartiality as editor.

"Why did it fail? We recruited new, young journalists and increased their salaries. We expected them to do a professional job, but they didn't. Although we pushed it as editor, we couldn't fulfill deadlines. First it was a few hours late, then a few days, and then it was week, and finally it was three weeks! So we started losing money. Imagine a weekly magazine that was late by a week. We lost billions of rupiah."

---

† Marcus W. Brauchli, "Magazine Long Critical of Suharto Finds itself looking for a New Role," *The Wall Street Journal* Interactive Edition, June 2, 1998).
†† Ibid

"Myself, I believe chief editor for 10 years is too long. After Suharto's downfall it was not challenging anymore," Susanto says. "At *Tempo* we learned about the four kinds of leadership: telling, selling, participating and delegating. So I started the fourth stage of management, which is delegation. I gave Endy (Bayuni) more authority. This was not disappearing, this was delegating. If we want new blood, you have to delegate. But some people could not understand this style."

It's not the kind of delegation technique usually recommended in management manuals, but Endy said he did not mind – too much. "I was happy. Me and Vincent (Lingga) were running the show. But sometimes we wondered where he was. Because there were times when we would need to consult him on personnel issues, for instance, and he was not around. That was a handicap."

Raymond, apparently, was the opposite. He trusted few people, had a highly personalized style of management and delegated very little. Unusually for a publisher, Raymond was quite active in the newsroom, often leading the daily news "budget" meetings and supervising training for new reporters, journalists at the *Post* said. The former Jesuit seminarian ordered his journalists to take classes in logic. "He had us go for training in logic with teachers of philosophy because he said some of us had a problem with logic, and this would make us write better," Ati Nurbaiti says. "He would go more thoroughly than *Pak* Santo did through the paper telling us where we should have given more background or insight to the readers. He directly led the training of new reporters."

The *Post* had saved money from its salad days in the 1990s to build a new office building that would finally allow it to come out from the *Kompas Gramedia* compound. But management was splurging on the doomed acquisition of *D&R,* buying an office building in Bali, and funding a distribution arrangement in Indonesia with the *International Herald Tribune.*

"We were cash flush and were about to start building a new office. It was not a good time to build property when prices were falling," Endy says. "At the same time, we started a spending spree. We bought property in Bali and bought a magazine with no assets and a lot of debt. We started printing in Bali and distributing the IHT. In 1998 when everybody stopped spending money, we were spending like crazy." The *Post* made no money on the IHT deal, the Bali printing venture folded after two years, the magazine was an unmitigated disaster – and the newspaper would have to postpone building that new office for another decade as it paid down debt.

The Jakarta Post had never had a professional finance manger. Purchasing and accounting practices were a little loose, to say the least. "Until about 2003, almost anybody could sign for and purchase something," Endy says. "You needed a camera? You bought it and then signed (an expense claim) for it. New laptop computer? Buy and sign for it. By 2003, we were practically bankrupt and this is what made Jusuf very angry at Raymond." It still rankles with the board chairman. "During the exuberant times you maybe can afford these stupidities, but afterward no. There was no accountability," Jusuf says.

There was no accounting either for all the unexplained bombings, looting and rioting across Indonesia that marked the first half of 1999. Christian-Muslim clashes were getting worse in the old Spice Islands of the Moluccas and on Sulawesi; violence had worsened in Aceh. Many Indonesians blamed disgruntled elements of the military, acting in concert with the Suharto family and other conservative former members of the ruling elite, for trying to thwart the corruption investigation and the drive towards greater democracy. The military was known to be unhappy with Habibie's efforts to pacify Aceh and East Timor, two places where it had extensive businesses. In March 1999, Habibie visited conflict-ridden Aceh province and apologized for years of military brutality there, promising it would never happen again. Two months later, the military fired into a crowd of unarmed protesters, killing more than 40. Claims of a shadowy conspiracy were nearly impossible to verify, but evidence could be found that much of the violence had been carefully organized and well funded.

Gen. Wiranto, who harbored ambitions of ruling the world's fourth largest nation, had made sweeping changes among his top officers to consolidate his position and reform the military, which was under huge public pressure to change from the often brutal body that underpinned Suharto's despotic 32-year rule. But he was having trouble controlling the opposing factions of the military and was coming under sharp criticism for failing to stem the savage sectarian and ethnic violence convulsing parts of the country. In February, Wiranto issued a blanket "shoot on sight" order to troops to combat the mayhem.

"We noticed that the bombings would often happen around the time a Suharto family member would be called in for questioning or making a court appearance, but we could not prove there was a link. We just knew it was too much of a coincidence," Endy Bayuni says. The newsroom was usually awash with rumors, much of it unpublishable, Susanto says. "We tried to cover the chaos by covering from both sides. We noticed there were new groups on the scene. We noticed radicalization among the students, and radicalization among Muslims. We knew there were certain persons behind them, but we could only publish the facts."

Habibie's government had been almost farcical in its public show of investigating the Suharto family's wealth when *Time* magazine came out with an explosive cover story in mid-May entitled "Suharto, Inc." The Indonesian media happily reported the juicy details of the *Time* story, including the bombshell allegation that Suharto had transferred $9 billion from a Swiss bank to an Austrian bank in July 1998 and that he and his six children had been worth $15 billion. Former *Jakarta Post* check editor Jason Tedjasukmana was one of the team of reporters who worked on the story.

One by one, Suharto's children were summoned to the attorney general's office for questioning and made carefully stated denials of the allegations in *Time*. "Most of the questions are incorrect and the most accurate fact is that I'm the daughter of *Pak* Harto," quipped eldest daughter Tutut, then 50, to reporters after eight hours of questioning over Time's report that put her wealth at $700 million.

On June 2, *The Jakarta Post* reported in an exclusive story that Suharto planned to sue *Time*, quoting his lawyer. That same story led with the Swiss justice minister and foreign minister telling Indonesia's visiting Attorney General Andi Ghalib, who had been dispatched to Switzerland and Austria to investigate the *Time* report, that they could freeze any asset of the Suharto family – if Indonesian authorities only made an official request. This was inexplicably never done.[4]

Tommy Suharto, who had gone on trial in April 1999 on graft charges over a land swap deal with the corruption-ridden national foodstuffs agency, Bulog, was questioned the day before his father filed the lawsuit against *Time*. The magazine had reported that Tommy owned 60 percent of Humpuss, a group with 60 subsidiaries in businesses ranging from construction to pharmaceuticals. *Time* estimated his wealth at $800 million. A spokesman for the Attorney General's office said Tommy acknowledged owning a golf club, a 22-room apartment in Ascot, England, three Boeing 747 airplanes and a ranch in New Zealand, but the value of his investments had depreciated considerably due to the rupiah devaluation and some of the assets had been sold to cover debts.

Having led the Suharto family on their "perp walk" before the national media, Habibie and his Golkar party were ready for their own parade in what was to be Indonesia's first truly democratic elections. On June 7, approximately 100 million Indonesians went to the milestone parliamentary polls, one of the most peaceful elections in Indonesia, and for once, a true "Festival of Democracy". The government imposed very little campaign restrictions and 48 political parties contested the polls, versus the three that were allowed to do so during the New Order. Though it took more than a month to declare, the final results showed Megawati Sukarnoputri's Indonesian Democratic Party-Struggle with 34 percent of the vote, Golkar with 22 percent, Abdurrahman Wahid's PKB with 13 percent and the Islamic-based People Development Party (PPP) with 11 percent.

Golkar had done surprisingly well outside Java in the remote regions of Indonesia where the other parties had little presence and where Golkar could deliver patronage. The results presaged a nasty political struggle among the factions supporting Habibie, Megawati

---

4 Ghalib would be sacked shortly after returning from his trip and finding himself charged with corruption. The charges were later dropped.

and Wahid, with the military and its guaranteed seats in the MPR, holding a trump card in the presidential battle in October.

Habibie had astounded people at home and abroad by announcing in December 1998 that East Timor could hold a referendum on self-determination, long the dream of the vast majority of East Timorese. But the United Nations wanted Indonesia's military to withdraw first in order to hold a fair and peaceful vote, a process that would take months, if not years. Habibie, however, said East Timor could be given independence as early as Jan. 1, 2000. He may have thought he was scoring a diplomatic coup, while getting rid of one intractable problem among many in his increasingly volatile country. And Catholic East Timor was not a good fit for predominantly Muslim Indonesia, as far as the devoutly Islamic Habibie was concerned. But the military, which had traditionally supplemented its meager budget allocations with a network of businesses in the territories it operated from, was deeply involved in East Timor's $400 million economy, particularly in the coffee business. Moreover, East Timor had for the past quarter-century been a strategic battlefield and training ground to groom its officer corps. The highly nationalistic military, which had always prioritized the territorial unity of the archipelago above all else, was not happy with Habibie's plan.

Jakarta Post reporter Ati Nurbaiti had gone to the picturesque seaside town of Liquica in early April 1999 with the National Human Rights Commission after reports that pro-Indonesian militias had killed five people near there. Indonesia had since the early 1990s opened East Timor to reporters. Jakarta genuinely thought it had a good story to tell about the development of its "province" despite the civil war. Ati, then 38 and a mother of two daughters, then 9 and 12, was feeling ill-prepared for the trip; she felt she had not done her research properly before rushing to East Timor. Ati had trained as a researcher before joining the *Post* in 1992.

Some 2,000 frightened people had taken refuge in a church compound in Liquica. A militia group known as Besa Mera Putih showed up at the church, and with Indonesian troops and police behind them, fired tear gas to flush out the people, before opening fire on those trying to flee, according to witnesses. An international police investigation later determined that up to 200 people had been massacred and charges were filed against 21 Indonesian officers and militia men.

The road to Liquica was lined with fresh graves, Ati recalls. This is what she remembers from reporting trips to East Timor and Aceh. You would pass a river bend, a scenic lake, a stretch of pristine shoreline and somebody would always point out where the bodies had been dumped, where the people were shot or where they had disappeared. "And in Jakarta we used to think these were exaggerated stories. That was the success of New Order propaganda." She interviewed residents who had taken refuge in the compound. "It didn't make sense that the military couldn't control the massacre," she said. "It didn't make sense if the military was there to secure the situation that so many deaths happened." It appeared that the military had acted quickly to clean up evidence of the slaughter. "Tiles were quickly painted over, but one bathroom was missed and you could see the blood stains."

If the Indonesian military had hoped to provoke Falintil rebels to launch an all-out attack in revenge, as some speculated at the time (and indeed rebel leader Xanana Gusmao, in detention in Jakarta, did call for a popular insurrection in response) it was a grave miscalculation. The rebels stayed in the forest and the Indonesian military was viewed as the sole aggressor in East Timor.

On May 5, Indonesian and Portuguese representatives signed an agreement at the United Nations that called for an Aug. 30 referendum in which East Timorese would choose either independence or autonomy within Indonesia. The agreement said Indonesian police would provide security in the territory and the Indonesian military pledged to stop arming militias. That would prove to be a feckless promise.

The August 30 balloting in East Timor was remarkably free of violence, and 98 percent of the registered voters turned out. But the militias were only waiting for the results to come out, and those were splashed in headlines around the world. "East Timorese say 'No'" was the banner headline on the *Sunday Post* on September 5. An overwhelming 78.5 percent had rejected Indonesia's offer of an autonomy package and chose independence. Habibie immediately announced that Gusmao would be released under a general amnesty. It was a rare moment of historical vindication and self-determination. "The history of the past 23 years has largely been a demonstration that between losing their lives and their homeland, the East Timorese people opted for the first. And this sacrifice of 250,000 lives was not in vain," Gusmao had said on the day of the referendum.

The backlash was swift and brutal. Pro-Indonesia militia set fire to a building on the grounds of the Dili bishop's compound housing 5,000 refugees, killing 25 and injuring dozens. On Sept. 7, after more than 100 people had been killed since the historic referendum, Indonesia imposed martial law. "It is scary to think we are giving *carte blanche* to an institution with a long history of human rights abuses not only in East Timor but elsewhere in Indonesia, including Aceh," *The Jakarta Post* said in an editorial. "TNI (the armed forces) seems to lack the political will to prevail over its self-created militias in East Timor from the beginning. This raises speculation that TNI may have its own agenda, different from the government. East Timor has been a military adventure all along from the 1975 invasion, the 1976 annexation, through all these years…It would not be surprising to see TNI doing all it can to prevent the inevitable separation and deprive the East Timorese of their hard-earned freedom."

The Jakarta Post's harsh editorials about the East Timor debacle could hardly have endeared the newspaper to the still powerful military, and did not go down so well with some of the readers, either, given the nationalist bent of most Indonesians. "They said we were anti-military and questioned our nationalism," Endy says. "And even within our own newspaper we had this debate. But in our defense, we were trying to promote universal values: the right to self-determination. This was not anti-Indonesian. These are universal values, which Indonesia as a democracy had to respect."

The newspaper had long tried to cultivate high-ranking officers as part of its "lobbying" efforts, Susanto says. The editors had prepared a book on the history of the Indonesian army around this time. In addition to its other business diversifications, the *Post* was publishing books, mostly about Indonesian culture, art and ethnography. But the book on the army was eventually shelved over financing issues and the controversies it might engender. The late Benny Murdani, who had fought in every Indonesian conflict since independence, was one who questioned the value of such a book. "He laughed when we told him we planned to publish a book about the Indonesian army," Susanto recalled. "He said: 'Why do you want to publish a book about the Indonesian army when the Indonesian army never won any war, though we always pretended to win.' We never did publish it because there was a big argument about whether to publish a book that would embarrass the armed forces. Some officers said, 'go ahead, it will be a good lesson for us,' but some others raised objections. And there was also the problem of funding."

The Jakarta Post was probably the least of Gen. Wiranto's concerns, with U.S. President Bill Clinton leading an international chorus calling on Indonesia to allow international peacekeepers into East Timor. Wiranto finally bowed to the pressure and agreed to that. On September 16, the Indonesian armed forces began an ignominious withdrawal, a day before an Australian-led multinational force came ashore. But the bloodshed continued. On Sept. 21, *Financial Times* reporter Sander Thoenes, 30, was shot through the chest on a motorcycle as he approached a militia roadblock less than two hours after he arrived. Australian troops the next day recovered his body still sprawled on the street. Wiranto, who like many in the military enjoyed *karaoke*, was shown on television singing the song "Feelings" after the East Timor carnage.

An East Timor tribunal issued an arrest warrant against Wiranto in May 2004, citing crimes against humanity for the deaths of more than 1,000 people in violence blamed on the pro-Jakarta militias. Wiranto was running for president at the time. Wiranto has consistently denied committing any human rights violations and says an Indonesian judicial panel found him innocent of such accusations. "I believe that the issue came to the surface again after I became a presidential candidate. I think this is an effort at character assassination," he told reporters then.

Golkar had nominated Habibie in May to be its candidate in

October's presidential election, which would take place in a vote by 1,000 members of the MPR. But the "reform wing" of the party led by Akbar Tanjung was having misgivings, believing the mercurial "mad scientist" was unelectable. The lawlessness unleashed in East Timor had shown the president had little control over the most powerful institution in the country and he had demonstrated few political skills as president. He was also linked to a scandal involving Bank Bali, which had paid a huge loan collection fee to a middleman who happened to be a senior Golkar official. The party and Habibie denied the money was earmarked for Habibie's campaign war chest, but the scandal had tainted the party and its candidate. Thus, the presidency was wide open for the first time in Indonesian history as the MPR convened to elect Indonesia's new leader. Megawati, whose PDI-P won a plurality of the votes in the June general elections, and who had a fervent mass following, was the clear favorite, though she had high negatives with the Islamic bloc because she was a woman – and an avowedly secular one at that – presiding over a party that had a strong Christian faction.

Habibie was fighting an uphill battle all along as the longest-serving and most indulged minister in Suharto's Cabinets. But his performance as President, *The Jakarta Post* suggested, doomed any chance he might have had at re-election: "Indonesia has seen its fortunes and its international reputation sink lower and lower into the depths of ignominy." The messy secession of East Timor had fueled similar demands for self-rule in other provinces. The Bali Bank scandal and Habibie's reluctance to investigate the Suharto family showed that the culture of corruption and abuse of power was still prevalent. The *Post's* judgment on the Habibie presidency was harsh. "In brief, to say that there has been no meaningful progress during the period that Habibie has been President is a gross understatement. In many respects, such as the prevalence of corruption, human rights abuses and security for investors, this country ranks among the lowest in the world."

When the House rejected Habibie's "accountability speech" defending his presidency, it basically consigned him to the dustbin of history, leaving the door wide open for Megawati. Instead,

Abdurrahman Wahid turned out to be Indonesia's accidental president. Despite misgivings in his own party about his credentials and his party's fourth-place showing in the June elections, he won with crucial support from an Islamic axis in the House.

Megawati's June victory did not give her enough seats to control the House, but she was reluctant to get into political horse-trading, and was keeping her usual – and to her supporters maddening – low profile. Former president Sukarno remained a popular figure with Indonesians, many of whom were not familiar with his disastrous economic policies and the confrontational foreign policy that led ultimately to his undoing. Megawati bathed in his reflected glory. With her supporters reportedly ready to rampage over Wahid's shock victory, parliament quickly elected her vice president. "I think we said from the beginning this would not work because, like Gus Dur himself said, we now have a president who is blind and a vice president who is mute," Endy says. "It was a challenge to explain to our readers how did 'Gus Dur' wind up as president. We felt there was a conspiracy to deny her the presidency."

Almost totally blind, enfeebled by illness, with only lukewarm support from his political allies and distrusted by the military, Wahid faced an uphill battle that would have challenged the most politically adept. His first months in power were marked by a contest of wills between him and his powerful minister for political affairs and security, Gen. Wiranto. Wiranto's exit was probably inevitable after an official inquiry into the East Timor violence implicated the former armed forces commander. But Gus Dur mainly wanted to get rid of him because the military strong man was a challenge to his own presidency which rested on a weak base.

But for several weeks, President Wahid, whose 20-month presidency was marked by a tendency to "shoot from the lip," sent contradictory signals about whether Wiranto should stay or go, apparently trying to get the general to stage his own retreat. Wahid finally just "suspended" Wiranto from the Cabinet. It was at the time seen as a courageous move against a military that had been taking the law unto itself, and a general who had harbored ambitions of following in Suharto's footsteps and ruling the world's fourth most-populous nation. Wiranto, his reputation in tatters at home and abroad over the atrocities his soldiers had committed in East Timor and during Indonesia's political upheaval, was out of the public eye for a long time afterward.

"Throughout this episode, Indonesia and the world have been presented with an example of Abdurrahman's peculiar style of getting things done," *The Jakarta Post* said in a February 15, 2000 editorial. The President had kept everyone guessing for a fortnight about what he would do. And when he did make the announcement, it was late on a Sunday night and missed the morning editions of newspapers. "A deliberate diversionary tactic? Hard to say," the *Post* said. "But anyone who has an interest in 'reading' Abdurrahman and his apparent inconsistencies had better beware that the Indonesian President has long had a reputation as a skillful politician. But what is more important is the job of removing Wiranto from the Cabinet has been achieved by a civilian, democratically elected President, with no shocks or upheavals."

This would prove to be the high point of the Wahid presidency. The NU leader who had long been at the forefront of preaching toleration and secular values in the highly diverse nation, won plaudits at the start of his presidency, after the sectarian slaughter in Spice Islands tailed off and a ceasefire with rebels in Aceh was secured.

But then came the embarrassments and opprobrium. The irrepressible Tommy Suharto was the first. He was sentenced to jail in October 2000 – winning accolades for the notoriously corrupt legal system – only to disappear, raining ridicule on the government. Wahid's new attorney general reopened the case against former president Suharto, then watched haplessly as a Jakarta district court ruled that the old dictator was too enfeebled and mentally incompetent to stand trial.

Initially enthusiastic international lending institutions – on which Indonesia was relying to survive – had become deeply skeptical over the government's erratic course. Finally in May 2000, seven months into his presidency, the "Buloggate" scandal surfaced – allegations that Wahid's people had misused around $6 million from the national food stocks agency, which had a long history as a personal piggy bank for politicians, and for the remainder of his presidency Wahid was mired in a tedious and unseemly battle to stay in power.

Indonesia was beginning to be a target of terrorism attacks as the new millennium dawned, and at first people thought it was yet another case of the military trying to sow fear and anxiety for political purposes. Thus, when a massive explosion in August 2000 hit the Philippine ambassador's car in leafy Menteng just as he was getting into it, blocks away from the U.S. ambassador's residence, suspicion first fell almost reflexively on the Indonesian military, which Indonesia's Human Rights Commission would conclude a year later was behind some of the atrocities perpetrated in the Christian-Muslim fighting in the Moluccas. In fact, an Indonesian court in 2003 convicted an Islamic militant with links to the shadowy Jemaah Islamiyah (JI) network and Muslim rebels fighting in the Philippines for the blast that killed two people and injured 21 others, including Ambassador Leonides Caday.

In September 2000, Wahid's government finally opened cases against the military, militias and civilians involved in the East Timor referendum violence a year earlier. Within days of the announcement, pro-Indonesia militiamen stormed the United Nations compound in Atambua, in Indonesia's West Timor province, and killed three foreign relief workers – an American, a Croatian and an Ethiopian. They dragged the corpses behind a vehicle before burning them in the street. The attack took place while Wahid was attending a special United Nations Millennium Summit in New York along with 154 other world leaders. Minister of Defense Mahfud M.D. only generated more outrage after blaming the United States itself for the attack, saying a U.S. embargo on military equipment for Indonesia had caused spare parts to dry up, thus preventing the speedy dispatch of men and equipment to Atambua. "This habit of blaming outsiders for everything that goes wrong in this country serves no real purpose other than soothing the bruised ego of the country's leaders who have failed in their jobs," a *Jakarta Post* editorial said. Criticism over Atambua could not be separated from the way Jakarta has handled the whole East Timor question, it said. "Clearly the world is not impressed by Indonesia's performance or lack of it."

Days after the Atambua killings, the Jakarta Stock Exchange was bombed, killing 15, injuring dozens, and striking terror into the heart of the business community. The bombing took place a day before Suharto was to go on trial for corruption. Attorney General Marzuki Darusman told reporters it looked like the work of Suharto supporters. The next day, Wahid came before reporters to announce he had ordered the arrest of Tommy Suharto and a member of the Islam Defenders Front (FPI), a vigilante group that emerged in the chaos of mid-1998 to enforce their interpretation of Islamic values. Tommy, however, saved them the trouble and showed up smiling for the television cameras at police headquarters the next day. The police chief warmly greeted Tommy and interviewed him briefly before sending him home – then was sacked by Wahid for failing to detain Suharto's youngest child, who was being investigated in connection with a land scam involving Bulog.

As for the father, two weeks after the stock exchange bombings a district court in Jakarta dismissed the corruption charges against him on the grounds he was too ill to stand trial. "If the chief goal of these legal exercises is to seek the truth and uphold justice, and not exact retribution, the South Jakarta District Court judges have now killed those hopes for good," the *Post* said in an editorial. "The nation will never learn the truth about many of the still unexplained events when they were ruled by Suharto." The ruling made it "difficult if not impossible for the government to prosecute other corruptors who benefited while he ruled the country," the editorial added.

In October, Wahid came back from a trip to Buenos Aires and, in one of the bizarre moves that were his trademark, met Tommy Suharto at the five-star Borobudur Hotel in Jakarta. A presidential spokesman later confirmed that Tommy had offered cash in exchange for a pardon, but the offer was rejected. Days later, Tommy was sentenced to 18 months in prison for the $11 million land scam deal with Bulog, becoming the first, and thus far the only, member of the Suharto family to be tried and found guilty of corruption. But when police came to Tommy's home in Menteng to arrest him, he was long gone, and would remain on the lam for more than a year. The new police chief, Gen. Suroyo Bimantoro, was pilloried in the press.

But Tommy's escape seemed to demonstrate that Wahid had little authority over the police or the military. Not long after this incident, the former commander of Suharto's presidential guard (Paspampres) was named the new army commander – against Wahid's express wishes.

If the center was looking pretty shaky, the provinces were becoming ever more lawless. Mining and plantation companies, especially those outside Java, had become victims of harassment at the local level since Suharto's fall. Local administrations, completely excluded from the decision-making process for 32 years, were now asserting their rights. Suharto's exit liberated a network of activists in the provinces that had been kept under the New Order thumb. Contracts concluded under the Suharto regime were now considered fair game, with Wahid unable to stabilize power at the center and the police and military too discredited and too distracted by political maneuverings to enforce the law. Companies such Kelian Equatorial in East Kalimantan, Freeport in Irian, Indorayon in North Sumatra and Caltex Oil in Riau had been subjected to arbitrary claims and harassment. The resentment was understandable, *The Jakarta Post* said in an editorial on May 10, 2000. Many businesses in the provinces had simply ignored local administrations, because their only requirement was to keep the central government in Jakarta happy. "Local people sometimes received almost nothing for their land that was appropriated for investors; the real payments having been given to official or political leaders in Jakarta." The *Post* called on companies to exercise "social responsibility" and hire local contractors, labor and suppliers. Foreign investors would learn that the hard way in years to come. In August of 2001, U.S.-owned Caltex Oil in Riau offered a package that included job offers for local residents and community development funds – to avoid a planned blockade by protesters who had demanded a 70 percent stake in the operations.

On December 24, 2000 a series of church bombings across Indonesia, including at Jakarta's Catholic Cathedral, raised fresh questions about who was perpetrating terrorist attacks in Indonesia and why. Police investigators said at least one of the suspects in the bombings that killed 16 people had been trained in Afghanistan. *The Jakarta Post*, reflecting a widespread assumption, jumped on that and pointed the finger in an editorial at Laskar Jihad, a group established earlier that year to send young volunteers to fight the Christians in the Spice Islands.

The lads at Laskar were vastly unamused by the insinuations in *The Jakarta Post* over their involvement in the church bombings. One day in January 2001, they arrived by buses at *The Jakarta Post* office in the *Kompas Gramedia* compound and invited themselves in. "They met some of our editors," Endy recalled. "They wanted an apology and a retraction of the editorial. Our argument was if you're not happy with our opinion, please write your own opinion and we'll publish that."

The next day the *Post* published Laskar Jihad's vehement denial of having anything to do with the Christmas Eve bombings. But Laskar was still not happy and came back a week later in the buses and met the editors again. They again demanded a retraction and public apology. "We said we can't retract an opinion. They said if not, then we'll move to 'plan B'. And we said, what's plan B? And they said we'll bomb your office. We took that seriously," Endy said.

So the *Post* printed a retraction of the editorial and apologized for offending anybody, including the United States, after its embassy called to complain about a line in the original editorial that said the CIA had trained the *mujahideen* in Afghanistan.[5] "But looking back, they had a right to be angry, because JI (Jemaah Islamiyah) was later found to be behind the Christmas Eve bombings," Endy said.

As the millennium drew to a close, Indonesia had reached a state of political stalemate amounting almost to non-governance. Wahid could not count on the police or the military. And it seemed like every time he tried to make a case against Suharto or his family members, something got bombed. Indonesia's three-year political conflict

---

5 The CIA, mainly working through Pakistan's military intelligence agency ISI, did in fact provide arms and training to the mujahideen under a 1985 National Security Directive authorizing covert aid to the guerrillas fighting the Soviet occupation of Afghanistan.

beginning with the decline and fall of Suharto had destabilized the center and unleashed a virtual free-for-all in the provinces, where Jakarta's writ not longer ran. Now the specter of an Islamic jihad had cast a further pall over the start to the millennium.

RESOLVING CHAOS: NEW BEGINNINGS

Rita Widiadana made it to Sanglah hospital in Denpasar, Bali just before midnight that Saturday night of October 12, 2002. The poorly equipped, under-staffed medical facility was already overflowing with wounded. Minutes earlier, she had heard the sound of the explosion followed by two other blasts at her home in Denpasar and knew something bad must have happened. Indeed, it had. A suicide bomber had walked into Paddy's Bar in Kuta Beach, 10 km from Rita's home in Denpasar, and set off a bomb in the middle of a crowd of customers. A second bomber waited for people to flee into the street before detonating a Mitsubishi van packed with more than a ton of explosives outside the Sari Club. The 202 dead included 88 Australians and 28 Britons. Hundreds were wounded and many had lost limbs. Only a few nurses and doctors were on duty that night, and their English was generally not good. "So everybody lent their hands to help families of victims and the victims communicate (with Indonesian staff)," Rita recalled. "All the journalists did everything they could to help mothers who had lost their children, lovers who lost their partners, friends."

Rita, who had moved to Bali two years earlier from Jakarta with her architect husband and their three teen-aged sons, had called the Jakarta newsroom shortly after the explosions with the initial police report that the blasts had killed at least a handful of people. The night editor had already put *The Sunday Post* edition to bed. He thought about stopping the press and ordering a redo of the front page to carry the breaking news item, but decided against it. Explosions had become all too routine in Indonesia in the post-Suharto political wars. It was Saturday night after a long week and he wanted to go home. So *The Sunday Post* came out the next day with nothing on the number one news story around the globe: the Bali nightclub bombings that would launch Indonesia onto the front lines of the U.S.-led global "war on terror". But *The Jakarta Post* did have a website, and that carried the story. Former managing editor Lela Madjiah had rushed to the office and spent the rest of the night and early morning in the newsroom feverishly updating thejakartapost.com.

Rita's *Jakarta Post* colleague Wayan Juniartha had gone to the scene of the bombings on Jalan Legian. Since he had a car, he began ferrying the wounded to Sanglah hospital, while trying to piece together the story. "We went online minute by minute with updates," Rita said, adding that *The Jakarta Post* was the first to have a report out on the Internet. "We received hundreds of calls that night from media and journalists around the world. Our small office became the media center for international media on the first night and day of the Bali bombing."

Rita and *Kompas* reporter Brigita Isworo Laksmi went down to Jalan Legian around 2 a.m. "Parts of bodies were scattered all over the narrow street. A number of wounded tourists were still there waiting for ambulances. Many foreign women and children looked scared. We transported some of the wounded victims to nearby clinics and hotels. We also drove some families with their small children to the airport. We just kept going back to the streets to find people who needed help and transportation to hotels or airports. Brigita and I were so angry knowing that many taxi drivers charged the victims high fees to the airport. We really had fierce arguments with those naughty taxi drivers." She kept phoning in the quotes and color to the Jakarta newsroom. "But, for sure, my mind and body focused only on how to help those victims, especially the elderly, women and children who were stranded in the middle of the chaotic Kuta, far away from their homes."

Jakarta Post Deputy Chief Editor Endy Bayuni was with other top Indonesian editors on a trip to Australia, where the Bali bombings were a huge story, and he was quickly besieged with interviews from the Australian media. He says his two Bali reporters were in a dilemma that journalists at the point of conflict and disaster often find themselves in: help victims or report the story. "As a human being and as a reporter, what's your call? Our journalists decided to do both. Though we were disappointed with missing the Sunday edition, we were very proud of our two journalists who filed throughout the night while helping victims." When it became clear by the following day that the bombing had been the work of Jemaah Islamiyah, Hindu Bali braced for a backlash against minority Muslims on the island. It never came "thanks to the active interfaith dialogue among members of the Balinese society," Rita says.

Jemaah Islamiyah had its antecedents in the old Darul Islam movement dating back to the 1950s, whose objective was to create an Islamic state in Indonesia. Its spiritual leaders, Abdullah Sungkar and Abu Bakar Bashir, had fled to Malaysia to avoid subversion charges during Suharto's crackdown on the Islamic right in the mid-1980s. In Malaysia they recruited Indonesians to fight with the mujahideen in Afghanistan, not so much to battle godless Soviet communists as to pick up guerrilla skills and bomb-making techniques. While Jemaah Islamiyah was often described in the aftermath of the Bali Bombings as al Qaeda's franchise in Southeast Asia whose goal was to set up an Islamic caliphate across swathes of the region, the group has since become more local than regional in focus, experts now believe.

The 2002 Bali nightclub bombings, and the bombing of the JW Marriott Hotel in Jakarta that killed 12 people in August of 2003, were "classic al-Qaeda type" operations, says Sidney Jones, who was then project director at the International Crisis Group in Jakarta and a leading expert on Islamist militancy in Indonesia. Those bombings were "part of the Bin Laden view of the Christian-Zionist conspiracy, part of his call to attack American interests all over the world."[1] Jemaah Islamiyah, which in 2001 had a broad network operating in Malaysia, Singapore, Indonesia, the Philippines, Pakistan and Afghanistan, has largely gone to ground after concerted and coordinated police crackdown on the group, including from the

---

1   "Sidney Jones on Jemaah Islamiyah", *Indonesia Matters*, January 5, 2006

U.S.-funded "Detachment 88" force in Indonesia.

In a country prone to conspiracy theories, some officials initially tried to deny a Muslim connection to the bombings. "At the time, there was a lot of denial that Muslims could have done something like this," Endy says. "You had statements that it was the CIA, the Israeli intelligence service Mossad, East Timorese – anybody but Muslims." Former president Abdurrahman Wahid even told Australian television that circumstantial evidence pointed to Indonesian police as the agent behind one of the Bali nightclub bombs.[2]

Wahid's strange presidency had stumbled to a humiliating denouement by the middle of 2001. The weakness at the center was contributing to conflict and chaos in the outer islands, particularly in Ambon, the capital of the Moluccas, and Poso in Central Sulawesi. Evidence that the military was arming and funding both sides of those sectarian conflicts was more compelling than Wahid's assertions about the Bali bombings.

The year had gotten off to another horrific start in Indonesia. Renewed fighting in Borneo between indigenous Dayaks and settlers from Madura had killed more than 300 people – again with widespread reports that heads had been taken from Madurese victims. A *Time* magazine cover that March showed nude, headless bodies and a caption that read: "Bloody Borneo: a massacre and cannibalism strike at the heart of Indonesia". Separatist conflicts had intensified in Aceh and Irian, which the military was determined should not go the way of East Timor.

For months, Wahid had been battling opposition in parliament, which in April threatened to impeach him unless he improved his performance in office. Parliament was also investigating him over "Buloggate" and "Bruneigate" – allegations he had taken a $2 million gift from the Sultan of Brunei on behalf of Aceh. He was taking heat as well over the government's inept handling of an economy still prostrate from the Asian financial crisis. Wahid's response was to first threaten to dissolve the opposition Golkar party, then to dissolve parliament itself and rule by decree until new elections. Wahid's NU

2 "Inside Indonesia's War on Terror", SBS Television Australia, October 12, 2005

vowed to send hundreds of thousands of its members to Jakarta for a "jihad" in support of his embattled presidency.

The president had even asked the military leadership, with whom he had been feuding, to support a state of emergency decree. He thought that would help matters, seeing as how it would have allowed him to dissolve the parliament that was howling for his head. Their refusal to do so only served to expose his political maladroitness and damage his reformist credentials. On July 23, it finally came to a sorry end when the MPR voted 591-0 to remove Wahid from office and Megawati Sukarnoputri was inaugurated as Indonesia's fifth president. Six weeks later, the September 11 attacks on the United States would spread shockwaves around the world. Indonesia would soon enough be seen as a "second front" in a U.S.-led war on terrorism.

It was clear after 9/11 that the United States would attack Afghanistan, and that in turn would provoke a reaction in Indonesia, the world's most populous Muslim country and one which had already seen a radicalization of Islamic movements since the fall of Suharto. Within days of the suicide airline attacks, Islamic radicals were conducting "sweeps" for foreigners, particularly U.S. citizens, in Central Java towns. Demonstrators outside the U.S. embassy in Jakarta called for the U.S. ambassador to be killed. Megawati's vice president, PPP leader Hamzah Haz, echoing a sentiment heard in other corners of the world, said America should examine its conscience after 9/11. "Hopefully, this tragedy will cleanse the U.S. of its sins," Hamzah declared.

Megawati's task was to defuse the dangerous anti-American sentiment, which she saw as being manipulated for political ends, while distancing Indonesia from the impending attacks against Afghanistan, and later on, the war in Iraq. *The Jakarta Post* thought she showed skill in doing just that. Her government barred the "sweeps" against foreigners, invoked a law banning the burning of foreign flags and effigies of foreign leaders, and took some steps to assure the safety of foreigners. While Indonesia condemned the 9/11 attacks and supported the campaign against international terrorism, Jakarta insisted that any action must be taken collectively and led by the United Nations. "This message is important for both the international and domestic audience," an Oct. 8 editorial said.

While the United States and the rest of the world were waking up to the threat of random terrorism, Indonesia had been dealing with it for years. Days after Megawati took office, Syafiuddin Kartasasmita, a Supreme Court judge who had impressed the Indonesian public by sentencing the smirking Tommy Suharto to 18 months in jail earlier that year for the land scam with Bulog, was shot dead by assassins on a motorcycle as he was driving in Jakarta. Two months after that, a panel of Supreme Court justices obligingly overturned Tommy's jail sentence, even though he was still a fugitive. The Indonesian judiciary had sunk further into disrepute.

But in the anti-terrorism climate that had begun to take hold after the 9/11 attacks, Indonesia's police made a fresh effort to capture Tommy and found him at the end of November 2001 in Tangerang, outside Jakarta. The Government said he would be charged in connection with the assassination of Judge Kartasasmita and a bombing at the Taman Mini Indonesia Indah theme park built by his mother, as well as possession of weapons and explosives found in his home and fleeing arrest. He would be only the third Suharto-era figure to face jail time. Bob Hasan was sentenced to six years in jail earlier that year for misusing reforestation funds, and a former Bulog head was given two years for colluding with Tommy in the land scam case. In July 2002, Tommy was sentenced to 15 years in jail for paying a hit man to murder Judge Kartasasmita. The sentence was reduced to 10 years on appeal and Tommy was paroled in October 2006, at the age of 44, after serving just four years in jail.

The chronic political wars at the center following Suharto's fall, and manoeuvring among factions of the police and military, had spawned many a conspiracy theory about who and what was behind the mysterious bombings and sectarian conflicts bedevilling Indonesia. Now attention was beginning to turn to radical Islam as a possible cause for some of the violence.

In February 2002, Singapore's Senior Minister Lee Kuan Yew criticized Jakarta, saying Jemaah Islamiyah and al Qaeda were operating freely in Indonesia. Singapore and Malaysia had rounded up a number of JI militants in the days after 9/11 over an alleged plot to bomb Changi Airport, the Singapore American School and The American Club on the island state. In March, Philippines police arrested three Indonesian citizens in Manila for possession of explosives and suspicion of planning terrorist activities. In March of 2002, Indonesian police revealed that five suspected JI members – including Indonesian born Mas Selamat Kastari – had arrived in Medan with Singaporean passports.[3]

Five months before the Bali nightclub bombings, Vice President Hamzah Haz had visited Abu Bakar Bashir at the latter's *pesantren* in Solo, in a show of support for the Jemaah Islamiyah spiritual leader. The two concluded that no international terrorist group was operating within Indonesia, he said. This perceived climate of complacency in Indonesia changed drastically after the Bali bombings. Indonesian police were now actively cooperating with U.S. authorities in tracking down al Qaeda and JI operatives in Indonesia. In June, police arrested Omar al-Faruq, a Kuwaiti citizen and high-ranking al Qaeda member, and handed him over to U.S. authorities who transferred him to Bagram air base in Afghanistan for questioning.

On October 10, two days before the Bali bombings, JI members held a news conference in Solo, saying if Abu Bakar Bashir was arrested, they would wage *jihad*. Bashir was arrested less than a week after the nightclub bombings in connection with the Christmas Eve 2000 church bombings and a plot to assassinate President Megawati. The next day, Megawati signed two new anti-terrorism decrees, giving police the ability to detain terrorism suspects for six months without trial and authorizing the death penalty for terrorist acts. Both the main Muslim organizations, the Nahdlatul Ulama and Muhammadiyah, expressed support for the measures.

Within weeks, police had arrested Imam Samudra, now 38, the chief planner of the nightclub bombings, and two others: Ali Ghufron alias Mukhlas, the financier, and Amrozi bin Nurhasyim, "the smiling bomber", a mechanic who bought the explosives and whose

---

3 Kastari was arrested by Indonesian police later that year and handed over to Singapore. He escaped detention in Singapore in early 2008.

van was used for one of the car bombs. The actual bomb-maker is believed to be Dulmatin, an alleged JI operative who may have been killed in a gun battle with Philippine forces on January 31, 2008. The three remained on death row in Bali, their execution imminent in 2008. Even in jail, they were thought to be dangerous. Police said that Samudra used a smuggled laptop computer to communicate with militants to organize another bombing in Bali's Kuta Beach in September 2005 that killed 20 people.

Megawati's Security Minister Susilo Bambang Yudhoyono, who had returned to the cabinet after his falling out with Wahid, was increasingly taking center stage to articulate government policy, given Megawati's famed reticence in public. In October 2003, it was Yudhoyono, not Megawati, who went to Bali for the first anniversary of the nightclub bombings. Coming after the August car-bombing of the JW Marriott hotel in Jakarta, Yudhoyono delivered a strong speech against terrorism, notable for using the kind of tough language well-accepted in the Western world, but not often heard in Indonesia.

Yudhoyono had trained at the U.S. Army's Fort Benning base and earned a Master's degree in the United States. He had fought in East Timor, served as head of a peacekeeping mission in Bosnia, and held top army staff positions and cabinet posts. He was now widely viewed as a candidate for the 2004 presidential election. A tall Javanese, with an intellectual bent and an aristocratic bearing, he certainly looked the part.

The Post-Suharto period was a huge let-down for *reformasi* advocates. First Habibie and then Gus Dur had been so consumed with their own political survival, and trying to put out the brushfires of conflict that kept erupting around the archipelago they paid little attention to political or economic reform. The economy was stagnant and the country was being run by many of the same old faces left over from the New Order. At the same time, however, the clamps had come off the press, which was free to report how and what it liked. Two generations of journalists had spent their careers probing the limits of press freedom and now it was like roaming a strange town after getting out of prison – the landscape was bewildering and daunting.

Ten years after Suharto ordered the closing of *Tempo,* the weekly magazine faced an altogether different kind of danger, one that threatened to put the magazine out of business and its editor behind bars. Tomy Winata, a construction tycoon with close ties to the military, brought a criminal defamation case against Bambang Harymurti, who had succeeded Goenawan Mohamad as chief editor of the influential magazine. *Tempo* reported in its March 3, 2003 edition that Winata had been awarded a contract to renovate the Tanah Abang market in central Jakarta before it burned down in a fire, a fortuitous accident that Winata had stood to benefit from. Winata, however, angrily denied to *Tempo* he had ever made a proposal to renovate the market.

Days after the magazine report appeared, some 200 demonstrators, many of them employees of Winata's company, showed up at Tempo's office and tried to force their way in through a cordon of anti-riot police. Several were eventually allowed in to meet Tempo editors and reporters with whom they loudly remonstrated. Eventually the argument was brought down to a local police station, where some of the protesters took the opportunity to beat Bambang soundly. The police failure to stop the violence spooked the journalistic community, which now feared that the mob had replaced official goons as the agent of oppression against the press in Indonesia.

The case brought *Tempo's* senior editor and *Jakarta Post* Director Fikri Jufri out of his semi-retirement. "They can destroy our assets, but not our idealism," he declared at a street rally. "There is only one word for such action, 'fight'". Though *Tempo* ran a correction in its next edition, Winata was far from placated. The case went to trial in September 2004. Bambang not only faced jail time: Winata was asking the court for enough in financial damages to bankrupt *Tempo* and its daily newspaper, *Tempo Koran.* At his trial in September 2004, Bambang argued that applying libel laws with criminal penalties dating from the Dutch colonial period amounted to a muzzling of the press. But it was all to no avail. A Jakarta district court acquitted the two *Tempo* journalists who had worked on the story, and placed sole responsibility on the chief editor, sentencing Bambang to a year in jail. Vindication came on Feb. 9, 2006, when the Supreme Court overturned the verdict and ruled that Bambang should have been tried under laws governing the press, not the criminal code. "We want to ensure that journalists are protected," the Supreme Court spokesman said.

It was one of several such "test cases" that the international community was using as yardsticks for legal certainty and the rule of law in Indonesia. Yet the case also pointed to a need for self-discipline and a professional code of ethics in the press, which itself was hardly immune from the corruption disease that afflicted so many other Indonesian institutions. Winata may have had a point when he argued that the *Tempo* article could have mobilized victims of the Tanah Abang fire to take revenge against him.[4] The sudden and rather unbridled freedom after decades of official browbeating and self-censorship had spawned charges that the Indonesian media had become reckless. To which editors not unreasonably responded by saying: Sue us, but don't jail us.

Post Senior Editor Harry Bhaskara says, however, that self-censorship was still the larger problem. "Censorship on the press still exists, post-1998. But it has moved from the government to the community. Anyone or any organization for that matter can lodge a protest against the press. Sometimes the protest can be violent, as was the ransacking of the *Jawa Pos* office in Surabaya several years ago by an Islamic group offended by a report in the newspaper. It is censorship in the form of communal pressure. Sometimes it is more formidable than the official government censorship under Suharto."

Endy Bayuni says threats and intimidation have become an all too frequent part of the job. "What has changed now is that the enemies of press freedom are no longer coming from the government, but are coming from individual politicians, individual businessmen or powerful political groups who are not happy about the way they are being portrayed in the media." And legal protection is weak. "When we're subjected to harassment or intimidation and we turn to police, the police do nothing about it."

Readers of *The Jakarta Post* had disappeared like tears in the rain

---

4 "*Tempo* fights for its life – again", Bill Guerin, Pacific Media Watch, March 14, 2003

during the financial and political crises that beset Indonesia in 1998. Circulation had fallen precipitously to 28,000 in 1999 from a peak of 51,000 in 1997. Staff morale had fallen steeply as well. The business was in trouble and Raymond decided to shake things up. He commissioned a management consulting firm run by an old colleague to do a bottom-up study of the *Post* in 2001. If he was hoping for some "shock therapy" to give the *Post* a new lease on life, he probably got more than he bargained for.

It's hard to imagine a report that could possibly be more critical of Raymond and Susanto and their management practices. This wasn't a report that the board had commissioned – Raymond was the client. And if he was expecting their barbed recommendations to give him ammunition to shake up the staff, he certainly wasn't prepared to have them flying at him like a barrage of arrows.

"Rampant office politics" had created problems between department heads, particularly between the heads of circulation and advertising, the report said. Raymond had created his "golden boys" and then applied "the concept of conflict management," giving authority to subordinates to create mini-kingdoms and then having them fight it out in debilitating turf battles, with Raymond watching from above the fray. The report referred to "office espionage" and "weekly intelligence reports." In fact, the management model described in the report was an eerily familiar one, since it could well have described Suharto's New Order in some respects.

"I suspect Raymond was aware about this similarity and we had a dark suspicion that he had deliberately copied it from the dictator," Harry says. "After all, this is an easier way to lead an organization because the 'people' are weak because of constant internal strife created by his cohorts."

The business was being run abysmally without any known management principles being applied, the report continued. "There is not prudent financial management, no financial planning and no business strategy." Cash management was "chaotic" – office supplies could be purchased by just about anyone.

"The problem of leadership at the *Post* was that management principles were not applied, but rather it was all about personal relationships. And if there were criticisms of management practices, it was always taken as personal criticism," the report said.

The report was equally merciless when it came to Susanto, pouring scorn over his idea of delegation through absenteeism. "The situation in editorial has worsened over the last several years... The high absenteeism of the chief editor without delegating full responsibilities to the managing editors on a daily basis has created internal problems. For the last six years, the chief editor has not written any articles. The absenteeism and the delegation without full responsibilities to the managing editors has created an even bigger gap between the chief editor and the rest of the newsroom," the report said, and bluntly recommended he be replaced.

"Maintaining the current chief editor in that position is impossible. The primary reason is the boredom factor after holding that job for the past 10 years." Low morale, high turnover, and giving the managing editors a chance to move up were other reasons to replace Susanto, the report said.

All in all, the report concluded somewhat pessimistically, "*The Jakarta Post* has a destructive culture that endangers all the capital and resources of the institution." The only saving grace was that the two competing English language newspapers in Jakarta had folded by 1999 and *The Jakarta Post* had a window of opportunity to overhaul itself before someone inevitably challenged its monopoly in that market.

Susanto felt he was misunderstood, though he did agree that 10 years was too long a tenure to stay engaged as a chief editor in Indonesia, given the constant flow of urgent news developments. He said he continued to write editorials from home, which he sent by email to the office, and thought too much of the report was based on staff evaluations of management. "They asked the staff to evaluate management, which was unheard of. Many on *The Jakarta Post* staff did not understand how a newspaper is run. They could not understand me and Raymond, how we individually involved ourselves in the struggle against the Suharto regime. They wanted to play it safe. We stressed to them this is a newspaper. It's different from a common factory. Our product is information and it's our responsibility to improve the community, build democracy. And some of our staff could not understand that."

Raymond tried to make lemonade with this lemon of a report, which also contained frank individual evaluations of most of the desk editors and senior reporters. He held meetings to disclose unflattering descriptions of staff, and it went over like a lead balloon in the newsroom. People felt humiliated by the public criticism and morale fell even further. "That (consultant) guy told us we were all shit," Harry Bhaskara said. "That was the word he used. And when we sought an explanation, Raymond explained that it was 'shock therapy.' I've never seen this in a management manual before."

Jusuf Wanandi was dismayed by the report, but not all that surprised, since he had been having qualms about management practices at the newspaper for several years. The report Raymond had commissioned himself ironically sealed his fate. Susanto was given the title "senior editor" and Raymond was reassigned as chief editor in 2002. Jusuf replaced Raymond as publisher, determined to right what was now evidently a sinking ship. "There were no rules on anything. So when we took over, it was really a mess. Mess, mess, mess!" Jusuf said, shaking his head.

Susanto roused himself from his sick bed and began travelling regularly with President Megawati after his demotion. The two had remained friends over the years, and she seemed to like to hear his take on things. Susanto wanted an ambassadorship, preferably to Australia, but some in parliament thought he was too soft-spoken to handle the hard-bitten Australian media. He was given the Moscow posting instead in 2003 and ended up missing the Presidential elections the next year. Megawati could have perhaps used his advice, because she was not playing a very smart game with her popular politics and security minister, Susilo Bambang Yudhoyono, who in the fashion of U.S. presidents of old, liked to go by his initials: SBY.

Megawati's presidency was a disappointment to those who hoped she would get the *reformasi* wagon rolling again. But she seemed incapable of articulating a social vision or pulling the economy out of the doldrums. Like her father Sukarno, however, she put a priority on national unity and endorsed the military's bid to crush separatist movements in Aceh and Papua. She also seemed reluctant to risk upsetting the Islamic right by cracking down on Jemaah Islamiyah, whose name means "Islamic Community". Banning the "Islamic Community" in Muslim Indonesia was risky politics.

Yudhoyono, meanwhile, was happily taking political center stage, a spot Megawati seemed reluctant to occupy. In May of 2003, he announced the imposition of martial law on Aceh, enabling a massive military operation to crush the Free Aceh Movement, after the collapse of peace talks in Tokyo. By March of 2004, his popularity beginning to soar, SBY launched an advertisement promoting peaceful elections. An annoyed Megawati, thinking he was jumping the gun on campaigning, began excluding him from Cabinet meetings. When her husband insulted him in public, SBY thought it best to resign. Indonesian voters sided with Yudhoyono in April's general elections. His new Democrat Party won more votes than even it could have imagined, while Megawati's Indonesian Democratic Party-Struggle came in second overall to a resurgent Golkar. After July's first stage of the presidential elections eliminated Wiranto, who was running on Golkar's ticket, Megawati and SBY faced off in a run-off in September. He won in a landslide.

Yudhoyono tried to set a "can-do" tone to his presidency in the beginning, giving Vice President Jusuf Kalla, a former business executive who had achieved some success as a mediator in conflict-ridden areas, extensive responsibilities. He also set out an ambitious agenda for investigating corruption, attracting foreign investment, and dealing with terrorism. But his cautious and sometimes indecisive approach disillusioned some of his early supporters, though his admirers defend him, saying he has taken a judicious and sensible approach to reform a fractious Indonesia. He hardly had a chance to get started on the plan for his first 100 days in office when the first of a series of disasters struck Indonesia on his watch.

On a bright Sunday morning on Dec. 26, 2004, a 9.15 magnitude earthquake spawned a record tsunami that swamped a dozen countries along the Indian Ocean, killing 230,000 people, including around 170,000 in Indonesia alone (See box story). Yudhoyono had

"The water is coming"

Sartinah Fatar was eating breakfast with her family in Kampong Java, a fishing village in Aceh, when the earthquake rattled the dishes off the table. They all ran outside, joining others racing in from the beach who were shouting strangely: "The water is coming". Bewildered by those cries, she ran with her husband to the elementary school next door, her 8-year-old daughter close on her heels and her 18-year old son helping his frail grandmother.

Sartinah was scrambling onto the roof of the school when the tsunami wave, taller than the palm trees in the yard and traveling at the speed of a train, slammed into her. She never saw her daughter, son and mother again. It was an all-too-sad and familiar story that bright, Sunday morning on Dec. 26, 2004, the day a 9.15 earthquake – the second-strongest on record – unleashed an unprecedented tsunami that swamped the Indian Ocean rim. More than 230,000 people were killed, including 170,000 in Aceh alone, and 2.3 million destitute survivors in 12 countries were now in desperate need of help.

"I was hanging onto the roof and thinking I never had a chance to ask for my mother's forgiveness," Sartinah said, tears flowing down her cheeks. "As a Muslim you have to ask forgiveness. If your mother doesn't forgive you, you can't go to heaven." She was speaking to me a year after the giant waves ripped apart families and left survivors scarred by guilt at having survived, at not being able to help more.

Within minutes, the wall of water had swept clean a strip of coastline 800 km long, or about the distance between San Diego and San Francisco. The waves swept people up and churned them along with debris as if they were in a washing machine. The relentless surge flattened buildings, ripped up trees and tossed cars and boats around like bath toys. In the town of Lampuuk, the tsunami traveled some 7 km (4 miles) inland until it smacked into steep hillsides that still show wave marks 10 meters high. The only building left standing in a vast sea of rubble in the town was a mosque.

The catastrophe took an appalling toll on children, many of whom were home that Sunday morning with their mothers. Scores of women who lost all their children to the waves clung to hope and underwent sterilization reversals. Others plunged into suicidal despair. Viyarseeli Nadarajalingam tried to kill herself after her six children drowned in front of her eyes in Vatharayan, Sri Lanka.[†]

Local journalists were among the first to arrive and the scenes of devastation were unlike anything anybody had ever seen, in real life or on the screen. Broken bodies were everywhere. The stench of death was omnipresent and overpowering. Survivors wandered like zombies among the wreckage in a daze, posting messages and photographs of family members on notice boards. In the days and weeks ahead, they would pour out their stories of confusion and despair, and also courage and selflessness.

"We were so shocked by the devastation and the bodies still not collected," says *Jakarta Post* managing editor Riyadi Suparno, who arrived several days after the tsunami. "It's affecting you emotionally." He went looking for an old friend from university days who had been living in Banda Aceh. He found the broken house, his friend's bedroom with familiar clothes and books. Nearly four years later his friend is still missing and presumed dead.

With all telecommunications down, and planes unable to land at Banda Aceh airport for the first 24 hours, Aceh was virtually cut off from the rest of the world, posing huge obstacles to reporters trying to get to the news story and then get the news out. And like everybody else, they had to scavenge for food and lodging those first couple of days.

The Jakarta Post newsroom first began to realize the scale of the disaster in Aceh after getting reports on Sunday afternoon that refugees from the northern part of Aceh were pouring into Lhokseumawe, an industrial town further to the south, Chief Editor Endy Bayuni says. "At the time, the whole world was still focusing on the devastation of the tsunami in southern Thailand, India and Sri Lanka. There were also some brief communications from the military, probably about the only institution that still had means of communications with the outside world."

Photographer P.J. Leo joined the Hercules transport plane that was taking Vice President Jusuf Kalla's delegation to the disaster, the first outsiders to reach Banda Aceh, some 24 hours after the tsunami. Senior reporter Ridwan M. Sijabat tried to get to the provincial capital by commercial flight. Like hordes of other reporters, he was stuck in Medan for two days waiting for a seat, but filing stories he was getting from the refugees streaming into that city, Endy says. Sijabat finally got on a flight taking reporters to Meulaboh, the town closest to the quake's epicenter and cut off for days. A third of its 120,000 people were killed in the waves, and the survivors mobbed the helicopters bringing in food and medicines.

As the unprecedented scale of the disaster became evident, the *Post* expanded its coverage team in Aceh. Riyadi was in charge of coordinating logistics for the team. Endy himself went up to lead the editing team. Veteran reporters of the Aceh conflict, Tiarma "Ade" Siboro and Tertiani "Baby" Simanjuntak, roamed the improvised refugee camps for survivor tales. Eventually, the *Post* had more than 10 people on the team.

For many journalists, it was the biggest story of their careers. The tsunami smashed up entire communities and slaughtered its inhabitants. The monster waves left thousands of orphans, "bachelor towns" where most of the women died, mothers who lost all their children, and the compounded grief from multiple deaths in families in its awful wake. Fishermen sat listlessly on the beach, their boats lost or destroyed, and began to fear the sea. The agent of horrific destruction had once been their livelihood. How to trust it again?

For 30 years, Aceh had been virtually off-limits to reporters, as the military prosecuted a dirty war against GAM insurgents that saw human rights atrocities on both sides. "One of the things that struck us in reporting the tragedy was the freedom we enjoyed in traveling inside Aceh, assuming that you could overcome the transportation problems," Endy said. "One third of the Aceh provincial administration officials perished in the tsunami, so there was no government to speak of in the first days of the tragedy. The Indonesian military was busy with moving the relief operation. There was a nightly press conference at the media center, but they were not all that useful. Without government restrictions and without government officials giving us directions, we were left to decide for ourselves to look for the stories to tell the rest of the world. This unrestricted access helped *The Jakarta Post,* as well as all other media who covered Aceh, to come up with some of the best reports ever seen in the coverage of natural disasters. The Indonesian government also decided to make it easier for foreign journalists and relief workers to enter the country," Endy says

"It's true that journalism works best when we don't see restrictions imposed on us. Stories from Aceh moved so many people around the world that they responded by showing their generosity. The international solidarity shown, unprecedented in scale, is in large part due the great work journalists put in in Aceh," Endy says.

The stunning television pictures of a phenomenon few people had ever seen, the fact it happened just after Christmas and that thousands of foreign tourists were among the victims, prompted an unprecedented outpouring of charity across the world. Charities, individuals and governments pledged more than $12 billion in cash or kind, and most of it was disbursed. That would be the equivalent of about $8,000 each for the estimated 1.5 million survivors around the Indian Ocean rim who needed help – an astounding number, aid experts say.

It was not all good, however. A lot of money was spent unwisely. Many of the well-meaning charities and individuals who converged on the disaster zone, networking through the Internet, and not unattracted to the possibility of doing good in exotic, albeit shattered, beach resorts, were not competent. Rivalries between aid agencies, delivery of inappropriate aid, and the sheer scale of the disaster sometimes overwhelmed the relief effort, a World Disasters report concluded in 2005. More than 300 NGOs, from established groups such as Oxfam, Save the Children and the Red Cross to a rainbow of spontaneous aid groups were on the ground in some areas. Many could hire their own helicopters and boats to do need assessments and were not inclined to share information. On the other hand, the overabundance of aid insured that basic needs of food, medicines and shelter were covered with the first month for even those in the most remote areas.

The disaster of biblical proportions drew a veritable Noah's Ark of faith-based groups, and good Samaritans to help the displaced in Indonesia, Thailand, India, Sri Lanka and other places around the

Indian Ocean to rebuild. Buddhists from Taiwan ran a camp for tsunami survivors in Islamic Aceh. Islamic charities such as London-based Muslim Aid were especially active in Aceh. Faith-based charities were among the first to come and last to leave; feeding the hungry, clothing the naked, sheltering the homeless, healing the sick and burying the dead. Some tsunami survivors wondered if God was angry: Why did the horrific quake and monster waves strike their communities and not others? Why take the children? Some Islamic preachers in Aceh blamed the catastrophe on morals becoming too lax.

The mantra of the rebuilding effort was to "build back better", and indeed life has largely returned to normal after the tsunami. The tattered tent communities and army barracks that once housed hundreds of thousands have closed down and almost all of the nearly half-million displaced in Aceh have moved into new houses of varying standards and sizes. Children are back in school. Jobs seem to be plentiful. Even the peace agreement between the military and the rebel Free Aceh Movement has been a success – former rebel spokesman Irwandi Yusuf is now governor of the province.

The Indonesian rehabilitation and reconstruction agency said that by April 30, 2008 a total of 108,756 permanent houses had been built for the victims to replace the 116,880 that had been destroyed, and just over 1,600 remained to be built. Some of the housing that aid groups built was not quite up to standard and did not contain the required public facilities, but still the Aceh reconstruction effort compares very favorably with those following other major disasters, the agency said. Nearly 1,000 schools and 781 clinics had been built as well, and more than 2,500 km of road, 255 bridges, 11 airports and 17 seaports had been constructed. To a large extent, local communities and governments themselves drove the rebuilding process. Sustainable livelihoods were reintroduced. And part of that rebuilding process now includes tsunami early warning systems and drills, so that one of the worst disasters in modern history will not wreak such havoc again.

† "Sri Lanka mother mourns six children lost to tsunami", Reuters, March 24, 2005

been president for less than 60 days. Another earthquake killed nearly 1,000 people three months later in Sumatra. Yet another strong quake in May 2006 devastated a wide area around the ancient city of Yogyakarta, killing more than 5,700 and destroying or damaging some 150,000 homes. And in July of 2006, an undersea earthquake triggered a tsunami that pulverized Pangandaran, a small resort and fishing village near Yogyakarta. A series of plane accidents, including one at Yogyakarta airport that killed 22 in March of 2007, raised questions about Indonesia's safety standards and prompted the European Union to ban all Indonesian airlines from its airspace.

The 2004 tsunami did have a silver lining, providing a window of opportunity to settle one of the world's longest-running separatist conflicts. The Free Aceh movement declared a unilateral ceasefire to allow the massive reconstruction job to proceed. The government and rebels quickly agreed to work for a lasting peace deal. By September 2005, the rebels had begun handing in weapons to foreign peace monitors, while Indonesia police and military began withdrawing forces. The process ended with the surprising victory in November 2006 of former rebel spokesman and veterinarian, Irwandi Yusuf as governor. Today, his government has invited foreign investment into resource-rich Aceh, touting it as one of Indonesia's safest provinces. Yudhoyono has been nominated for a Nobel Peace Prize for presiding over this unlikely development, though as a former general in a military that has been highly tainted by human rights abuses, the prize itself has proven elusive.

On January 1, 2001, Indonesia began what has sometimes been called the "big bang". This was an ambitious plan to devolve power to local governments from what had been a highly centralized government in an archipelago spanning the width of North America and containing around 300 ethnic groups in a population of 230 million.

The many actual "bangs" from the chronic separatist and sectarian conflicts that afflicted the post-Suharto period made this initiative for local empowerment all the more imperative. Resource-rich provinces had long complained they were providing far more in revenues to the government in Jakarta than they were getting back in development funds. Decentralization was meant to address that concern, though it devolved power primarily to district governments, because Jakarta feared that empowered provincial governments and state assemblies might lead to even greater separatism.

Decentralization was also meant to curtail corruption by sending money, programs and civil servants directly to regional governments, before bureaucrats, politicians and cronies could get their greedy hands on all that swag in Jakarta. The idea was that a network of activists and NGOs might keep an eye on misfeasance better at the local level. A 2007 World Bank report noted that regional spending did indeed rise, and more than 16,000 public service facilities were handed over to the regions. An inter-governmental fiscal system was put in place without disrupting government services too much.

But while Indonesia became one of the most decentralized countries in the world, at least in structure, it remained ensnarled in corruption and red tape. The World Bank report said Indonesia had the slowest business start-up time of any country in Asia, taking 105 days compared with just five in Singapore. Corruption remained widespread, except now the axis of graft had moved to local legislatures and politicians, instead of the ones in Jakarta. But at least a stronger civil society resulting from decentralization had led to a higher number of cases being uncovered, the World Bank said.

Indonesia was also struggling to instill the "rule of law" as opposed to the "law of rulers" that pertained under Suharto's New Order. The Tommy Suharto case had already made Indonesia's police and judiciary look foolish. Tackling Suharto's wealth was seen as a crucial test of Yudhoyono's promise to curb corruption after his landslide election in 2004. But SBY's government finally had to throw in the towel in 2007, stating some months before Suharto died in January 2008 that he was too old and sick to prosecute anymore for any ill-gotten gains. Suharto and his family have always denied any wrongdoing. In fact, the former general was more successful than his opponents in the battles over his wealth. *Time* magazine had to appeal a 2007 Supreme Court ruling in favor of Suharto's libel suit against the magazine that ordered the U.S. weekly to pay more than $100 million in damages and to print apologies over its May 1999 cover story.

Yudhoyono met World Bank officials in the United States in 2007 to discuss a new U.N.-World Bank initiative to help developing countries recover stolen assets. The initiative cited Suharto and the former Philippines presidents Ferdinand Marcos and Joseph Estrada among "10 of the notorious cases of the past few decades," and quoted a report by Transparency International that put Suharto's assets at $15-$35 billion, or as much as 1.3 percent of Indonesia's gross domestic product. In an effort to tackle Indonesian criminals who have hidden their money abroad, Yudhoyono has pushed – without much success – for an extradition treaty with Singapore and an agreement allowing the pursuit of misappropriated funds held in Hong Kong bank accounts. "Indonesia is undergoing a process of reform, but that process is very slow, almost glacial," said Damien Kingsbury, an associate professor at Australia's Deakin University. "The judiciary and the military are two areas which most need reform but which have been the least touched by the process, and these are two areas where the Suharto clan has strong links."[5]

The mysterious murder of Munir Said Thalib in September 2004 raised fresh questions about the rule of law and the lingering influence of a shadowy military power in Indonesia that seemed to be still at war with human rights activists despite the march of democratization in Indonesia. Munir, an outspoken critic of Indonesia's military and its methods of crushing dissent and separatists in places such as Aceh and Papua, was poisoned with arsenic while flying from Jakarta to Amsterdam on the state-owned airline, Garuda Indonesia.

It took more than three years, but the Supreme Court in January 2008 sentenced a former Garuda pilot to 20 years for the murder, in a case regarded as one of those "tests" of the government's determination to uphold the rule of law and make state agencies, including the espionage bureau, accountable. Pollycarpus Priyanto was convicted of serving Munir an arsenic-laced drink in the transit lounge at Singapore's Changi Airport.

But *The Jakarta Post*, among others, believed he was being made a scapegoat. The former president of state carrier Garuda, Indra

---

5   Reuters, October 11, 2007

Setiawan, had testified that before Munir's death, he had received a letter from the State Intelligence Agency (BIN) asking him to allow Priyanto to be a security officer on Munir's flight. "Very few people believe that Pollycarpus acted alone. This was also the conclusion of a government-sanctioned fact-finding in its report," the *Post* said in a September 7, 2006 editorial. "This was a premeditated murder perpetrated by criminals who want to keep the nation ignorant of their past brutalities," the newspaper said, noting speculation that Yudhoyono's government has been pressured to drop the case by "those who insisted Munir had to die."

Those who believed that was the case were therefore surprised when former State Intelligence Agency deputy chief Maj. Gen. Muchdi Purwopranjono was taken into custody on July 10, 2008 after he was named a suspect in Munir's murder case. National Police spokesman Inspector-General Abubakar Nataprawira said Muchdi, who once headed the covert operations wing of the intelligence agency, could be charged with premeditated murder, which carries a maximum penalty of death.

Though *The Jakarta Post* had been floundering in its management morass in the years after Suharto's downfall, the newspaper had developed a set of values and principles that stood it in good stead as it navigated the unexplored shoals of Indonesia's expanded press freedom.

The late Amir Daud, *The Jakarta Post's* first managing editor, brought with him from *Tempo* certain standards and practices for newsroom behavior, including a strict prohibition on accepting "envelopes." These were packets of money, ostensibly for lunch and transport, which flacks gave out to reporters at press conferences, product launches, and other events. *Jakarta Post* reporters were instructed to refuse acceptance of the envelopes. But if that caused any awkwardness (with colleagues from other publications for instance), or there was chance the flacks would just end up pocketing the money themselves, then reporters were told to bring the envelopes back to the newsroom secretary, who would keep them and record the amounts on a spreadsheet. "We still tell all our reporters don't accept envelopes, and if you do, you're fired," Endy Bayuni says.

At the end of the year, the accumulated stash is donated, usually to a local orphanage.[6] The money given out is not extravagant – about Rp 20,000-Rp50,000 ($2-$5) for most events, and maybe five times that or more for an election campaign event or a big grand opening. But for reporters making around Rp 250,000 a month in the mid-1980s, it could represent up to a quarter of a month's pay and that was mighty tempting.

Harry Bhaskara explains: "The first time you get an envelope, it's hard to reject, because it's just you and the briber. But the next time gets easier and easier. And I'm very happy that I could avoid this scourge afflicting Indonesian journalists. It was hard to resist at first. And maybe some did (take the money), but most of us stuck to the rule."

Nan Achnas, the well-known Indonesian documentary maker, who worked at the *Post* for a year, recalls being given an assignment to cover a sewing machine exhibition at the annual Jakarta Fair in the mid-1980s. The following day, the person Nan interviewed phoned her and asked her where she should send the sewing machine. "I was incredulous. I had come from an Anglo-Saxon education system," said Nan, who grew up in Malaysia and went to a British international school. "I said no thanks, I don't sew, and my paper doesn't allow us to accept gifts. It was so absurd. But that was my first exposure to corruption in Indonesia."

Over the years, the practice of refusing gifts and envelopes has been acculturated and the *Post* has earned a reputation as a "clean" newspaper. One *Jakarta Post* reporter was fired in the mid-1990s for asking a hotel in Bali for money to buy souvenirs for his children. The hotel was so flabbergasted it called the newsroom and reported the case.

Reporters and editors, past and present, often cite the value creed of *The Jakarta Post* as perhaps its single biggest asset. Riyadi Suparno, now a managing editor at the *Post*, says the pluralistic environment of the newspaper changed him personally and has created a unique newsroom culture. "I think the strongest element of *The Jakarta Post*

6   In 2007, the total came to Rp 7.5 million or about $850

is its values. In our recruitment, after a certain probation period, usually you can tell if a person is open enough to accept differences and that is part of our consideration of whether to confirm them.

"When I joined *The Jakarta Post*, I was kind of a fundamentalist type of person. In university, I was with a group of people that thought killing a *khafir* (disbeliever) was acceptable, and I used to be in that situation. And *The Jakarta Post* changed me a lot. I think many people who join the *Post* have to change their values or sooner or later they will quit. If you talk to ex-*Jakarta Post* journalists, they will share certain values – pluralism, democracy, equality, diversity – global values. There have been people, especially Muslims, working at *The Jakarta Post* who were not comfortable with these values and they had to quit. They didn't feel that *The Jakarta Post* was the right place for them; that it was not Islamic in its values."

But Harry Bhaskara says institutional values are not necessarily set in stone and those at *The Jakarta Post* are vulnerable to change. "To nurture a set of values in an organization you need a continuum, a thread that binds people from the past to present. It is here that JP is failing," he said, referring as did many others to the constant problem of staff turnover. "Most of the people who joined JP in its earlier years have all gone. The paper is increasingly manned by people who are new and who do not have any knowledge or emotional attachment to the history of the paper. It is like a man without a backbone. *Kompas* and *Tempo* have a strong corporate culture. This partly explains why they are market leaders."

Endy Bayuni, the main link between the newspaper's beginnings and its present, returned in 2004 from a year's sabbatical at Harvard as a Nieman Fellow to take over from Raymond Toruan as chief editor. Jusuf Wanandi had by then grown totally disillusioned with Raymond and had thrown him off the Board of Directors as well. Although Raymond had his detractors as well as supporters in the newsroom, the Indonesian staff felt uneasy about the unhappy ending. Says Raymond today: "I think they kind of got fed up with me after 20 years, with my independence and this Fabian socialism that I brought in."

He was a gonzo figure in the newsroom, a former Jesuit seminarian enamored with "liberation theology," plotting with activists and student leaders while drinking strong coffee and chain-smoking unfiltered *kreteks*. In 2000 he was photographed delivering a speech to a crowd of people from the back of a Sumatran elephant at the Senayan Sports complex on the 17th anniversary of the *Post*, trying to call attention to the plight of the endangered pachyderms.

"I think that the inherent values of JP journalists of my generation were really shaped by the idealism which Susanto and Raymond embedded," says Managing Editor Dymas Suryodiningrat. "Our beliefs and ethics are a product of the Susanto era. It is something that we, the senior editorial staff, try to continue today and instill amongst our younger reporters. I recall being National Desk Editor during the East Timor crisis in 1999 and somewhat indecisive about when to actually pull our three or four reporters/photographers out of Dili in anticipation of impending violence. For two or three days the question would be "should we pull them out now or let them hang on another day to get the biggest news event happening in the world at the time?" Then on the third or fourth day Pak Santo came up to my desk and gave me a direct order: "Get them out of there now! Sure enough, within a day the worst of the violence erupted."

Endy, a bright, affable and popular figure in the newsroom, set about healing the newsroom in the wake of Susanto and Raymond's departure, bringing a more professional approach to the newsroom.

He also has brought to the position a strong conviction that Indonesia's multiculturalism should be reflected in the newsroom. "It remains a consistent standpoint which we are proud of, and will continue to propagate, in line with the overall mission as set by Raymond to create a more humane civil society," Dymas said.

"Mas" Endy was the first of the four chief editors of *The Jakarta Post* to come up through the ranks of the newspaper. The 51-year-old father of two grown sons, an ethnic Minang from West Sumatra, was born in Jakarta. But he spent a considerable time of his childhood abroad as the son of a diplomat – Burma, Thailand, Argentina, Switzerland and finally England, where he earned a BA in economics from Kingston University in Surrey in 1981 before joining the *Post* two years later. Growing up in different cultures abroad, integrating them into his own worldview, must have contributed greatly to his pluralist outlook.

"Endy was able to garner a profound respect from the editorial staff for several reasons," Dymas said. "First he rose to become one of the best and most consistent writers at the *Post*. His articles and writing style were a standard which younger journalists aspired to. Everything is printed in the paper for all to judge and everyone could see how good he was as a writer, editor and journalist. I think it was an assumed natural evolution that he would become chief editor. His somewhat soft-spoken character was also acceptable to most.

"Second, Endy was also the first home-grown chief editor. So I think we were also quite proud of that fact. After more than two decades, here was someone who began his career at the Post, grew up at the *Post* and became a quality journalist – albeit the fact he did leave for several years in the middle of career to work at AFP and Reuters.

Staff say the other big change Endy has brought in was a renewed emphasis on writing. "He has ushered in an era of narrative journalism, a community newspaper," Dymas said. "As an accomplished writer he pays great attention to this aspect of journalism. As a consequence, the *Post* has been able to produce a greater stock of in-house op-ed writers. During the Suharto era, opinions were sometimes wrapped as news content to allow escape from censors. When Endy took over, it became a natural progression to adapt the *Post* from a simple newspaper to a 'views paper' with a clearer demarcation of news and opinion."

The presentation of news and views is something media organizations across the world are trying to balance in an Internet Age that has begat the blogosphere.

CHAPTER NINE

GATHERING TOGETHER: THE POST COMMUNITY

The Jakarta Post moved to a spacious five-storey office building on April 24, 2008, the eve of its silver anniversary celebrations. "After 25 years, we finally settle down in our own office," President Director Jusuf Wanandi said at the ribbon-cutting ceremony. A quarter-century earlier, *The Jakarta Post* began life in a converted laundry warehouse with the lofty ambition of being Indonesia's face to the world, but its own façade tucked away in the mighty Kompas complex, was humble indeed.

The Post had been dreaming about this building for years, buying both the land and the cinema house that stood on it in 1996, when revenues and circulation were nearing peak levels. Then came the 1997/98 financial crisis that sent the newspaper into a downward spiral that nearly led to bankruptcy. It would be another decade before the new building, a monument to the newspaper's resilience, would be completed. The movie theater went bankrupt due to fierce competition from cinema chains. *The Post* had survived the economic storms of the late 1990s in large part because its competitors had gone out of business. That was about to change, however.

Jakarta Governor Fauzi Bowo, who came to inaugurate the building, joined Jusuf and other board members on a tour of the Rp 35 billion ($3.8 million) building and I followed them in. My, how things had changed. The newsroom on the second floor was at least 10 times the size of our original home in the ersatz laundry room.

The décor was white and minimalist, as quiet as a library, and, in keeping with the newspaper's online ambitions, totally Wi-Fi.

The governor paused before a framed edition of the first copy of *The Jakarta Post* on April 25, 1983. The lead photo showed the rubble of the U.S. Marines barracks in Beirut after it was bombed by what the late U.S. president Reagan called "barbarians". The lead story under the headline "Islamic fanatics indicted" was about Darul Islam leaders being charged with subversion in court. A story below the fold had the attorney general warning of corruption. "See that?" Fauzi said, chuckling and pointing to the page. "Nothing has changed in 25 years."

Many things had, of course, changed, though some had not. The autocratic Suharto has been ousted and since died, but the political elite were still in power. The first family and their cronies were no longer gouging the economy, but corruption remained endemic. The military was retreating from politics and business, but had not yet fully come under civilian control and human rights abuses continued. Separatism had subsided, but religious extremism was still a problem. The economy had regained pre-financial crisis levels of per capita income, but Indonesia was still under-performing against its peers.

Jusuf tells me that holding together a nation of more than 230 million people spread across the 13,000 islands of an archipelago that straddles strategic sea lanes linking the Indian Ocean to the South China Sea and the Pacific has been the biggest achievement of the post-Suharto era. "Without democratization and promoting regional autonomy, the country could most probably not have survived as one nation after Suharto stepped down, but instead would have broken into four or five nations or states," he says. "What has been achieved thus far with democracy and regional autonomy, however slow and weak, has been a salvation for the unity of Indonesia."

Indonesia's military, so long the bane of civil society, has a long way to go towards reform, he says. "Their territorial role has been maintained and their structure has remained the same, including the existence of military districts. Moreover, they continue to oppose the intervention by civilian leaders in military affairs. They preserve their impunity by tightening up their ranks in cases of abuses against human rights and humanity. They do not allow any high-ranking officers to be made accountable in a judicial case of human rights violations. Instead, it is always the underling that has to bear the burden. Restructuring of the Armed Forces to be able to perform its main role in defending the country has not happened."

But the military no longer has the capability of returning to politics, because a new generation of officers is not steeped in that tradition, he says. "One of the reasons why the danger of a military coup has decreased is because even the military has no sense of patriotism left. They individually are only thinking about their pockets. That has been caused by Suharto's policy to make them his Praetorian guard in the last 12 years of his regime, following Gen. Murdani's demotion, and when he no longer trusted the Army."

By the end of 2008, the military was supposed to have emptied its pockets and sold a veritable bazaar of enterprises ranging from golf courses and offices to taxi firms, shipping lines and airlines. Since the founding of the armed forces in the fight against Dutch colonial rule, it had been common practice for the armed forces to find ways of making money on the side, often in partnership with opportunist Chinese businessmen.

The businesses, foundations and cooperatives were used to supplement meager salaries – soldiers typically earn about $100-$300 a month. But for top officers, such as Suharto and his ilk, it could be a gravy train leading to undreamed of wealth. Yudhoyono's government estimated the military's 1,500 businesses were worth about $110 million in 2008.

Getting the army out of its legal businesses will be one thing. Squeezing them out of their black market activities – smuggling, illegal logging, prostitution camps, racketeering, freelance security deals – could be another challenge altogether. "Income from illegal businesses is probably double that of the legal ones, so it is a much bigger problem. It could take 10-20 years to tackle those areas," said Damien Kingsbury, head of international studies at Australia's Deakin University and a leading expert on Indonesia.[1]

---

1 "Indonesia's army to bid farewell to business" by Sara Webb, Reuters, May 15, 2008

Along with a free press and a vibrant democracy that percolates down to the village level, this predominantly Muslim country also seems committed to pluralism and secularism, despite the rise of political Islam and Islamist radicals in recent years. Muslims are divided politically between nationalists and those who make Islam the basis of their party. In the 2004 elections the latter received 37 percent of the votes and won two gubernatorial races in 2008. But these results seemed to reflect more of disenchantment with the same old faces in the two main political parties – Golkar and PDI-P – than any swing towards politicized Islam, Jusuf says.

Indeed, an Indo Barometer opinion poll, conducted in June 2008, showed that only 21 percent of respondents would vote for Islamic parties, while 49 percent said they would support secular-nationalist ones. Megawati Sukarnoputri's PDI-P topped the table with 23.8 percent support, with Golkar trailing in second place with 12 percent.

Jusuf worries, however, that the Yudhoyono administration has not tried to stop a trend toward local governments declaring Sharia law in their districts: 55 out of 440 *kabupaten* have done that so far but, lacking legal and administrative structures, have not implemented it. "However, extremist groups continue to pressure for their implementation," he says.

The rising influence of the small but influential PKS party, a chief advocate of Sharia law, has engendered fears that Indonesia will tilt toward more conservative policies such as Islamic laws requiring women to wear head-coverings, permitting polygamy, curbs on minority religions, and possibly a cooler welcome to foreign investors. The PKS aims to win a fifth of the votes in the 2009 general election and perhaps field a candidate in the presidential poll that follows later in the year. Inspired by Egypt's Muslim Brotherhood, the PKS has won support for its focus on clean government and an effective grassroots organization.

Yudhoyono, worried about the rise of Islamic hardliners in Indonesia, has turned to conservative Muslim groups for support. But some commentators worry that support is coming at the expense of Indonesia's long-standing commitment to multiculturalism

– its "unity in diversity" and may deepen rifts between religious communities. Yudhoyono came under strong pressure in 2008 to ban the minority Ahmadiyah faith, an Islamic offshoot that differs with other Muslims as to whether Muhammad was the final prophet. The group was attacked several times by local mobs who destroyed homes and mosques. Police regularly failed to respond to the attacks.

Yudhoyono's government at first seemed to be considering proposals to ban the group. Other religious organizations, worried that banning Ahmadiyah would only embolden hardliners to persecute other minority faiths, held an inter-faith rally in May 2008 that was attacked by the Islam Defenders Front (FPI) causing 70 injuries. Squads of FPI members in the past have forced gambling dens, bars and nightclubs to close and have attacked Christian churches. After an outpouring of public outrage, police arrested 57 FPI members. Finally in August 2008, Religious Affairs Minister Maftuh Basyunui said the government would not issue a presidential regulation disbanding Ahmadiyah, as demanded by conservative groups, though they would be restricted from spreading their teachings.

Jusuf, however, believes Muslims are generally not inclined to establish a theocracy in Indonesia. "If there is a group amongst them that would like to establish Sharia, other groups will oppose them." All the main political parties profess pluralism, democracy and secular laws – even PKS says it wants to shake off its Islamist reputation and adopt a more pluralistic approach. Nevertheless, the move toward Islamic conservatism has been steadily growing in Indonesia, facilitated in part by an increasingly globalized media. The issue of religious tolerance is one that will continue to be closely followed in the world's most populous Muslim country, which has become something of a beacon to democratic Islamic movements elsewhere in the world. Indeed, Indonesia has gotten better marks of late on its drive towards democratizing its institutions following Suharto's autocracy. The U.S. think-tank Freedom House, impressed with the country's freewheeling press and political life, ranked Indonesia as the only "free" country in Southeast Asia in its annual country report in January 2008.

Indonesia's courts, police and prosecutors, however, can be subject to political meddling or corruption, posing fundamental uncertainties for foreign investors as well as ordinary citizens. Jusuf points to Lapindo, an oil and gas company indirectly owned by Social Welfare Minister Aburizal Bakrie, which has been blamed for a bizarre "mud flow", a volcanic caldera in the making, that has displaced tens of thousands from their homes in East Java. The "mud volcano" first erupted in 2006 from a well Lapindo was digging in an explosion that killed 13 company workers at the site. The company blamed the Yogyakarta earthquake that year for triggering the disaster, but independent researchers say it was probably due to drilling. The government has yet to investigate the initial explosion. Bakrie, ranked by *Forbes* magazine as Indonesia's wealthiest man, has been able "to avoid paying the reparation and compensation to the victims and instead has successfully shifted the burden to the state," Jusuf says.

The Jakarta Post as a newspaper has changed considerably along with the country. A quarter century ago, *The Post* was a scuffling outfit consisting of a couple of dozen employees putting out an eight-page broadsheet with almost no ads for 5,000 readers. Now the newspaper had a staff of 250, plus another 50 on retainer, producing a 24-page daily – 27 percent of it advertising – with a circulation of 40,000. In 1983, it was founded as the face of Suharto's Indonesia to the world. Today, it aims to be the portal to Indonesia for the world (see box).

Daniel Rembeth, who took over as Executive Director in December 2005, has been given the task of implementing the board's strategy of embracing the Internet Age. He began his career in magazines, hired as an intern by Time-Warner in San Francisco after graduating from the University of California at Berkeley with a business degree. The 48-year-old from Jakarta worked in the advertising industry in Indonesia and with Megawati Sukarnoputri's 2004 election campaign conceptualizing campaign promotions before joining *The Post*. He was also the first manager at *The Jakarta Post* with a background in international media marketing. *The Post,* he felt, had not taken a hard-headed business approach in its strategy in the past. "Much of it was emotional decisions without market research. I wouldn't say we were in dire condition, but if you saw the books, if it wasn't for *Pak* Jusuf and the board's leadership, this newspaper would have been closed long ago. My first presentation to them was that I'm going to grow the value of *The Post* to all stakeholders – not just a return on investment, but the intrinsic good will. We were a good company. We had a good product. But we didn't expand in a way to become a library of products. *The Jakarta Post* had been a single-product company for far too long. In fact, you can't compete by being just a single-product company."

With that in mind, *The Post* launched a slick Sunday magazine called *Weekender*, the first companion product to the newspaper. Edited by former copy editor Bruce Emond, *Weekender* debuted in January 2007, featuring columnists, trend and lifestyle stories, profiles and reviews. The 60-page monthly also features plenty of display ads for the upscale audience that makes up a big chunk of *The Post's* demographics. Not enough, however, to allow the magazine to appear weekly, its ultimate ambition. The magazine aims to appeal to a broad range of subscribers: Indonesians and expats from many lands, with different backgrounds and interests, Emond says. "Our articles are about the shared experience of living in Indonesia, for Indonesians and those transplanted here," he says.

Most importantly, it is an English-language product, which is still the company's calling card in Indonesia. "Up until now, I keep wondering, why the heck did they invest in *D&R* magazine?" Daniel says, referring to the failed acquisition of the Indonesian-language magazine in 1999. "It was not in English. I keep saying if we expand our products we have to do so in our core competence. And to back it up, we have to do research, research, and research. Coming from the ad industry, I always based my decisions on research. I have to know the market."

The second new product, a monthly supplement called *Youthspeak*, was not aimed at making money, but is part of the newspaper's "corporate social responsibility". Spearheaded by Marketing Manager Yulia Herawati, the 12-page supplement is inserted into the newspaper print run of around 40,000. Another 5,000 copies are sent to schools throughout Indonesia, sponsored by multinational companies doing business in Indonesia.

Youthspeak, which first came out in November 2007, is designed to be an English-language and current events teaching aid in the classroom. Part of the U.S. Newspaper in Education (NIE) initiative, teachers make lesson plans based on what is in the newspaper, which bridges the gap between the classroom and the "real world" while improving reading skills, Yulia says. *The Post* sponsors workshops to show teachers how to use the supplement interactively. Much of the space is devoted to young readers' opinions, columns on online games, and lessons on current events lessons similar to those in textbooks. The first edition won an award for best special coverage at the annual Asia Media Awards in Macau in 2008.

The Post has resumed printing a Bali edition since 2006, reaching a break-even point in only seven months, and started printing in the country's second-largest city of Surabaya in June 2008. The newspaper, meanwhile, is trying to reorient its coverage to suit the 21st-century demands of its readership. The last survey found that *Jakarta Post* readers liked the opinion page best, followed by the business page, and the city page. The readers liked views, financial information, and news about the place where they live – pretty much what newspapers around the world have also discovered. "Our readers' constraint is not money," Daniel says. "It's time. We have to adapt to their lifestyle. Nobody reads long copy anymore."

While the Post may hope its *Youthspeak* readers will grow up with the habit of wanting to "read the paper" every day, *The Jakarta Post* – like other newspaper industries around the world – has to wonder how long these ink-on-paper products will be around. Newspapers across the world have seen advertising revenues steadily decline. In the United States, ad revenues had fallen 12 percent in the first five months of 2008 following an 8 percent decline last year, raising questions about the survival of some papers. Newspapers have been cutting costs by shedding thousands of workers, shrinking distribution routes and printing fewer pages. The Internet is grabbing an ever-increasing share of ad revenue and advertisers have many more choices online. But newspaper websites are only getting a small portion of that revenue stream and digital advertising pays less than newspaper display ads.[2] With newsprint paper prices soaring, the prognosis cannot be optimistic. On the other hand, the Internet is drawing new readers to newspapers and content is still king on the Internet. With that in mind, *The Post* launched an ambitious portal on its 25th anniversary on April 25, 2008 (see box on following page).

If you're stuck in traffic in Jakarta, which is pretty much all the time, you will undoubtedly be besieged by *tukang koran,* the newspaper vendors who amble through the gridlock displaying an array of newspapers and magazines. Newspapers may be a dying industry elsewhere in the world, but for now at least they are alive and well in Indonesia. More than 800 newspapers are in circulation throughout the country, almost four times the number that existed during the dying days of the New Order.

Many of them are owned by conglomerates or business houses, prompting journalists to worry about the growing influence of big business on the media. "The line is getting blurred between the editorial side and the marketing side," *Tempo* Senior Editor and *Jakarta Post* Director Fikri Jufri says. "You have a lot of soft advertisements, advertorial now. Now the money coming into the press these days… they have their ways," he says, fluttering his fingers.

Post Managing Editor Ati Nurbaiti says many Indonesian newsrooms are dealing with this kind of pressure. "For every newspaper now, government is not the issue; it's the business people, including their own shareholders. And it's up to the editorial board to maintain that independence as much as they can. The advertising department gets pressure from clients to use handout photos of their products on the business page. Or they don't want the word "advertorial" or "advertisement" to be placed on top of one of their testimonials. And we have to tell them our rules; that every ad has to be labeled advertisement – even if it's in very small type. Now, the business side says the clients do understand that if it's not credible, the public won't buy the newspaper, and in the end, their products

---

2 "Papers Facing Worst Year for Ad Revenue", by Richard Perez-Pena, *The New York Times,* June 23, 2008

The New Portal Paradigm

The Jakarta Post spent its first quarter-century as an ink-on-paper product. It does not expect to survive in that form a quarter-century later. By 2033, the newspaper expects its portal (thejakartapost.com) will be the company's flagship product. And the print edition of *The Jakarta Post*? Well, that could go the way of codpieces and doublets, which were the height of fashion in 1575 when the first newspaper was published.[†]

The Post, of course, is not unique in that respect. Newspapers are dying around the world, and those that do survive are shrinking. Yet this is happening at a time when newspaper readership around the world is growing – through their websites. Newspaper websites in the United States lured more than 66 million unique visitors in the first quarter of 2008, a 12 percent increase over the previous year. The problem is the business model: Newspaper websites only account for a fraction of total ad revenue.

The Web 2.0 version of *The Jakarta Post* was a little slow in coming, but its debut on April 25, 2008 was welcomed in a country that had no other English-language, multimedia news site. *The Post* portal features a clean layout with a banner headline up top for easy navigation. Stories on the front page invite readers to post comments. The site also has RSS (Really Simple Syndication) to let readers track related stories and postings. The portal followed on the success of *The Jakarta Post* online edition, whose revenue from advertising had been doubling every year, albeit from a fairly low base.

In an April 25, 2008 editorial that echoed the newspaper's original ambition to be the "Journal of Indonesia Today", the newspaper announced the portal would "represent Indonesia to the world". It's a lofty ambition that will have to be realized in stages, says Managing Director Daniel Rembeth. "Our portal is still under development, but we decided to launch it in several phases. The portal will carry us beyond our traditional distribution area. It will also open new markets/readers for the Post. However, we – the board – need to be fully committed to embrace this. We have to agree to strategically set out a plan –mid- and long-term – for digital to be the main channel for the organization. How I see it, it's the future and the future is now. Digitalization will be progressing rapidly. We need to get ready for Web 3.0, after watching Web 2.0 pass by so quickly."

The Jakarta Post, like other newspapers, has had to deal with an inherently frustrating development for the industry: the popularity of Internet-based news means people have come to expect to get news and information free of charge. Some publishers have introduced free newspapers funded entirely by advertisers in response. "This may extend the life of newspapers by a few more years, but it won't be enough to convince today's younger generation to start reading newspapers every day," *The Post* said in its April 25 editorial.

The portal represents a paradigm shift, which recognizes that readers are no longer passive consumers of the product but actually are part of the product itself. *The Post* portal aims to be more than just an extension of the previous online version of the paper. It will provide not only news and information, but also a range of other services including podcasts, videocasts and even e-transactions for the general public, *The Post* editorial said. This implies that reporters themselves will be undergoing transformation, packing smartphones, video cameras and digital recorders along with their satellite phones and cleft sticks[‡] to cover stories that must now be presented in three dimensions.

The Jakarta Post said it is looking to partner with other companies and organizations to provide a panoply of information and services for the public, but will stick to its "core competencies", including providing news and information in English. "We understand that one day, in the not-too-distant future, the portal will take over from the printed newspaper as the company flagship," *The Post* editorial declared.

The acerbic Indonesia media blog "Unspun", often critical of *The Jakarta Post,* gave the portal a thumb's up, calling it "a good start." But the blog also said "the folks at *The Post* are still stuck in thinking of their website as a newspaper, or the reflection of one…Done well, *The Post's* interactive strategy would create communities among its readers." The blog recommended that *The Post* get journalists or guest writers to do blogs on the site, and also do more with its RSS feeds to better alert readers when the website runs news about a particular issue or company. Daniel says a blogging culture does not yet exist in *The Post,* but is something the newspaper wants to cultivate in the future.

The Jakarta Post, like other media organizations, is grappling with a changing business model: how to deal with a future in which the consumer is taking over the printing press, the news photo desk, and the news television studio. It is the era of the "two-way pipe", the conversation of reader and his chosen medium. The defining issue is trust. Who will consumers trust as the medium for their information and services? Yet even in the era of Internet-based communications, someone must still do the work that has traditionally been the domain of journalists: to gather and compile facts and information, verify their accuracy, sort out the essential from the non-essential, edit and package, do it in a way that is easy for people to understand (either through text or audio-visual means), and finally deliver it via the medium of the day. "Today it is newspapers and radio/television. Tomorrow, it could all be online," *The Post* said in its 25th anniversary editorial. Daniel calls it "creative destruction" and says the days of one-way communication and journalists' monopoly on truth are over. "Newspapers must establish a dialogue with readers to get a true multi-dimensional product."

This is a far cry from the New Order when the "dialogue" was between the authorities and the media over what the people needed to know. It tended to be a one-way pipe. "At least there is this openness, we're on the right path," says *Post* Director Fikri Jufri. "Before, in Suharto's time, they said go right, go left, now go straight. Now what you have is 'being lost in the right way'. You used to be directed, but now you're free, and you may stumble along the way, but the road to democracy is there. And we have to hold onto it. It's like Thomas Jefferson said: 'If I had to choose between a government without newspapers, or newspapers without a government, I would not hesitate a moment to choose the latter.' We have to hold onto it, because if you're going back to the old way, oh my gosh… It's a less repressive society today. Is it less corrupt? I don't think so."

[†] It was called *Relation aller Fürnemmen und gedenckwürdigen Historien*, or Collection of all distinguished and commemorable news, published by Johann Carolus in Germany.

[††] In Evelyn Waugh's famous satirical novel of foreign correspondents, "Scoop", the protagonist packs "cleft sticks" to send his dispatches from North Africa back to London. It's actually an idiomatic phrase meaning a very difficult problem

won't sell either. But that message has to be repeated over and over, not just with the business side, but in the newsroom as well. And this at a time when the press is free."

Fellow Managing Editor Riady Suparno also sees editorial's independence a continuing challenge. "The independence of the editorial department is an issue because the intervention of the owners is getting more frequent. A couple of the board members are intrusive. They may sit on the board of a company and they want us to cover something and that is a problem for us. (Former chief editor) Susanto, though his physical presence in the office was minimal compared to the others, could prevent the intrusiveness of the owners in the newsroom. At least, the employee foundation is there to maintain the integrity of the newspaper, because it is nonpartisan."

Those pressures certainly are not unique to Indonesia – big business firms own much of the world's media. But in Indonesia a strong strain of *pers perjuangan*, or the battling press of Indonesia's struggle for independence, still courses through newsroom. Adherents believe they have more integrity, more independence and are more engaged in the struggle for the common good than the *pers industrial* or industrial press. Raymond and his espousal of "Fabian socialism" saw himself in this tradition as did many other journalists at *The Jakarta Post* over the years. *The Post,* which seems to have had a foot in both streams over the years, is now facing strong competition from the "industrial press".

For most of the past decade, *The Jakarta Post* had enjoyed virtually a monopoly in the English-language newspaper market, following the demise of the *Indonesia Observer* and *Indonesia Times* in the aftermath of the financial crisis, a hiatus that helped the newspaper consolidate following the management mess it had gotten into. But in 2006, a new English-language newspaper called *The Point* came out. And in 2008, the *Jakarta Globe* announced plans to aggressively take on *The Post* with a newspaper financed by James Riady, whose family owns the Lippo Group, a major Indonesian conglomerate with interests in banking and property. *The Globe* has hired a former *Newsweek* correspondent and a former AFP reporter to run the newspaper.

Suharto's death on January 27, 2008 was a historical milestone for Indonesia, though not necessarily a turning point. His stamp on Indonesia was certainly strong, but even a few months after his passing it seems to be fading – like the Cheshire cat's grin, or perhaps Semar's, the former president's favorite *wayang* character. "The Father of Development" kept economic growth humming for 32 years, and largely kept a lid on communal conflict. But he also bequeathed a brutal army, a shattered economy, a neutered political system and dysfunctional institutions when he quit the presidency during a popular uprising in May 1998. Much of his rule was peaceful, but stability came at the cost of repression. Up to a half-million Indonesians suspected of being communists or sympathizers were slaughtered in an army-inspired bloodbath in the months before he took power from an ailing Sukarno. And over the next three decades, his army continued to kill – students, labor activists, human rights campaigners, journalists and criminals in "mysterious shootings", and in the rebellious provinces of East Timor, Aceh and Papua.

Indonesians tend to remember the good things about his rule, especially the 25 years of economic growth, even if that came at the expense of depleting the country's oil reserves and forests. Over the past decade since his ouster, Indonesia has managed to right many of the wrongs of his regime. East Timor is independent now. Aceh is ruled by a former rebel. Papua has been given special autonomy. The over-centralization has dissipated into devolution. Authoritarianism has given way to perhaps the freest democracy in the region. But graft remains widespread and Southeast Asia's biggest economy ranks among the most corrupt in the world and is a deterrent to foreign investment. The 2008 case of an Indonesian lawmaker who said he took bribes to vote for the senior deputy central bank governor illustrated how endemic the problem is in Southeast Asia's biggest economy. Agus Condro Prayitno, 46, of the PDI-P, admitted that he and some other legislators each took 500 million rupiah ($54,620) after Miranda Goeltom was elected to the central bank's board in 2004. "My thought at that time was, there's 500 million rupiah. I can change my car, and so I bought a Mercedes, secondhand, but still in good condition. My driver used to be ashamed to drive in a cheap Soluna. He was thrilled when I bought the Mercedes."

But he didn't think his case was extreme or that he was irredeemable. "Like walking in the middle of the ricefield, there's mud on my pants and shoes, but it hasn't reached my kneecap. I can correct myself as a politician, and hope others will follow." He also disclosed that he, like other legislators had to "donate" $500-$600 a month to his PDI-P party, a practice, analysts said, that encourages them to look for extra-curricular sources of income.[3]

If many Indonesians are inclined to forgive and forget Suharto's venality, they are having a harder time getting past the human rights abuses. In March of 2008, Indonesia's Human Rights Commission opened inquiries into the mass killings and abuses that tainted Suharto's 32-year rule. Four teams have begin collecting evidence in the 1965-66 communist pogrom, alleged atrocities by Indonesian soldiers in Aceh and Papua and the hundreds of killings and abductions blamed on security forces in the 1980s and 1990s.

Sabam Siagian, 76, who remained a director after his return as ambassador to Australia in the mid-1990s, is still a frequent visitor to his old newsroom, writing the occasional editorial, usually on foreign affairs, on the same ancient Olympia typewriter next to his little-used computer work station that he has pecked on for the past quarter-century. He likes to keep a big picture in his frame, and says it is important for *The Jakarta Post* to plan for dynamic changes ahead. In another quarter-century Indonesia will have a population of 400 million, and if it continues to grow at an average of 5 percent a year, Indonesia's GDP will be about $1.4 trillion – about the same as Canada's today. By 2043, Indonesia and its neighbors in the 10-member Association of Southeast Asian Nations may well have achieved their EU-style political, economic and security community and will have an important geostrategic role as a balancing power between China, Japan and India, and a key component of an Asia-Pacific free trade area.

As the world gets smaller and Indonesia's profile becomes larger, new English language news products, both printed and increasingly

---

3 "Indonesia MP admits taking bribes, embarrasses party", August 26, 2008, Reuters

in digital forms, will appear in the Indonesian market "not necessarily propelled by the usual profit motive", Sabam says.

"This future projection of the media industry in Indonesia, with the coming generation changes – which for sure will be impacted by the increasing intensity of the globalization process – has been the topic of discussion in our recent board meetings", he says. "We do not exactly know what the future holds for *The Jakarta Post* but at least we have made the essential preparations to position ourselves as advantageously as possible. Twenty-five years ago on blind faith we decided to publish *The Jakarta Post*. We could not possibly fathom then what the future would hold for this dubious experiment. Probably now we at *The Jakarta Post* are better prepared to cope with a rapid changing future since there is this inner confidence and solidarity through our editorial and business team members to face what possibly could be a radical new media world."

Newspapers across the world see their future in portals, but they still have a core readership that reads their print editions. Newspapers may be dying, but they were still bringing in more revenue than their online incarnations into the first decade of the 21st century and two decades into the Internet Age. "The Internet is replacing newspapers and that is happening quicker than people think," Endy says. "The price of newsprint has increased by 50 percent (in the first half of 2008), but you can't raise subscription prices by that. Newspapers will cease to exist in 10 years, but journalists' skills will still be in demand. You're still going to need news gatherers, with skills in accuracy and knowing what's relevant and how to package and present that information…What no one has found, to this stage, is how to make money on the Internet. But that's not my job; that's the job of the business department. My job is to make sure reporters and editors are trained up for this new model. Who will end up paying our salaries? I think in the next 10 years someone will figure that out."

The paradigm change is not just the medium, but the audience. They are deciding how and when to access information, what to save and what to have pushed to them. They are participating in the information revolution. They have views and reviews. For news organizations, the audience is now a consumer, a partner and a potential competitor. A blog is created every second, according to one estimate. That is constructing a towering Babel of fact, fiction, half-truths and opinion. Truth and fact-based, unbiased, old-fashioned journalism can be lost in this cacophony. Gaining trust and credibility with the audience will be the differentiator for news organizations.

In the "message from the publisher" in the inaugural edition of the newspaper, *The Jakarta Post* said it aimed to have a two-way communication with its readership, "to reach and touch you, the reader. And we earnestly ask that you keep in touch with us, too, by writing us letters for our letters column, and suggesting or contributing stories for our news and opinion pages. And so together we can take the pulse of Indonesia today." In a world of many choices and voices, *The Jakarta Post* is betting that its brand as a trusted source of news, information and services, with values that reflect those of its community of readers, will keep the newspaper going in one form or another when it marks its centenary 75 years from now.

AUTHOR'S NOTE

This book uses modern spellings of Indonesian names, using *u* instead of *oe* for names such as Suharto and Sukarno. I generally refer to Indonesians by their first name on second reference following the local practice. Many Indonesians in any case use only one name. The historical record largely comes from the archives of *The Jakarta Post*, except where footnoted. I take full responsibility for the interpretation of that record (except where otherwise attributed), as well as any errors or ommissions.

ACKNOWLEDGEMENTS

My mother Kathleen, who encouraged me to write practically from the moment she began reading to me as a child, kept every card and letter I had sent home since college, before giving them all back to me in a spring-cleaning fit a few years ago. Those letters home from the 1980s were exceptionally helpful in trying to reconstruct some of the personal events in the early chapters of this book. My brother Jim's letters, recollections and editing pointers were also valuable. My younger brother David offered narrative writing tips. My wife Mohini and daughters Tavleen and Jasleen have my deepest love and thanks for allowing me the time and space for this book.

The editors and board members of *The Jakarta Post* were generous with their time and access. President Director Jusuf Wanandi spent many hours over a number of interviews with me and remained deeply committed to an independent book written about his newspaper. Chief Editor Endy Bayuni is a walking archive of the history of Indonesia and the *Post*, as well as an incisive commentator of his times. Former chief editor Sabam Siagian was a fount of anecdotes and ideas for the book. Former chief editors Raymond Toruan and Susanto Pudjomartono were of vital help in reconstructing the dramatic events of the 1990s. Vincent Lingga, Harry Bhaskara and Maggie Agusta have been with the newspaper from its early beginnings and their recollections helped create the picture of *The Jakarta Post*'s past and present.

I owe thanks to many others for their support and advice including two old friends and acclaimed authors of Indonesian books, Adam Schwarz and Michael Vatikiotis. Many others also contributed stories and anecdotes including Fikri Jufri, Sofyan Wanandi, Debra Yatim, Nan Achnas, Bambang Harymurti, Jason Tedjasukmana and Aristides Katoppo. Lena and Pranajaya at the *Post* provided administrative support. Special thanks to Soetoyo and his colleagues in the Post photo department for the outstanding pictures in the book.

Jeremy Wagstaff was the ideal editor – an experienced book editor, who was a correspondent in Indonesia for Reuters and the then *Asian Wall Street Journal* in the 1990s and who himself has authored a book (*Loose Wire*). I was fortunate to have Equinox, the leading English-language publisher in Indonesia, for this my first book. Equinox founder Mark Hanusz was totally professional and supportive, with the added value of being fine company in a Jakarta watering hole.

Finally, I wish to express gratitude to my employer Reuters for allowing me to write this book and putting up with my distractions in doing so.

-Bill Tarrant

SELECTED BIBLIOGRAPHY

Anderson, Benedict R. *Language and Power: Exploring Political Cultures in Indonesia,* Cornell University Press, Ithaca, 1990

Conboy, Ken. *The Second Front: Inside Indonesia's Most Dangerous Terrorist Network,* Equinox Publishing, Jakarta, 2005

Crouch, Harold. *The Army and Politics in Indonesia,* Cornell University Press, Ithaca, 1988 (revised edition)

Hughes, John. *Sukarno: A Coup That Misfired: A Purge That Ran Wild,* John Hughes, Archipelago Press, Singapore, 2003

Maher, Michael. *Indonesia: An Eyewitness Account,* Penguin Books Australia, Ringwood, Victoria, 2000

Mallet, Victor. *The Trouble with Tigers,* HarperCollins, London, 1999

McDonald, Hamish. *Suharto's Indonesia,* Fontana Books, Blackburn, Victoria, 1980

O'Rourke, Kevin. *Reformasi,* Allen & Unwin, Sydney, 2002

Robison, Richard. *Indonesia: The Rise of Capital,* Allen & Unwin, Sydney, 1986

Schwarz, Adam. *A Nation in Waiting,* Allen & Unwin, Singapore, 1999

Soeharto. *My Thoughts, Words and Deeds: An Autobiography,* Citra Lamtoro Gung Persada, Jakarta, 1991

Sukarno. *An Autobiography as told to Cindy Adams,* Bobbs-Merrill co., Indianapolis, 1965

Vatikiotis, Michael. *Indonesian Politics Under Suharto,* Routledge, London, 1993

INDEX

An asterisk indicates a photograph.

OTHER TITLES BY EQUINOX PUBLISHING

ILLUSTRATED

MUSEUM PASIFIKA:
Selected Artwork of Asia Pacific
Philippe Augier and
Georges Breguet, Editors
978-979-3780-70-2
2009, hardcover, 288 pages

INDONESIAN ODYSSEY:
A Private Journey Through
Indonesia's Most Renowned
Fine Art Collections
Helena Spanjaard
978-979-3780-64-1
2008, hardcover, 320 pages

MODERN MALAYSIAN:
A Tribute to Felda's
Craftspeople
Sakinah Aljunid
979-3780-32-0
2006, hardcover, 160 pages

MADE IN INDONESIA:
A Tribute to the Country's
Craftspeople
Warwick Purser
979-3780-13-4
2005, hardcover, 160 pages

BANGKOK INSIDE OUT
Daniel Ziv & Guy Sharett
979-97964-6-6
2005, softcover, 176 pages

A CUP OF JAVA
Gabriella Teggia & Mark Hanusz
979-95898-9-4
2003, softcover, 144 pages

JAKARTA INSIDE OUT
Daniel Ziv
979-95898-7-8
2002, softcover, 184 pages

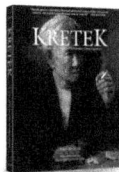

KRETEK:
The Culture and Heritage of
Indonesia's Clove Cigarettes
Mark Hanusz
979-95898-0-0
2000, hardcover, 224 pages

NON-FICTION

**ELITE: The Special Forces of
Indonesia 1950-2008**
Ken Conboy
978-979-3780-60-3 (text version)
978-979-3780-59-7 (color version)
2008, softcover, 148 & 64 pages

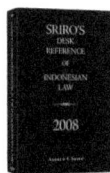

**SRIRO'S DESK REFERENCE
OF INDONESIAN LAW 2008**
Andrew I. Sriro
978-979-3780-61-0
2008, softcover, 672 pages

FAMILY BUSINESS
Asih Sumardono & Mark Hanusz
978-979-3780-58-0
2007, softcover, 192 pages

LOOSE WIRE
A Personal Guide to Making
Technology Work for You
Jeremy Wagstaff
979-3780-39-8
2007, softcover, 368 pages

PEACE IN ACEH
A Personal Account of the
Helsinki Peace Process
Damien Kingsbury
979-3780-25-8
2006, softcover, 236 pages

**THE LEGACY OF THE
BARANG PEOPLE**
György Busztin
979-3780-37-1
2006, softcover, 120 pages

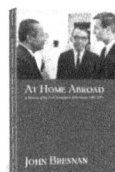

AT HOME ABROAD:
A Memoir of the Ford
Foundation in Indonesia
John Bresnan
979-3780-34-7
2006, softcover, 236 pages

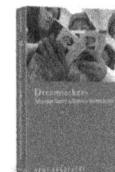

DREAMSEEKERS:
Indonesian Women as Domestic
Workers in Asia
Dewi Aggraeni
979-3780-28-2
2006, softcover, 272 pages

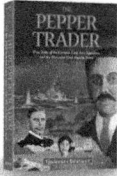

THE PEPPER TRADER
Geoffrey Bennett
979-3780-26-6
2006, softcover, 392 pages

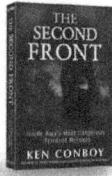

THE SECOND FRONT
Ken Conboy
979-3780-09-6
2006, softcover, 256 pages

SIDELINES
Goenawan Mohamad
979-3780-07-X
2005, softcover, 260 pages

**BULE GILA: Tales of a
Dutch Barman in Jakarta**
Bartele Santema
979-3780-04-5
2005, softcover, 160 pages

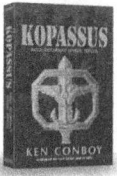

**KOPASSUS: Inside Indonesia's
Special Forces**
Ken Conboy
979-95898-8-6
2003, softcover, 352 pages

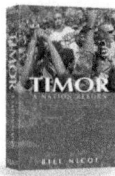

TIMOR: A Nation Reborn
Bill Nicol
979-95898-6-X
2002, softcover, 352 pages

**GUS DUR: The Authorized
Biography of Abdurrahman Wahid**
Greg Barton
979-95898-5-1
2002, softcover, 436 pages

**NO REGRETS: Reflections
of a Presidential Spokesman**
Wimar Witoelar
979-95898-4-3
2002, softcover, 200 pages

FICTION

ELLIPSIS
Laksmi Pamuntjak
979-3780-30-4
2006, softcover, 98 pages

SAMAN
Ayu Utami
979-3780-11-8
2005, softcover, 184 pages

**THE INVISIBLE PALACE:
The True Story of a
Journalist's Murder in Java**
José Manuel Tesoro
979-97964-7-4
2004, softcover, 328 pages

**INTEL: Inside Indonesia's
Intelligence Service**
Ken Conboy
979-97964-4-X
2004, softcover, 264 pages

THE SPICE GARDEN
Michael Vatikiotis
979-97964-2-3
2004, softcover, 256 pages

**THE KING, THE WITCH AND
THE PRIEST**
Pramoedya Ananta Toer
979-95898-3-5
2001, softcover, 128 pages

IT'S NOT AN ALL NIGHT FAIR
Pramoedya Ananta Toer
979-95898-2-7
2001, softcover, 120 pages

TALES FROM DJAKARTA
Pramoedya Ananta Toer
979-95898-1-9
2000, softcover, 288 pages

ENVIRONMENTAL POLITICS AND POWER IN INDONESIA
Hariadi Kartodihardjo & Hira Jhamtani
978-979-3780-66-5
2009, softcover, 292 pages

SOCIAL SCIENCE AND POWER IN INDONESIA
Vedi R. Hadiz & Daniel Dhakidae
979-3780-01-0
2005, hardcover, 304 pages

PEOPLE, POPULATION, AND POLICY IN INDONESIA
Terence H. Hull
979-3780-02-9
2005, hardcover, 208 pages

**INDONESIA:
THE RISE OF CAPITAL**
Richard Robison
978-979-3780-65-8
2008, softcover, 452 pages

GANGSTERS AND REVOLUTIONARIES
Robert Cribb
978-979-3780-71-9
2008, softcover, 248 pages

**DUTCH CULTURE OVERSEAS:
Colonial Practice in the
Netherlands Indies 1900-1942**
Frances Gouda
978-979-3780-62-7
2008, softcover, 316 pages

**THE ROMANCE OF K'TUT
TANTRI AND INDONESIA**
Timothy Lindsey
978-979-3780-63-4
2008, softcover, 406 pages

**THE PRESS IN NEW ORDER
INDONESIA**
David T. Hill
979-3780-46-0
2008, softcover, 188 pages

**INDONESIAN FOREIGN POLICY
AND THE DILEMMA OF
DEPENDENCE**
Franklin B. Weinstein
978-979-3780-56-6
2007, softcover, 388 pages

**THE ARMY AND POLITICS
IN INDONESIA**
Harold Crouch
979-3780-50-9
2007, softcover, 592 pages

VILLAGES IN INDONESIA
Edited by Koentjaraningrat
979-3780-51-7
2007, softcover, 460 pages

**CULTURE AND POLITICS
IN INDONESIA**
Edited by Claire Holt
978-979-3780-57-3
2007, softcover, 368 pages

INDONESIAN POLITICAL THINKING
Edited by H. Feith and L. Castles
978-979-3780-52-8
2007, softcover, 524 pages

OPIUM TO JAVA
James R. Rush
979-3780-49-5
2007, softcover, 256 pages

THE ECONOMY OF INDONESIA
Edited by Bruce Glassbuner
978-979-3780-55-9
2007, softcover, 460 pages

**CHINESE POLICY
TOWARD INDONESIA**
David Mozingo
978-979-3780-54-2
2007, softcover, 308 pages

**MEDIA, CULTURE AND
POLITICS IN INDONESIA**
Krishna Sen and David T. Hill
979-3780-42-8
2006, softcover, 256 pages

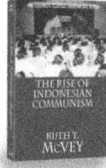

**THE RISE OF INDONESIAN
COMMUNISM**
Ruth T. McVey
979-3780-36-3
2006, softcover, 510 pages

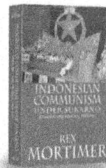

**INDONESIAN COMMUNISM
UNDER SUKARNO:
Ideology and Politics 1959-1965**
Rex Mortimer
979-3780-29-0
2006, softcover, 464 pages

**JAVA IN A TIME OF
REVOLUTION: Occupation
and Resistance 1944-1946**
Benedict R.O'G. Anderson
979-3780-14-2
2006, softcover, 516 pages

**LANGUAGE AND POWER:
Exploring Political Cultures
in Indonesia**
Benedict R. O'G. Anderson
979-3780-40-1
2006, softcover, 316 pages

**AN INTRODUCTION
TO INDONESIAN
HISTORIOGRAPHY**
Edited by Soedjatmoko
979-3780-44-4
2006, softcover, 468 pages

**POPULATION TRENDS
IN INDONESIA**
Widjojo Nitisastro
979-3780-43-6
2006, softcover, 292 pages

**THE DECLINE OF CONSTITUTIONAL
DEMOCRACY IN INDONESIA**
Herbert Feith
979-3780-45-2
2006, softcover, 644 pages

CUSTOM PUBLICATIONS

**TWENTY YEARS OF
WELCOMING THE WORLD
Melia Bali Villas
& Spa Resort**
2005, hardcover, 160 pages

**CELEBRATING INDONESIA:
Fifty Years with the
Ford Foundation 1953-2003**
Goenawan Mohamad
979-97964-1-5
2004, hardcover, 240 pages

www.ingramcontent.com/pod-product-compliance
Lightning Source LLC
Chambersburg PA
CBHW031500270326
41930CB00006B/176